The Complete Heretic's Guide to Western Religion

The Mormons

by

David Fitzgerald

The Complete Heretic's Guide
to Western Religion: The Mormons

Published by David Fitzgerald
Copyright 2013 David Fitzgerald
Cover design by Casimir Fornalski
Cover Art by Matt Burns
Interior layout: www.formatting4U.com

Printed in the United States of America

Praise for
The Complete Heretic's Guide to Western Religion (Book One)

"David Fitzgerald explains religion in a way pastors rarely do: by telling the truth. Along the way, we find ourselves laughing—partly because he's hilarious and partly because we're horrified by the beliefs that millions of people hold. If the first step to curing the Religion Virus is to understand the disease, I, for one, am glad to have David as my teacher."

- Hemant Mehta
TheFriendlyAtheist.com

"In the last several years, David Fitzgerald has emerged as one of the few authors who can discuss the academic particulars of history in a fashion that makes them accessible and entertaining. I learned quite a bit about the outlandish and immoral history of the Mormon Church by reading the Mormon installment in David's collection on Western religion. This new work continues in the same engaging vein that made *Nailed* a success and departs from his old style only in ways that make this book the best in his, thankfully, still-growing collection... Even the proof version of the book is stellar. David has a real gift for writing about academic material in a way that a music major like me can not only 'get it' but also in a way that makes it not stiff as a freaking board, the way a lot of informative literature is written."

- JT Eberhard
Co-founder of Skepticon, Blogger (*What Would JT Do?*)

"David Fitzgerald's *The Mormons* is an excellent primer for anyone interested in this strange and secretive religion. The chapter on archaeological difficulties should close the door for anyone wondering if the Book of Mormon is actual history, or corresponds to anything found in the real world."

- Former Mormon elder (for 28 years) Brian Dalton
star of "Mr. Deity"

"If you find history boring, it's because you haven't heard it from David Fitzgerald. The quote, 'History is the autobiography of a madman,' was surely talking about Joseph Smith and the Mormons. Fitzgerald captures those ravings perfectly. (If you read Fitzgerald's previous book, *Nailed*, you may be disappointed to learn that Joseph Smith was in fact a real person) Fitzgerald has an affable personality and is always quick with a joke and a smile. When he talks about history he is able to direct that charm like a laser while delivering top notch scholarship. Also, most historians don't wear kilts. This is a problem I'm glad Fitzgerald is addressing. If you only read one book this year that was translated from gold tablets written in reformed Egyptian, make it this one!"

- Steven Olson
author of *Unbelievable History*

"I've been an atheist for awhile, but it's David Fitzgerald's fault that I no longer believe in Jesus. His first book, *Nailed*, was simply amazing, and now he's putting Mormons front and center in this hilarious, yet informative and influential look into the Church of Latter Day Saints. This is a must read for every BYU student."

-David Smalley
Dogma Debate Radio

"When discussing religion David Fitzgerald has the unbridled enthusiasm of the geekiest kid you knew in high school describing a favorite episode of Dr. Who, but this enthusiasm is oddly and delightfully paired with the confidence and efficiency of words you'd find in a seasoned stand up comedian. He is therefore perfectly suited to entertain while educating the masses. If I believed in God I'd thank her for giving us David Fitzgerald."

- Keith Lowell Jensen
Comedian/sex god

To Don Havis, who knows all this already;
Andrea Moore-Emmett, who knows all this and much, much
more;
and to all the wonderful Mormons and ex-Mormons
who shared their stories, doubts, advice, knowledge and love
of,
as well as escapes from, Mormonism with me.

Contents

"Each of us has to face the matter—either the Church is true, or it is a fraud. There is no middle ground. It is the Church and kingdom of God, or it is nothing."
- Mormon President Gordon B. Hinckley
LDS General Conference, April 2003.

"I will tell you who the real fanatics are: they are they who adopt false principles and ideas as facts, and try to establish a superstructure upon a false foundation... If our religion is of this character we want to know it; we would like to find a philosopher who can prove it to us."
- Brigham Young, *Journal of Discourses*
vol. 13, p. 272

"It is better not to have so much faith as to believe all the lies."

- Hyrum Smith
brother of Joseph Smith

Introduction: Meet the Mormons

Religion has been a huge force throughout human history. Western religion has shaped western civilizations, given hope, comfort and inspiration to millions, and just like Eastern religion, all of its sects are ultimately based on wishful thinking, bad guesswork concerning the nature of reality and in all too many cases, crazy nonsense. But if all the major religions today held a competition to see which was the goofiest, most blatantly, most demonstrably well-documented pile of sheer unflinching bullshit, who would win? It's a tough call, but in this little book, I'd like to make a heartfelt argument on behalf of the Church of Jesus Christ of Latter-day Saints, a.k.a. the Mormons!

Now, I know there are some who will criticize this book for being mean-spirited for picking on a much-maligned group. Nothing could be further from the truth. Mormons are a fascinating bunch, and I sincerely adore them. They are some of the most upbeat, generous, good-hearted folks I know, and it's because they *don't* have a small army of vicious lawyers or issue fatwas for blasphemy (unlike *some* religions we know) that I even have the *cojones* to write such a book in the first place.

Others may feel it's religious bigotry to criticize someone else's religion, but frankly, that's condescending crap.

1

Religious opinions should be no more immune to discussion and criticism than scientific or political ones. I respect Mormons and believers of every other stripe enough to take their assertions seriously enough to point out where they are untrue. That is not bigotry. As the late Senator Daniel Patrick Moynihan said, everyone is entitled to their own opinions, but not their own facts.

Anyone interested in the truth of Mormon claims will find this book a useful resource, but do be aware that the audience will be assumed throughout to be nonbelievers: atheists, agnostics and other freethinkers. If you are a Mormon who leads a happy and fulfilled life in your faith, I'm sincerely happy for you, and I have no bone to pick with you. I will not think less of you for not wanting to read any further.

But other Mormons secretly go through life under tremendous pressures: pressure to conform, pressure to get married in the Temple, pressure to have lots of children, pressure to be the perfect wife/husband/child, pressure to be straight, pressure to squelch doubts, pressure to devote all their free time to the church, pressure to uphold untenable dogma, pressure to be financially successful, pressure to maintain appearances, pressure to always say that you're happy. I know this because a lot of them tell me so. This book is written for them as well; they are not alone.

And the difficulties may not be confined to members of the church. Utah ranks number one in incidents of depression and suicides, nationwide. One study reported: "In Utah, 14 percent of adults and adolescents reported experiencing severe psychological distress, and 10 percent said they'd had a major depressive episode in the past year. Bad mental health days come three times a month for those living in Utah."[i] Incidentally, Utah leads the nation in fraud (see "God is Not a Good Investment Advisor," chapter 8) and pornography consumption[ii], too.

Mormons don't always show a live and let live attitude when it comes to non-Mormons, as witnessed by their recent aggressive campaign to pump money and volunteer hours into the notorious anti-gay Proposition 8 in California, as well as their less visible decades-long efforts against lesbian and gay rights, documented in films like *8: The Mormon Proposition* (2010).

The simple fact that the LDS church, like every other religion on the planet, h demands moral authority over any of us is more than enough reason to examine their claims about reality—and oppose them if they are wrong. Sex researchers Darrel Ray and Amanda Brown compiled a tremendous amount of data on the impact of religion upon sexuality. Unsurprisingly, their findings demonstrated that fundamentalist religions employ more guilt than liberal ones. Slightly more surprising was that the Mormons topped the list for levels of guilt about sex over all other denominations, even significantly above Catholics.[iii]

As I write this in early 2012, two of the leading Republican presidential candidates are Mormons, which would seem to imply that a significant number of Americans feel okay with a leader of the free world wearing sacred undergarments. I have a problem with this.

And let's face it, Mormonism is hilariously entertaining to outsiders, as *South Park's* Trey Parker and Matt Stone have long known. The 2003 *South Park* episode "All About Mormons" was a spot-on look at Mormon doctrine and origins, and their 1998 comedy *Orgazmo* featured an LDS missionary turned pornstar. But it's their Broadway smash *The Book of Mormon* that has really shown off the entertainment value of Mormon doctrine and practice.

A word of caution: No one likes a jerk, even if—maybe especially if—they're right about what they're talking about. So the information presented here is not just so that you can be a wiseass about it to your Mormon acquaintances (though that is an option), but so that you'll be equipped for a good conversation the next time a pair of LDS missionaries come knocking on your door. If, instead of telling them to shove off, you invite them in for an enjoyable and enlightening chat, then I will be a very happy author indeed. And you will have made the world a better place.

David Fitzgerald

Some Fun Facts

The Church of Jesus Christ of Latter-day Saints reports[iv] a worldwide membership of over 14 million, including 28,660 congregations organized into stakes, wards and branches, along with local auxiliary organizations (Relief Society, Sunday School, Young Men, Young Women and Primary), as well as a Church-operated educational system, welfare system and missionary program. Few American religions can match them for sheer devotion and manpower.

It's not uncommon for members to spend up to twenty hours a week in unpaid church work. They give up two meals a month and give the money saved on food to fund the Church's internal welfare system for members in need. When other mainstream faiths are losing the younger generation, Mormons continue to build a hard-working, committed workforce by placing high expectations and a demanding schedule on their young people. Throughout high school, they are required to spend an hour a day in church classes, on top of their regular schoolwork.

Every year, over 52,000 self-funded volunteer Mormon missionaries (most between the ages of 19 and 25, but retired couples as well) are active across nearly 350 missions around the world, distributing church materials translated into over 166 languages. It claims to be the fourth largest religion in the United States and the sixth largest Christian denomination internationally—even if the overwhelming majority of Christian denominations don't consider them Christian at all.

Mormon Royalty

Ultimately, the church is controlled by fifteen old white men. The supreme leader is the President, also known as the First Elder, the Presiding High Priest, and the "President, Prophet, Seer and Revelator." According to Mormon scriptures, he is the only living prophet on earth; no one may receive commandments and revelations but him. He has been given the keys of the mysteries and the revelations which are sealed, and authority to counsel and dictate to the Saints on all matters from the greatest to the most trifling. His word even takes precedence over earlier prophets, and he can clarify, correct or change any prior prophet's teachings, even those of Joseph Smith himself.

His number 2 and 3 men are the First Counselor and Second Counselor. Together, this holy trinity is referred to as the First Presidency. Directly below them is the Quorum of the Twelve Apostles. All fifteen men hold their positions for life; when the President dies, the longest serving apostle becomes the new President. The church leadership is often referred to as "the Brethren," an apt name, seeing that there are no women in any quorum; females are officially forbidden from the priesthood and positions of authority. Nonwhite men are unofficially forbidden from the two highest quorums, though there are a handful of non-Caucasians in the next lowest tier of general authorities, the Quorum of Seventy.

Apostles in the top two tiers of church power come from a very rarified pool of candidates: virtually all have come from so-called "Mormon Royalty"—a handful of profoundly interconnected power families with impeccable pedigrees. Though not acknowledged openly by most Saints, nepotism runs fast and furious throughout the church. Those Mormons with an ancestor like Joseph Smith or Brigham Young stand a much greater chance of being considered more spiritual and getting a good power position. The same holds for those who marry into the big name families of the church, revered names like Smith, Young, McKay, Pratt, Kimball, Benson, Hinckley, Monson, Leavitt, Lund, Richards, Romney, Lee, Packer, and others, all deeply intertwined through marriage.

How connected are they? In 2004, when two relative outsiders were admitted into the Quorum of Twelve Apostles, all fifteen leaders of the church were related to current or former general authorities of the church. Five were directly related to each other, and four others were related to each other by marriage. Four were directly related to former LDS Presidents, five to former apostles. Two had wives who were direct descendants of former presidents, five had wives directly related to former apostles, and seven had wives who were related by blood or marriage to current general authorities. In 2004, only one apostle had no blood ties to any other general authority—though his wife was related to several current general authorities and was the direct descendent of a former apostle. Like any corporate entity, it has its internal squabbles, power struggles, and office politics, but at heart, the Mormon Church is very much a family-run business—and it is a big business...

Show Me the Money

Although the church does not disclose its finances, it has long been widely recognized as the wealthiest church per capita in America.[v] *Time* Magazine put the church's total assets at "a minimum of $30 billion" in 1997; in their 1999 book *Mormon America* investigative journalists Richard and Joan K. Ostling conservatively estimated church assets at least $25-$30 billion, adding it was likely "well beyond that." The church criticized these numbers as excessive—but without offering any hint of what the real figures might be. The church's financial growth is fueled by "sacred taxation," i.e., tithing. To be in good standing, all faithful Mormons must tithe, that is, give 10 percent of their gross (*not* net) income to the church, and it's not unheard of for some Mormons to pay a double tithe. The Ostlings' research concluded that as of the mid-1990s, annual tithing revenue was likely between $4.25 and $5.3 billion. That's billion, with a "b," not an "m." Annually.

The Ostlings also found that in addition, the church owns a surprisingly large number of lucrative commercial investments, managed mostly through its Deseret Management Corporation. These holdings bring in another estimated $600 million annually. They include an estimated $6 billion or more in stock and bonds; several insurance companies, including Beneficial Life, a company with $16 billion in insurance and assets of $1.6 billion; media holdings including Bonneville International Corporations, which owns a chain of twenty-five radio stations (seventh-largest in the country), a television station and other media operations; Hawaii Reserves, which manages extensive real estate developments in Hawaii, such as the Disneyesque tourist trap Polynesian Cultural Center, the major source of PCC's labor force, Brigham Young University Hawaii, and nearly every development in the Mormon island town of Laie; and more than 150 farms and ranches (including the largest cattle ranch in America), making the LDS church one of the biggest landowners in the nation, with around 1 million acres of farm and ranch land, roughly equal to the size of the state of Delaware.

Incidentally, the church's religious buildings and property, like the magnificent Salt Lake City Temple, are considered expenses and not sources of revenue. A big focus for church funds is on their humanitarian efforts. Every year tens of millions of dollars are donated to carry out outreach activities in 178 countries, which also happen to contribute to church growth. And like many religions, Mormonism claims to be the fastest growing religious sect in the world. But where did this tax-exempt multi-billion dollar multinational corporation come from?

Endnotes: Introduction

[i] "How sad is your state? Depression rates ranked" Melissa Dahl, msnbc.com, Dec. 4, 2007

[ii] "Porn in the USA: Conservatives Are Biggest Consumers," *New Scientist*, Ewen Callaway, Feb. 28, 2009

[iii] Rey, p. 180. The Mormons beat out everyone in sexual guilt, with Jehovah's Witnesses, Pentecostals and Seventh-Day

Adventists just behind them. Incidentally, the lowest rates of sexual guilt were found in atheists, agnostics, Jews and lowest of all, those frisky Unitarians.

[iv] Source: LDS Newsroom (http://newsroom.lds.org/facts-and-stats); updated April 2011

[v] Source on finances: http://www.pbs.org/mormons/faqs/structure.html

[vi] *Mormon America*, Ch. 7, particularly pp.124-127, and Appendix B

Part One

**A Short, Juicy
and Sometimes
Not Too Pretty
History of the
Church
of Jesus Christ of
Latter-day Saints**

Chapter 1

Angels and Devils

The Burned-Over District

Never in American history has so much religious mania been packed into a single time and place as upstate New York during the 1820s through the 1840s, a time later christened "The Second Great Awakening." The region itself became known as the "Burned-Over District," in honor of the way it was repeatedly overrun by one religious craze after another.

It was an exciting time of promise for a generation still reeling from the fresh new world and unfettered religious liberty created by the American Revolution and exhilarated by the country's "second war of independence" against Britain in 1812. The millennium had never seemed closer at hand, and new religious movements were popping out all over: Jemima Wilkinson, a feverish Quaker woman, became a visionary and founded a celibate colony called Jerusalem at Seneca Lake. Her flock thought she was the Christ; she governed them through regular revelations from heaven and swore she would never die. A modern-day John the Baptist named Isaac Bullard, clothed only in his beard and a bearskin girdle, gathered a following of pilgrims in Woodstock, Vermont, before crossing into New York. As perhaps befitting a hippie from Woodstock, he championed free love and decried both private property and cleanliness— calling washing a sin and bragging he had not changed his clothes in seven years.

Following the biblical scholarship of William Miller, a farmer and uneducated Baptist lay minister, the Millerite sect proclaimed Christ was coming back to end the world on or before 1843. This was later updated to some time between March 21, 1843 and March 21, 1844. After that date came and went, the date for Jesus' return was re-recalculated to April 18, 1844. Then to October 22, 1844. Following the "Great Disappointment" of this day, Millerite scholars continued to predict still more dates while the group repeatedly hemorrhaged disappointed followers, who left in droves. Other bewildered Millerites began to expect Christ's second coming at any moment, day after day after day, until they finally gave up and become Adventists (the Seventh-Day Adventist Church is the biggest surviving descendent of the movement).

The Shakers had come to New England and set up a communal farm in central New York where they prepared for the coming kingdom of God with spirit-driven dancing, shaking, singing and shouting (and furniture making). While the Shakers ensured their eventual extinction by giving up sex and marriage, not too far away, the utopian collective Oneida Community pretty much encouraged everyone to sleep with everyone, a doctrine their leader, John Humphrey Noyes, called "Complex Marriage" (he also coined the term "Free Love"). Noyes often determined who would sleep with whom, and would pair up the less devout members with more faithful members in hopes that their devotion would rub off on them. Older men and women were also encouraged to introduce teenagers to sex, at least until Noyes was tipped off about a warrant for his arrest on charges of statutory rape and fled the country in the middle of the night, never to return.

Another utopian colony was the socialist commune Community Place in Skaneateles, New York, inspired by the French philosopher Charles Fourier. In addition to all these nonconformist religious movements and utopian experiments, it was also a time of social radicals like the pioneering feminist Elizabeth Cady Stanton. Even the old-line mainstream faiths were not immune to the revolutionary new mania in the air; the

Methodists, Baptists and Presbyterians were constantly splitting off into new splinter groups.

But even while some were boldly marching towards the glorious new future, your average early 1800s American still lived in a surprisingly rich world of pervasive superstition and widespread folk belief in the occult. Spirits, ghosts and spooks haunted the backwoods. Hedge-wizards, treasure-hunters and dowsers employed divining rods, magic amulets and talismans to uncover Indian treasures and lost Spanish gold. People thrilled to the New England ghost stories of Ichabod Crane being chased by a ghostly headless horseman, and Rip Van Winkle encountering the little people of the mountains and sleeping for 20 years. The mysterious stranger you met at the crossroads by moonlight might later turn out to be an angel, or the Devil himself.

Out of this giddy free-for-all of philosophical/religious upheaval and rustic folk magic came Joseph Smith.

Meet Joseph Smith

In March 1826, a court in Bainbridge, New York,

convicted twenty-one-year-old Joseph Smith, Jr. of being "a disorderly person and an impostor." Smith admitted at his trial to defrauding citizens being a "glass-looker"—organizing gold-digging expeditions and also to claiming to possess dark or "necromantic" powers, namely, being able to use a magic "seer-stone" to find hidden treasure, a not uncommon practice at the time.

"Jo" Smith, as he was known, along with his father and brother Hyrum, had been members of a small band of "money-diggers," treasure-hunters who made their living searching for ancient treasures, buried coins, lost property and the like. Joseph didn't do any of the actual digging; his specialty was more delicate, as his unhappy future father-in-law and brother-in-law later described:

"...his occupation was that of seeing, or pretending to see by means of a stone placed in his hat, and his hat closed over his face. In this way he pretended to discover minerals and hidden treasures."[vii]

"Joe Smith never handled one shovel of earth in those diggings. All Smith did was to peep with stone and hat, and give directions where and how to dig...Smith said if he should work with his hands at digging there, he would lose the power to see with the stone."[viii]

In October of 1825, Joseph had put on a demonstration of his clairvoyant powers for Josiah Stowell (19-century spelling is a bit idiosyncratic—some sources spell the name Stoal or Stowel), an elderly, well-to-do farmer, and a relative of one of his gold-digging partners. Using only his peep stone (and perhaps information fed to him by his partner), Joseph described Stowell's farm so accurately that the farmer, convinced of his psychic abilities, asked him to come to Pennsylvania, where local legend said there was a long-lost Spanish silver mine. A hunter by the name of Isaac Hale boarded the diggers at his home, and initially helped subsidize the expedition, but he was swiftly disillusioned with the group's chief treasure-detector, Joseph. He contemptuously described him as a careless young man, not very well educated, and very saucy and insolent to his father. He remarked that Joseph gave the 'money-diggers' great encouragement at first, but each time they dug where he assured them an immense treasure lay buried, he would then declare that the enchantment on the Spaniards' riches was so great he could not see, or that an angel or mischievous ghost had spirited the treasure further away through the earth. Soon the diggers had become sick of the wild golden goose chase, and began to leave. But the treasure hunt went on for another several months before Stowell's relatives caught wind of the situation and had Joseph arrested for fraud.

According to the trial record, Joseph did not deny that he used a peep stone to search for treasure. On the contrary, he attempted to defend himself by claiming his crystal-gazing powers were genuine and he was not out to deceive anybody. Josiah Stowell and another witness fervently vouchsafed for his psychic abilities, but the court was not impressed and found him guilty. For decades Mormon scholars denied the occurrence of this court trial. Dr. Francis W. Kirkham stated:

"If any evidence had been in existence that Joseph Smith had used a seer stone for fraud and deception, and especially had he made this confession in a court of law as early as 1826, or four years before the Book of Mormon was printed, and this confession was in a court record, it would have been impossible for him to have organized the restored Church."
(*A New Witness For Christ In America*, vol. 1, pp. 385-87)

Then, in 1971, the original 1826 court record was discovered in the basement of the County Jail in Norwich, New York.

In the court record, Joseph confessed that he had been offering his services as a seer for the last three years, which put his money-digging activities from 1823 to 1826. To put it another way, Joseph was operating as a con artist, during the same time he would later claim he was preparing himself to be worthy of receiving the gold plates that an angel had told him lay buried near his home. [ix]

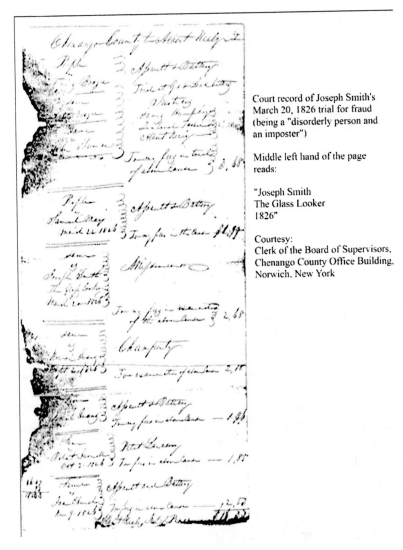

Court record of Joseph Smith's March 20, 1826 trial for fraud (being a "disorderly person and an imposter")

Middle left hand of the page reads:

"Joseph Smith
The Glass Looker
1826"

Courtesy:
Clerk of the Board of Supervisors, Chenango County Office Building, Norwich, New York

Mormon spin doctors like Gordon Madsen and LDS Historical Department Manager Richard Turley tried to mitigate the damage from this discovery by pointing to Stowell's adamant refusal to admit he had been deceived or defrauded. They even contended that Smith was found not guilty and discharged, echoing statements by early Mormon leaders like Oliver Cowdery, who in 1835 said that although Smith had been accused, the charges were groundless and "he was honorably acquitted."[x]

Cowdery was only telling half the truth. In 1830, Smith was twice re-arrested for failure to abide by the conditions of his release, and at both legal proceedings was acquitted on the grounds that the statute of limitations had run out on the original charges. Besides, if they had known about Cowdery's 1835 statement, it's difficult to accept their longstanding insistence that there had never been a trial at all in the first place! But the facts of the trial records are indisputable: Joseph was found guilty of fraud.

From Prisoner to Prophet

Despite this, within four years he was back in the local newspapers as the discoverer of the "Book of Mormon." Smith had several advantages for the prophet biz. He had a pedigree—his maternal grandfather Solomon Mack was a religious dissenter and a mystic haunted in his old age by heavenly lights and voices. Mack published a poorly spelled autobiography of his troubled life and extraordinary visions, complete with some original hymns. His father, Joseph Sr., also had a series of seven visions from 1811 to 1819 that convinced him there were no true religions. Joseph's mother, Lucy Mack Smith, had visions of her own, as did her sister. Her brother was a professional faith healer.[xii] Lucy spent much time in prayer and reading the Bible, but no one church could keep her affections. In her biography, she wrote:

> "If I remain a member of no church at all religious people will say I am of the world; and if I join some one of the different denominations, all the rest will say I am in error... This makes them witnesses against each other."[xiii]

Like many of their generation, neither of Joseph's parents had much use for established religion. They never joined any denomination or showed much interest in any of them during his youth. Lucy briefly found Methodist tent revival meetings exciting, but they only further convinced her husband, Joseph Sr., that church people didn't know any more about God than the unchurched. Like her father, Lucy had a strong mystic bent and believed in an intimate, homespun personal god who was always close at hand, speaking to them in dreams, providing everyday miracles or blighting the crops of sinners. She would talk to God as if he were a member of the family. With a family tree so rooted in mysticism, it's no wonder Joseph never had much in the way of reality checks.

Young Joseph Jr. was tall, good looking and charming, with a charismatic presence that filled the room every time he came through the door. His beautiful blue eyes and ready, infectious smile disarmed everyone he met. He had a lively imagination and despite a limited education and poor grammar, had a powerful voice and could transfix listeners with his conviction. He was also fascinated with Indian relics and ruins. Western New York was rich with archeological sites, and there were eight Indian burial mounds near the Smith family farm, which when ransacked were found to contain not merely bones but also quite sophisticated artifacts of stone, copper, and beaten silver. Two equally stupid groups took an interest in them: the first were the gold-digging treasure-seekers armed with witch-hazel divining rods, magic crystals and stuffed toads; the second, religious crackpots who sought the lost tribes of Israel in the New World. Joseph, luckily enough, was a member of both groups.

Joseph's mother wrote that as a youth, young Joseph loved to spin theories about the Moundbuilder Indians:

"During our evening conversations, Joseph would occasionally give us some of the most amusing recitals that could be imagined. He would describe the ancient inhabitants of this continent, their dress, mode of travelings, and the animals upon which they rode; their cities, their buildings, with every particular; their mode of warfare; and also their religious worship. This he would do with as much ease, seemingly, as if he had spent his whole life among them." [xiv]

The First Vision

Every Mormon can tearfully recite the details of Joseph Smith's "First Vision" as laid down in the *History of Joseph Smith, the Prophet* (*History of the Church*, vol. 1, ch. 1-5) and included in every copy of the LDS scripture, *The Pearl of Great Price*. The *Pearl*, in a nutshell, tells us that during a great revival in his area in 1820, 14-year old Joseph was torn between the feuding Baptists, Methodists and Presbyterians, and wondered how he could know which of them was the correct faith. After reading James 1:5 ("If any of you lack wisdom, let him ask of God, that giveth to all men liberally, and upbraideth not; and it shall be given him"), he decided he would put the question to God. So, on a beautiful clear morning in the early spring of 1820, he set off into the woods near his house and for the first time in his life, prayed aloud.

But before he could even ask God which church was the one true faith, he was immediately seized by a malevolent power that completely overcame him. Thick darkness gathered around him, and fearing for his life, he desperately prayed for God to save him. Just when his doom seemed certain, a pillar of light appeared overhead, brighter than the sun, descending gradually until it fell upon him. Instantly he found himself free from the terrible entity. He looked up to see two Personages, indescribably glorious and bright, standing above him in the air. One of them called him by name and pointing to the other, said "This is My Beloved Son. Hear Him!" Joseph immediately asked Jesus which church was right, for it had never occurred to him that they might all be wrong. But the Lord answered that he should join none of them, for all of them were corrupt and their creeds were an abomination to him—well, maybe Jesus didn't say *exactly* that...

You see, it may *not* have been God the Father and Jesus— it could have been two angels, or many angels, or just Jesus, or just a lone angel, or just a spirit. And he may not have been only 14 years old—it may have been when he was 15, or perhaps it was when he was 16. Or 17. Or 21. And it may not have been in response to a local revival in 1820—since records show there was none in the area then. It may have come about from his own personal Bible study convicting him of his sins. Or from uncertainty over whether God existed. Or from no reason at all—he was the lucky one to whom a spirit appeared with news of a hidden golden treasure. Or maybe there was no spirit at all, and he discovered the plates during his gold-digging career using a magic "seer-stone" he discovered while digging a well. Or perhaps it wasn't a magic sorcerer stone he used, but nothing less than an ancient holy relic, the Urim and Thummim. All these possibilities have been floated at various times.

And speaking of seer-stones, there may not have been any Urim and Thummim at all—it wasn't until 1833 (in *The Evening and Morning Star*, Jan. 1833) that Joseph Smith's scribe and famous Mormon hymnist William W. Phelps first suggested that perhaps the seer stones were the Urim and Thummim described in the Old Testament. Church historians were happy to rewrite the official church history to make it seem that the peep stone Joseph used to translate the Book of Mormon had been referred to as the Urim and Thummim all along. It gave Joseph's story more credibility to say venerable Old Testament artifacts were used to translate the Book of Mormon instead of a magical peep stone Joseph had found while digging a well... [xv]

There are in fact at least ten different—some radically different—known versions of the "First Vision."* Although Joseph claimed he was persecuted when he told people of his heavenly vision, in reality there is no evidence that Joseph told *anyone* about the vision until after the Book of Mormon was published many years later. There are no accounts in local newspapers, by neighbors, preachers or even by the members of Joseph's own family.[xvi] The familiar official version above wasn't even written until 1838, and didn't finally appear in print until 1842. It is, in fact, the fourth version of the story Smith told.

*And incidentally, all the different vision accounts are similar to other early 19th century accounts of religious visions that appeared in print before Joseph began his career. See "Having Visions in the Early 1800s Wasn't That Strange" on the MormonThink.com website. (http://mormonthink.com/firstvision web.htm#having)

The *First* First Vision: The "Strange Account"

The earliest known version was found in Joseph Smith's personal letterbook, written in 1832, ten years before the official account of the First Vision, but still 12 years after the fact. It is the only version handwritten by Joseph Smith himself—complete with bad grammar and spelling errors. In this unfinished version, sometimes referred to as "Joseph's Strange Account," young Joseph searches the Bible from the age of 12 to 15 and decides (all on his own this time) that all of the Christian churches have strayed from the truth. There is no word of him going to the grove near his home, or of a struggle with any forces of darkness. Instead, while he is praying from an unspecified locale, a pillar of light [in the manuscript Joseph first wrote "a piller (sic) of fire" but crossed out 'fire' and replaced it with 'light'] brighter than noontime sun comes down and fills him with the spirit of God. The heavens open and Joseph sees Jesus alone, who tells him his sins are forgiven. [xvii]

This alternate version never saw the light of day; for 130 years it was locked away in the vault of the LDS Church Historian's Office. The rare researchers who actually knew of its existence, and could obtain the necessary permission to see it, were forbidden to copy it or disclose its contents. [xviii] But the document was eventually forgotten, and unfortunately for the church, so was its security risk... It first appeared quite by accident in 1965, in a BYU student's graduate thesis— ironically enough, he was trying to gather information to support the first vision story. Not realizing the dangerous implications, he included it as an appendix to his thesis. [xix] It was swiftly seized upon and published as *Joseph Smith's Strange Account of the First Vision*. Four years later, the church historical department at last reluctantly released a public statement confirming the manuscript's authenticity. [xx]

Joseph Smith's 1832 "Strange Account" of his First Vision.

This earliest known version (and the only one handwritten by Joseph Smith himself, complete with bad grammar and spelling errors) contradicts the official version on several points. You can also see the changes he's making to the story as he goes along; for instance, in lines 14 & 15, where he has replaced "a piller (sic) of fire" with one of "light."
Source: *Brigham Young University Studies,* Spring 1969 issue, page 281

The Even Stranger Account

An acquaintance of the Smith family, Willard Chase, related an even stranger story of the first vision, told to him by Joseph Smith's father, set down in an 1833 affidavit and published in Eber Howe's *Mormonism Unvailed* (sic). In this downright spooky account, there are no appearances by Jesus, God, or fiery pillars of light. Instead, the story is filled with black magic, ghosts and D&D-style run-ins with shape-shifting monsters:

"I became acquainted with the Smith family, known as the authors of the Mormon Bible, in the year 1820. At that time, they were engaged in the money digging business, which they followed until the latter part of the season of 1827.

"... In the month of June, 1827, Joseph Smith, Sen. related to me the following story: 'That some years ago, a spirit had appeared to Joseph his son, in a vision, and informed him that in a certain place there was a record on plates of gold, and that he was the person that must obtain them, and this he must do in the following manner: On the 22 of September, he must repair to the place where was deposited this manuscript, dressed in black clothes, and riding a black horse with a switch tail, and demand the book in a certain name, and after obtaining it, he must go directly away, and neither lay it down nor look behind him.

"They accordingly fitted out Joseph with the suit of black clothes, and borrowed a black horse. He repaired to the place of deposit and demanded the book, which was in a stone box, unsealed, and so near the top of the ground that he could see one end of it, and raising it up, took out the book of gold; but fearing someone might discover where he got it, he laid it down to place back the top stone, as he found it; and turning around, to his surprise there was no book in sight.

"He again opened the box, and in it saw the book, and

attempted to take it out, but was hindered. He saw in the box something like a toad, which soon assumed the appearance of a man, and struck him on the side of his head. – Not being discouraged at trifles, he again stooped down and strove to take the book, when the spirit struck him again, and knocked him three or four rods, and hurt him prodigiously. After recovering from his fright, he inquired why he could not obtain the plates; to which the spirit made reply, because you have not obeyed your orders.'"

Long story short, Joseph eventually prevailed over the gold book's toad-man spirit guardian. He then met Martin Harris, who would prove very useful in the translation efforts, thanks to traits like those shown here:

"… He met one day in the streets of Palmyra, a rich man, whose name was Martin Harris, and addressed him thus: 'I have a commandment from God to ask the first man I meet in the street to give me fifty dollars, to assist me in doing the work of the Lord by translating the "Golden Bible".' Martin being naturally a credulous man, hands Joseph the money."
(cited in Eber D. Howe, *Mormonism Unvailed*, 1834, pp. 240-248)

The Indiana Jones Account

Joseph Smith's new friend Martin Harris, a rich man who would not be staying rich for much longer, had a very different story of his own to tell: According to Martin, Joseph Smith had been a member of a seven-man treasure-hunting party searching for ancient Indian gold. For this work, Joseph had a special tool—a mystical peep stone that Willard Chase had uncovered while digging a well. When he peered into it, "he could see many things." Using this magic seer stone, on the dawn of September 22, 1827, 21-year old Joseph discovered an amazing treasure atop a hill two miles north of Manchester. The find was not buried, but simply hidden within a modest pile of stones: four stones set up and covered by a flat stone.

Amazingly, this modest pile of five stones atop a hill just two miles from town had apparently remained undisturbed for thousands of years, because under the capstone were gold plates, and under them, two stones set in a little silver bow like a pair of spectacles. The plates would later turn out to be the Book of Life, or the Book of Mormon, and the spectacles to be the Urim and Thummim, a magical translation device.

When his fellow gold-digger partners learned of this find, they were furious and called Joseph a traitor for holding out on them, claiming that as his cohorts they had a right to the treasure, too. Afraid of his partners, Joseph hid the plates in various places, until an anonymous angel warned him to remove them and to have nothing more to do with his band of money-diggers, because they were wicked. The angel then told him to go look in the spectacles, and he would show him the man who would assist him: Martin Harris.

Joseph sought out Martin and told him all this. But clearly no dummy, Martin went and investigated Joseph's story first by going to Joseph's wife and family, talking with them separately to get the truth of the matter. It checked out: their stories agreed. Convinced, he returned to the village, only to find the town was in an uproar over the discovery, and a mob threatened to tar and feather Joseph, demanding that he couldn't leave until he showed the plates. Martin saw it was not safe for Joseph to remain, so he advised him to pay all his debts and hide out at his father-in-law's in Pennsylvania. But as Joseph was temporarily low on cash, Martin paid them for him, and furnished him with still more money for his escape.

What First Vision?

Needless to say, none of the flock was ever given the spooky voodoo version or the occult treasure-hunter version. In fact, for over a decade, no one seems to have been told about the First Vision at all. Assistant LDS church historian Dr. James B. Allen made some startling revelations in a 1966 article (*Dialogue: A Journal of Mormon Thought*, Autumn 1966, pages 29-45), where he admitted that for the entire decade of the 1830s, the First Vision was inexplicably absent from every Church publication, all the available contemporary writings about Joseph Smith, every contemporary journal or correspondence yet discovered, and that "the general membership of the Church knew little, if anything, about it."

The 1833 *Book of Commandments*, forerunner to the *Doctrine and Covenants*, made no mention of Joseph's first vision, despite having several references to the Book of Mormon and its origin. When the *Doctrine and Covenants* itself came along two years later in 1835, the first vision was still conspicuously absent, even though its preface declared that it contained "the leading items of religion which we have professed to believe." Interestingly, the D&C contained a series of seven "Lectures on Faith," which discuss the church doctrine that God and Jesus are two separate personages of the Godhead—but oddly, makes no mention of them appearing to Joseph Smith.

The First Vision never appeared in the early Mormon periodicals of that time like *The Evening and Morning Star* or the *Latter-day Saints Messenger and Advocate*—not even when Joseph's no. 2 man Oliver Cowdery published a series of letters dealing with the origin of the church, with Joseph's approval. Nor did it make it into the *Voice of Warning*, the church's first important missionary pamphlet, even though it featured long sections of information for missionaries on basic topics like fulfillment of prophecy, the Book of Mormon, external evidence of the book's authenticity, the resurrection, and the nature of revelation—virtually everything *except* the first vision.

A Second First Vision

Stranely enough (or perhaps not so strangely by now), Joseph Smith also completely neglected to mention his First Vision when he wrote the first LDS church history three years later in 1835. Joseph Smith and Oliver Cowdery wrote a history of the church meant to highlight all of the important points of its beginning.

Cowdery insisted that Joseph's vision occurred in 1823 and that his age at the time was 17, not 15. He blamed a printer's typo for the "error," contradicting both Joseph's earlier account and the official version today. In this first official church history, [xxii] young Joseph longed to discover which church, if any, he should join. This was inspired by the local religious revival in Palmyra (which really did happen in 1823, contrary to his first account which falsely claimed it had happened in 1820). Unsure if there was a god, but paradoxically, anxious to have his sins forgiven, he began secretly calling for a sign from heaven. Then, on the evening of September 21, 1823, as he lay in bed praying, a sudden brilliant burst of light filled his room. It was an angel in dazzling white raiment with a special message for Joseph: the Lord had chosen him to be his instrument to restore the true faith. He also told him of ancient scriptures written on gold plates buried nearby...

These are only half of the versions we know of, not even counting the ones that were later told by others like Brigham Young and other church leaders. But if you're already confused over all these differing accounts, you're not alone. Members of the church didn't even hear about the First Vision until 1842, and even then it wasn't given much importance. Researcher David Persuitte noted that even after the story of the "first" vision was finally published, there was lingering confusion among many Mormons over just what *was* Joseph's first vision. For several decades after his death, Mormon writers didn't refer to the 1820 appearance of God and Jesus as Joseph's first religious experience. Instead, they pointed to Joseph's 1823 vision of an angel—an angel named Moroni... [xxiii]

***

For further reading:

Two must-reads for anyone interested in Mormonism:

For the definitive biography of Joseph Smith: Fawn M. Brodie, *No Man Knows My History: The Life of Joseph Smith* (New York: Vintage, 1995)

For an engrossing history of Joseph Smith and the early Mormon church, and a searing look at the current-day polygamist fundamentalists, including a grisly double murder committed by members of one Mormon splinter group: Jon Krakauer, *Under the Banner of Heaven* (New York: Anchor, 2004)

For authoritative and balanced analysis of Joseph Smith's trial from an LDS scholar that repudiates other LDS attempts at sanitizing Smith's guilty verdict: Dan Vogel, "Rethinking the 1826 Judicial Decision,"
www.mormonscripturestudies.com/ch/dv/1826.asp

For more discussion on Joseph's evolving story of the founding of the church, and the parts of the story that don't hold up (and much more), see "The First Vision" on the excellent Mormonthink.com website:
http://www.mormonthink.com/firstvisionweb.htm
#therareseveral

Endnotes: Chapter 1

[vii] Isaac Hale's affidavit, published in the *Susquehanna Register*, May 1, 1834
[viii] Alva Hale, to his cousin Joseph Lewis, in *Amboy Journal*, June 11, 1879
[ix] "Joseph Smith's 1826 Trial: The Legal Setting," *Brigham Young University Studies* 30, Spring 1990, p.105
[x] *Latter Day Saints' Messenger and Advocate*, October 2, 1835, p. 201
[xi] Persuitte, pp. 96-97
[xii] Brodie, pp. 411-412

[xiii] Lucy Smith, *Biographical Sketches of Joseph Smith the Prophet and His Progenitors for Many Generations,* Liverpool, England, 1853 p. 37

[xiv] Brigham H. Roberts, *Studies of the Book of Mormon,* Salt Lake City: Signature Books, 1992, p. 243

[xv] Jerald and Sandra Tanner, *The Changing World of Mormonism,* pp. 80-83. See also B.H. Roberts' comment in *Comprehensive History of The Church of Jesus Christ of Latter-day Saints,* vol.1, page129—thanks to MormonThink's Ken Clark for this point

[xvi] http://mormonthink.com/firstvisionweb.htm#significant

[xvii] *BYU Studies,* Spring 1969, pp. 278ff; it can also be found in Dean C. Jessee's *The Personal Writings of Joseph Smith,* Salt Lake City: Deseret Books, 1984, pp. 14ff

[xviii] Tanner, *The Changing World of Mormonism,* pp. 150-151

[xix] Cheesman, Paul R. "An Analysis of the Accounts Relating Joseph Smith's Early Visions," M. A. thesis, Brigham Young University, 1965. The 1832 account appears in Appendix D

[xx] *Brigham Young University Studies,* Spring 1969, pp. 277-78

[xxi] Interview with Martin Harris, *Tiffany's Monthly,* 1859, New York: Published by Joel Tiffany, vol. v.—12, pp. 163-170

[xxii] LDS *Messenger and Advocate,* Kirtland, Ohio, Dec. 1834, vol.1, no.3

[xxiii] Persuitte, p. 23; for a list of statements from church leaders, see http://mormonthink.com/firstvisionweb.htm#thefirstvision

Chapter 2

Dropping the BOM

From Psychic to Prophet

Despite the guilty verdict at his 1826 trial, Joseph Smith continued to work for Josiah Stowell and occasionally still search for the Spaniards' fabled silver mine; old Stowell never lost faith in Joseph's psychic powers. Joseph also continued to make visits to Emma, the daughter of his former host, Isaac Hale. As a boarder in Isaac's house, Joseph had fallen hard for his quiet, dark-haired daughter. Unfortunately, Isaac despised him, and when young Joseph asked for her hand in marriage, the burly Vermonter threw him out of the house. But Isaac was frequently out hunting, and Joseph stole away to visit her as often as he could when her father was away. On January 18, 1827, he finally convinced her to run away and elope with him.

They lived with Joseph's parents for eight months before they dared return to face the wrath of her father. Joseph's friend and neighbor Peter Ingersoll drove them there in his wagon, and reported what happened: Isaac, normally a big bear of a man, met them in tears, saying "You have stolen my daughter and married her. I had much rather have followed her to her grave." He accused Joseph of being a feckless charlatan who spent all his time trying to deceive people with his crystal-gazing scam. In response, Ingersoll said:

"Joseph wept, and acknowledged he could not see in a

stone now, nor never could; and that his former pretensions in that respect, were all false. He then promised to give up his old habits of digging for money and looking into stones."[xxiv]

Isaac, somewhat mollified, told Joseph if he would give up his crazy schemes and start working hard to earn an honest living he would help him. Joseph readily agreed.

Touched by an Angel

About a year later, a new rumor spread through town: local boy Jo Smith had discovered an incredible ancient treasure atop the big hill on the turnpike just outside Manchester township. No two people in Palmyra had the same version of the story,[xxv] and for a long time Joseph himself was extremely reluctant to talk about the discovery; it wouldn't be until he set out to write the official church history in 1838 that the details would finally come out.

To make a very long, convoluted and contradictory story short, one day Joseph Smith announced to his family that he had been visited three times in a single night (September 21, 1823) by a white-skinned native American angel named Moroni. The angel had told him of a fabulous book, written upon gold plates, which explained the origins of the Indians as well as the truths of the gospel. Conveniently, the treasure trove was atop a nearby knoll just outside of town, the "hill Cumorah," which incidentally was also the site of an ancient battlefield. Joseph found it hidden just where the angel said— in a crude stone box under a large stone, where it had lain undisturbed for fourteen hundred years. Using a lever, he pried open the lid and gazed inside.

The book was there, made of thin gold plates about eight inches square, painstakingly engraved with ancient characters and bound together with three huge metal rings. Along with the marvelous golden book was the Sword of Laban, a fine-honed blade made of precious steel with a hilt of pure gold, an ancient breastplate and two magic stones, the Urim and Thummim, that would enable Smith himself to translate the

31

book. But before he could remove them, the angel forbade him, and warned him that the time to bring them forth would not be for another four years. First, Joseph would have to return there on precisely the same day each year to be instructed by the angel about the Lord's plans for the coming kingdom. So Joseph obeyed, and after more visions over several years, he was finally permitted to bring the golden book and its attendant treasures home with him on September 21, 1827, about eighteen months after his conviction for fraud.

Then again, it may have not happened that way at all. Joseph's longtime childhood friend Peter Ingersoll had an interesting insider's account of how these events had unfolded. According to Peter, Joseph told him one day he had brought home a bundle of fine white sand tied up in his frock. When his family asked him what he was carrying, a mischievous impulse entered his mind. Joseph told him:

"At that moment, I happened to think of what I had heard about a history found in Canada, called the "Golden Bible," so I very gravely told them it was the "Golden Bible." To my surprise, they were credulous enough to believe what I said. Accordingly I told them that I had received a commandment to let no one see it, for, says I, no man can see it with the naked eye and live. However, I offered to take out the book and show it to them, but they refused to see it, and left the room. Now," he concluded, "I have got the damn fools fixed and will carry out the fun." [xxvi]

Joseph took his fun game a step further. He made a box from clapboards as a chest for his "Golden Bible," and put it in a pillowcase for a covering. He let people lift it and feel it through the case. But he was forced to refuse to show the "Golden Plates" to anybody and change their hiding place frequently, since if anyone else so much as laid eyes on them they would instantly die.

This did not stop others from trying to get their hands on the gold plates. Willard Chase brought in a conjure man from sixty miles away and hired him to divine their hiding place, which alarmed Joseph so badly he moved them from under the family hearthstone to a spot under the floorboards of a cooper's shop across the street. But Chase's sister Sally had better luck, and found this new hiding spot with nothing but her own green seer stone (and perhaps some feminine wiles). Willard and his cohorts descended upon the hapless barrelmaker's shop, tearing up the floor in their efforts to root out Joseph's homemade clapboard treasure chest. But when they found it, the chest was empty. Furious, they demolished it. Joseph later announced that he had seen all this trouble coming, and had removed the treasure, renailed the box and replaced it back under floorboards. The plates were still safe and sound underneath a pile of flax.

Joseph's game continued to swiftly gain momentum; soon it had snowballed beyond the point that he could stop it. Virtually everyone in town seemed to believe his story. Martin Harris not only accepted the story, he freely elaborated on it and began talking excitedly about financing the publication of the "Golden Bible," even promising to pay Joseph's considerable debts so he would be free to take on the great work. If Joseph hadn't already been planning on taking his stunt to the next level all along, this promising development removed all doubts.

Stepping Up to the Plates

Between the curiosity seekers and the angry mobs threatening to tar and feather Joseph if he didn't pony up the "Golden Plates", it was impossible for Joseph to get any work done at home. So with Martin Harris' financial backing, Joseph and Emma fled his nosy family and rapacious neighbors (according to one account, the plates were hidden in a barrel of beans during the trip), and moved to a house owned by her father in Pennsylvania. He then set about translating "the "Golden Bible" into English. Old timey, King James English, oddly enough. Lo and behold, the book turned out to contain an unbelievable tale. As the Book of Mormon's official introduction puts it today:

"The book was written by many ancient prophets by the spirit of prophecy and revelation. Their words, written on gold plates, were quoted and abridged by a prophet-historian named Mormon. The record gives an account of two great civilizations. One came from Jerusalem in 600 BC, and afterward separated into two nations, known as the Nephites and the Lamanites. The other came much earlier when the Lord confounded the tongues at the Tower of Babel. This group is known as the Jaredites. After thousands of years, all were destroyed except the Lamanites, and they are the principal ancestors of the American Indians."

Translating the ancient text was quite a remarkable process. Initially, the prophet faced a serious problem: he was only semi-literate. He could read a little, but he could not write well. So he needed someone better educated to take down his inspired dictation. His first scribe was his wife Emma. She was amazed by his ability to translate the ancient inscriptions without even looking at them. He was able to read them perfectly well just by peering through the stones of the Urim and Thummim, even though the plates were wrapped in a small linen tablecloth.

Martin Harris, Joseph Smith's secretary, witness to the plates, and frequent financial patron. Harris was the perfect storm of credulousness and credit rating.

After Emma, the next secretary would be their patron Martin Harris. Harris had a reputation as a strong believer in "dreams, ghosts and hobgoblins,"[xxviii] already well experienced with things other folk might find extraordinary. He met Jesus one day in the shape of a deer, and walked and talked with him for a few miles. He also had to often contend with the Devil, who looked like a jackass, with very short, smooth hair like a mouse.[xxix] In April of 1828, he came down from Palmyra and moved in with the Smiths to help with the great work. He sat on one side of a blanket hung across the kitchen, and Joseph sat on the other with his translation stones, speaking at him from behind the curtain. The blanket was there for Harris' safety-like Emma, Joseph warned him if anyone tried to catch a glimpse at the plates, or the prophet at work, God's wrath would strike them dead instantly.

Harris obeyed, but doubts still troubled him. His wife also troubled him. For some reason, Mrs. Harris feared her husband was an idiot being played by a con artist for all his money. But how could he prove to her that the plates were real if he couldn't examine them for himself? Then he (or, maybe, she) came up with a great idea. He asked Joseph to write down some of the characters in the inscriptions. He would show them to the leading scholars in New York, so that they could verify the letters were genuine Hebrew. Once noted authorities gave their stamp of approval, their "Golden Bible" would be the archeological discovery of the century. Wasn't Joseph excited?

Shifty Characters

It was a solid plan, but as Joseph explained, the problem was that the plates were not written in Hebrew, but in an altered or "reformed" form of Egyptian. Since engraving on gold plate was such a tedious chore, the Nephite prophet Mormon had chosen to write in that language instead of Hebrew; it required less space. Undeterred, Harris continued to insist anyway. Eventually Joseph gave in and handed over a sheet with some of the ancient characters. Exposing the text to expert examination was a relatively safe risk for Joseph. After all, no one knew how to read ancient Egyptian. He had no way to know that in less than a decade, Champollion would crack the hieroglyphs via the Rosetta stone, so ancient Egyptian would've made a safely undecipherable choice. The assumption would come back to haunt him later more than once.

Harris showed the page to Charles Anthon, Professor of Greek and Latin at Columbia College. According to Joseph's autobiography, Harris' meeting went like this:

"Professor Anthony (sic) stated that the translation was correct, more so than any he had before seen translated from the Egyptian. I then showed him those which were not yet translated, and he said they were Egyptian, Chaldeac, Assyriac, and Arabic, and he said they were the true characters." [xxx]

Harris said (at least, Joseph *said* Harris said) the professor also gave him a certificate of authenticity verifying the translation, but before he could leave with it, Prof. Anthon asked him where the gold plates came from. When Harris began to excitedly tell him about the angel, Anthon asked for his certificate back, ripped it up in disgust and suggested that the plates be brought to him for a translation. Harris told him it was forbidden—that part of the record was sealed. Anthon curtly replied, "I cannot read a sealed book," and showed him the door. [xxxi]

Crestfallen, Harris returned to Joseph with the bad news, but after he mentioned Anthon's parting words, Joseph pulled out his Bible and opened it to Isaiah 29:11, where he read: "And the vision of all is become unto you as the words of a book that is sealed, which men deliver to one that is learned, saying, Read this, I pray thee: and he saith, I cannot; for it is sealed." Martin Harris was dumbfounded—he had fulfilled a prophecy!

When Anthon later learned the Mormons were saying he had verified the writings as authentic, he wrote a furious denial. He had never written any such certificate. There was no such thing as "reformed Egyptian hieroglyphics," and at that time no one had yet translated Egyptian, so it was perfectly ridiculous for Joseph to have him say 'the translation was more correct than any he had ever seen'! In fact, Prof. Anthon had suspected a hoax as soon as he laid eyes on the paper. There were no Egyptian hieroglyphs whatsoever; Joseph's sheet of characters was a mishmash assembled from imaginary figures and garbled letters from a mix of Greek, Hebrew and Roman alphabets, some drawn backwards or sidewise. At the bottom there was a crude drawing of a circle filled with strange markings, as if trying to resemble the Aztec calendar. He had initially thought the letter was an academic hoax, but when he heard about the angel and the magic spectacles, he quickly suspected it was a scheme to milk the farmer for his money, and told him so.*xxxii* But unfortunately for Martin Harris, he would never doubt Joseph again.

The two worked together on the translation for two long months. Progress was excruciatingly slow; it would take all day just to crank out a page or two. By the middle of June, Harris was tired of taking dictation and begged for a break. They had written a grand total of 116 pages, and he was eager to go show them to his wife back in Palmyra. At first Joseph flatly refused, but he finally gave in and let Harris go with the manuscript. Several weeks later, when he still hadn't returned, Emma begged him to go back to New York and find them before something terrible happened to their only copy of the manuscript.

Too late.

Into the Devil's Hands

Joseph returned to Palmyra to find that the manuscript was gone. Harris had arrived to show his wife the first 116 pages of the great work. She was not as impressed with the book that he had staked their entire farm on. As soon as his back was turned she promptly stole all 116 pages. Harris had spent all the weeks since literally tearing up the house to find them, with no luck. She refused to admit where she had hid them, or to even confirm that she hadn't just chucked the whole thing in the fireplace as a work of the devil (which, according to her descendants, is exactly what she did). *xxxiii*

Wretched, Martin Harris bawled, "I have lost my soul! I have lost my soul!" and Joseph cried, "Oh my God! All is lost! What shall I do?" He wept, he groaned, he paced back and forth frantically, he tried to make Harris go and keep looking for it, but he had already looked everywhere. Neither their tearful pleas nor furious outbursts could budge Harris' wife so much as an inch. She simply stood her ground and challenged Joseph to just re-translate those pages—if he could. Surely it would be a snap for a genuine prophet. On a personal note, I have to say I know very little about Lucy Harris, and to be perfectly honest she seems to have been a dreadful harpy. But just for this alone, I think I will always love her... It would seem she really did destroy the manuscript, because it was never seen again. *xxxiv*

After some of the most miserable weeks of his life, Smith announced his first divine revelation. The Lord had told him he could not replicate the original, which, after all, might be in the devil's hands by now and could be corrupted. Sadly, because of one evil woman, that portion of the "Golden Bible," the Book of Lehi, was lost forever. But God in his infinite wisdom had foreseen all this pesky business, and had a backup plan ready to go. He divinely provided a new set of some other, smaller gold plates—the plates of Nephi. Luckily, this second set covered exactly the same time period as the lost manuscript pages; they told a different story, but one that was still *pretty* close. Once Joseph translated the plates of Nephi, he could go back to the original set of plates and carry on—presumably starting with page 117...

Time for a Few Little Changes

With that crisis managed, translation resumed. Unfortunately, the output remained sluggish; despite all his holy resources,

Joseph's work progressed as unevenly as that of, say, any non-divinely inspired novelist. Some days he found that he was 'spiritually blind' and couldn't translate. When this happened, he would tell his secretary that he needed to go out and pray until he was sufficiently humble before God, but Martin Harris noted when Joseph became worn out from translating he would just go out back and throw stones on the river. *xxxv*

A lingering problem was Martin Harris himself. God became displeased with Harris' job performance as a scribe, and in March 1829 gave Joseph another revelation to pass on to him: "...When thou hast translated a few more pages, thou shalt stop for a season..." The Lord even had a replacement lined up: Oliver Cowdery, a gentle, lanky schoolmaster who somewhat resembled a young, better-looking Abraham Lincoln. Cowdery was a distant relation of Joseph's, they were third cousins.*xxxvi* Like Joseph, he was also a former treasure hunter, though he preferred to employ a dowsing rod instead of a seer stone.*xxxvii* This young schoolmaster would go on to become, for a while at least, second in authority over the entire church.

Cowdery stepped in as Joseph's third secretary on April 7, 1829. He was a remarkable improvement from dim Martin Harris, who still kept coming back around to make sure he didn't get left out of the action. The young schoolmaster was serious and bright—and it appears he also had helpful material to supplement the divine revelations (see ch. 9). A few other changes also helped speed things along: by this point, Joseph became tired of using the divine but unwieldy Urim and Thummim, and went back to peering at his trusty seer stone in a hat, just like in his old money-digging days. Fortunately, it worked just as well.*xxxviii*

Joseph had also become bored with working from behind a curtain, and dispensed with it. Since he didn't have to have the plates physically there to translate from them, there was no safety need for a curtain. In fact, it makes you wonder why there had to be any gold plates in the first place if he could just mystically tune in on them from anywhere with his peep stone all along... From here on, work on the book raced along at an impressive clip. Just three months after Cowdery began, they finished the 275,000 word manuscript in the first week of July 1829.

Printer's Devils

After a couple of tries, Joseph found a printer who agreed to print 5000 copies of the book, for $3,000. (To give some perspective, $3,000 in 1830 would be around $73,200 in adjusted dollars today.) Martin Harris guaranteed the money for the printing, even promising to mortgage his ten-thousand-dollar farm to finance the publication of the "Golden Bible," if necessary. His wife had no problem with this, as by now Harris had left her and started an affair with a neighbor's wife. In exchange for her husband, Lucy Harris received a house and eighty acres in the settlement—a real bargain. But printing ground to a halt once an angry committee of concerned citizens caught wind of the project and organized a pre-emptive boycott of the book. The alarmed printer refused to resume work until he had been paid in full.

But there was no money to pay him, nor would there be until Martin Harris mortgaged his farm. Joseph looked in the Urim and Thummim for guidance, and got a revelation to send Oliver Cowdery and Hiram Page, a close friend, to Toronto, where they would find a man eager to buy the copyright for more than enough money to ensure publication. They didn't. It was the first of Joseph's revelations that flat-out failed. Fortunately, the next one didn't. It was a fire-and-brimstone command directly from God almighty to Martin Harris, extorting him to pay the printer's bill. Some highlights:

"I command you to repent—repent, lest I smite you by the rod of my mouth, and by my wrath, and by mine anger, and your sufferings be sore...

I command thee that thou shalt not covet thine own property, but impart it freely to the printing of the Book of Mormon...

And misery thou shalt receive if thou wilt slight these counsels; yea, even the destruction of thyself and property...

Pay the printer's debt! Release thyself from bondage."*xxxix*

Terrified by the surprisingly specific word of the Lord, Harris scrambled to sell his farm and the printer was paid in full. At long last, the "Golden Bible" was published and on March 26, 1830, appeared for sale in the Palmyra bookstore as *The Book of Mormon: an Account Written by the Hand of Mormon, Upon Plates Taken from the Plates of Nephi.*

And that wasn't all.

Joseph's Witnesses

On May 15, 1829, a month before completing the manuscript, Cowdery and Smith had a visit from John the Baptist, who bestowed upon them the Aaronic priesthood. They baptized each other in the Susquehanna River, and then had yet another heavenly visit by the apostles Peter, James and John (incidentally, the apostle John had been alive and on earth all this time, according to later LDS doctrine). Later, Cowdery and a close friend, David Whitmer, announced they had a vision of an angel who showed them the "Golden Plates"; and later that afternoon (or as late as three days later*xl*), Martin Harris told them the same thing happened to him, too.

The trio signed their names to "their testimony," a blanket statement written by Joseph Smith, and became revered by Mormons as "The Three Witnesses"—although in person, all three reportedly told conflicting accounts of what they had seen,*xli* and over time their stories grew more and more elaborate with each retelling. As late as 1882, David Whitmer was still insisting, "These hands handled the plates, these eyes saw the angel, and these ears heard his voice,"*xlii* but when asked if the witnesses actually did "touch" the "real metal," he admitted, "We did not." In another interview he presented an interesting bit of doublespeak, vowing "that he did see and handle the plates," but he did not handle the plates *physically.*[xliii]

Along with Martin Harris, the other two of the "Three Witnesses" to the Golden Plates.

(left) Oliver Cowdery

(right) David Whitmer

Martin Harris didn't take nearly so long to spill the beans. Questioned by a lawyer who asked him outright if he had really seen the plates and their engravings with his own eyes, Harris confessed, that... well, he didn't actually *see* the plates—at least, not with his physical eyes:

"I did not see them as I do that pencil-case, yet I saw them with the eye of faith; I saw them just as distinctly as I see anything around me—though at the time they were covered with a cloth." [xliv]

Joseph must have foreseen that his three witnesses apparently wouldn't quite be up to snuff, since he felt the need to bring in eight *more* witnesses to put their names on another oddly-worded prepared statement pre-written by Joseph himself, testifying that they handled the plates and saw their strange inscriptions. The eight weren't exactly objective outsiders: they were Joseph's own father and two of his brothers, and four brothers and a brother-in-law of David Whitmer. Mark Twain was not terribly impressed by Joseph's selection. In his book *Roughing It* he quipped:

"...when I am far on the road to conviction and eight men, be they grammatical or otherwise, come forward and tell me that they have seen the plates too, and not only seen those plates, but hefted them, I am convinced. I could not feel more satisfied and at rest if the entire Whitmer family had testified."[xlv]

The Emperor's New Witnesses

Martin Harris caused a scandal a few years later, when on March 25, 1838, he publicly let it slip that none of the eleven witnesses saw or handled the physical plates. Martin hastily tried to backpedal from his gaffe, but he only managed to dig the hole deeper. He apologized for calling the testimony of the eight false and insisted that he still knew the Book of Mormon was true—because even though he never saw the plates directly, only as one might see "a city through a mountain," he hefted them repeatedly while they were in a box covered by a handkerchief. But the damage was done. His bombshell caused five high church authorities, including three Apostles, to immediately get up and leave the room—and the church. One of them, former Mormon High Priest Stephen Burnett, wrote three weeks later:

"I have reflected long and deliberately upon the history of this church & weighed the evidence for & against it—loth to give it up—but when I came to hear Martin Harris state in public that he never saw the plates with his natural eyes only in vision or imagination, neither Oliver nor David & also that the eight witnesses never saw them & hesitated to sign that instrument for that reason, but were persuaded to do it, the last pedestal gave way, in my view our foundations was sapped & the entire superstructure fell a heap of ruins..." [xlvi]

Years later, after half of the witnesses had left the church, they gave more details of their "testimony" to Thomas Ford, the Illinois governor. Joseph had first "set them to continual prayer and other spiritual exercises" and then assembled them in a room and produced a box, which he said contained the plates. The lid was opened, the witnesses peeped inside—and the box was ... empty.

The perplexed would-be witnesses said, "Brother Joseph, we do not see the plates." Joseph answered, "Oh ye of little faith! How long will God bear with this wicked and perverse generation? Down on your knees, brethren, every one of you, and pray God for the forgiveness of your sins, and for a holy and living faith which cometh down from heaven." So they dropped to their knees and prayed "for more than two hours with fanatical earnestness" (direct quote) and afterwards, looking into the box, "they were now persuaded that they saw the plates"—again, direct quote. [xlvii]

Incidentally, once the Book of Mormon was translated, all the "Golden Plates", far too holy to remain on earth, were transported back to heaven by the angel Moroni, where they apparently remain to this day. But back on earth, things were only just getting started.

***

For further reading:

D. Michael Quinn, *Early Mormonism and the Magic World View*, (Salt Lake City: Signature Books, 1998)

David Persuitte, *Joseph Smith and the Origins of the Book of Mormon*, 2 Ed., Jefferson, NC: McFarland & Co., 2000)

Grant Palmer, *An Insider's View of Mormon Origins*, (Salt Lake City: Signature Books, 2002)

Jerald & Sandra Tanner, *Changes in Joseph Smith's History*, (Salt Lake City: Utah Lighthouse Ministry, 1965)

Again, Fawn Brodie's *No Man Knows My History* and Jon Krakauer's *Under the Banner of Heaven* are highly recommended (see ch. 1 endnotes)

The *South Park* episode "All About Mormons" (Season 7, episode 12) is a dead-on hilarious and reasonably accurate depiction of Joseph Smith's account of the creation of the Book of Mormon.

Mark Twain's autobiographical *Roughing It* contains some amusing accounts of his run-ins with Mormons.

Endnotes: Chapter 2

[xxiv] cited in Brodie, pp. 438-439

[xxv] ibid., p.37

[xxvi] ibid.

[xxvii] ibid., p. 41

[xxviii] Palmer, 177

[xxix] Vogel, *Early Mormon Documents*, p. 271 —interview with an Episcopal priest in Palmyra in April 1831; two Ohio newspapers printed Harris' description of Jesus and the Devil

[xxx] "History of Joseph Smith," *Times and Seasons*, vol. 3, no. 13, May 2, 1842, p. 773

[xxxi] ibid.

[xxxii] Anthon's letter to E. D. Howe, February 17, 1834, cited in *Mormonism Unvailed*, pp. 270-2

[xxxiii] Stillitoe & Roberts, p.154

[xxxiv] Brodie, p. 55

[xxxv] ibid., p. 61

[xxxvi] Bushman, *JS:BoM*, p. 222; Bushman, *JS:RSR*, p. 578, n.51.

[xxxvii] Vogel, *EMD*, vol. 1: pp. 603-05; 619-20; see also: Quinn, *Early Mormonism and the Magic World View*, pp. 36-39

[xxxviii] Brodie, p. 43; David Whitmer describes, p. 61, pp. 412-413. And again, this assumes that Joseph ever used the "Urim and Thummim" in the first place, which cannot be assumed with any certainty. There are indications that he only ever used his trusty "seer stone" and the "Urim and Thummim" only came into the official story much later.

[xxxix] *Book of Commandments*, Ch. 16, pp. 40-41

[xl] Metcalf, pp. 70-71

[xli] Palmyra *Reflector*, March 19, 1831; cited in Brodie, p.77

[xlii] David Whitmer interview with J.W. Chatburn, *Saint's Herald*, June 15, 1882

[xliii] Nibley, pp. 94-95

[xliv] As per J. A. Clark, *Gleanings by the Way*, Philadelphia, 1842, pp.256-7; cited in Brodie, p.78

[xlv] Twain, *Roughing It*, University of California Press, 2003, p.58

[xlvi] Stephen Burnett, letter to Lyman E. Johnson, April 15, 1838; cited in Vogel, *EMD*, 2:288-93

[xlvii] Gov. Thomas Ford, *History of Illinois*, Chicago, 1854, p.257

Chapter 3

The Saints Come Marching In

The angel Moroni whisked Joseph's "Golden Plates" back up to heaven as swiftly as if they had never been here at all. But back on Earth, their story was just beginning. On April 6, 1830, Joseph formally organized his new church, which Jesus commanded him to call "The Church of Christ." Despite Jesus' explicit instructions, four years later Joseph changed their name to "The Church of the Latter Day Saints," and another four years later, changed it again to "The Church of Jesus Christ of Latter Day Saints." About a century later the church corrected the spelling to "The Church of Jesus Christ of Latter-day Saints." Regardless, most outsiders originally referred to them as "Mormonites."

Less than 50 attendees were at the new faith's first meeting, held in a private house. The church grew rapidly, though Smith wound up eventually excommunicating almost all the men who had been his first disciples and who had sworn they too, had seen the "Golden Plates". Of the eleven official witnesses, two soon died and six either left the church or were excommunicated (three eventually returned). Only Joseph's father and two brothers remained steadfast. And the church faced constant opposition. Then, as now, mainstream Christians lumped them together with the other weird new-fangled religious movements coming out—and for every person Joseph Smith baptized, there were a dozen who remembered his trial for fraud (which incidentally, occurred during the time he was supposed to be preparing himself for receiving the "gold plates").

True to form, the church wasted no time sending out missionaries to proselytize heavily. An eloquent and enthusiastic twenty-three-year-old, Parley Pratt had only been a convert for three weeks when he began spreading the word. He would go on to be nicknamed "The Archer of Paradise," gaining new converts all over the globe for decades (he would also be ancestor to 2012 presidential hopefuls Jon Huntsman and Mitt Romney). One of his early converts was Sidney Rigdon, a fiery, humorless Campbellite Baptist preacher who had been bitterly quarreling with his fellow churchmen and was nursing a grudge when Parley Pratt arrived with perfect timing. Ironically enough, it had been Rigdon who had first converted Pratt to Campbellism; Parley returned the favor. Rigdon was a fervent believer in the impending apocalypse and prone to "nervous spasms and swoonings," which he attributed to the Holy Spirit. The Book of Mormon excited him; it dovetailed nicely with his conviction that the new millennium was nigh. He fasted and prayed for days to determine whether Mormonism was the one true faith, until finally he suffered one of his swooning fits, saw an angel and was converted.[xlviii] He brought along over a hundred members of his congregation, more than doubling the size of the fledgling church.

Rigdon quickly wormed his way into Joseph's confidence, muscling out Oliver Cowdery to become the number two leader of the church. This didn't sit well with everyone. Many Saints became alarmed at Rigdon's new influence over Joseph (David Whitmer griped that the church's first name change was all due to Rigdon's machinations). Their fears appeared justified when Rigdon began to push Joseph to move the church to Ohio, only to have the Prophet shortly thereafter receive a revelation that the whole church was to pack up and assemble there. Joseph had to argue with his suspicious flock for weeks before he could convince a majority that Kirtland, Ohio, was the eastern edge of the Promised

Land, which stretched from there to the Pacific Ocean.

To the Promised Land (Take One)

And at first, Kirtland was indeed full of promise.

In January 1831, Joseph convinced about seventy-five followers to move with him to Kirtland, where they set about building a grand temple. The great work would last three years, with each Saint dedicating one day out of the week to work on the construction. It was a massive, three-story, 13,000 square foot stone edifice, in a hodgepodge of architectural styles, and dominated the landscape for miles. When the Temple was finally consecrated in 1836, some thousand men packed into the lower court for the dedication service, with another thousand Saints eagerly crowded around outside hoping to catch a spiritual contact high. For two days and two nights, the favored men inside prophesied, spoke in tongues and saw glorious visions. Joseph proclaimed that he could see the sanctuary was filled with angels, and shared reports from neighboring townsfolk who saw a bright light like a pillar of fire falling upon the Temple. [xlix]

The Temple's construction had cost the Saints between $60,000 and $70,000, an astronomical sum for the impoverished settlers, most of whom were living in shanties. There was not a great deal of money in Kirtland. Shortly after arriving, Joseph had announced a new revelation from God instituting the United Order of Enoch, which consecrated belongings with an unbreakable covenant and deed, just as the early church in Jerusalem had done in the days of the Apostles—in other words, Communism. Private property was now church property; a new convert was required to "consecrate" his all to the church, and was only given back what the church deemed "sufficient for himself and family;" the rest went to the Church storehouse and treasury. He then became "steward" of his former land and property, on behalf of the church, who reclaimed it when the steward died or left the church.

The church was experiencing growing pains. By 1836,

Kirtland's population had swelled to 3,000, which inflated the price of land. The church had plenty of real estate, but was short on financial liquidity to repay all its outstanding loans. What the church needed was a bank. So, deep in debt, the church organized the Kirtland Safety Society Bank Company in November 1836, with Sidney Rigdon as President and Joseph as Cashier. They expected the bank would solve the debt problem with a simple plan—just print out more money.

Ohio's banking system was already a chaotic mess. There were at least three hundred different kinds of authorized banknotes floating around (not to mention loads of illegal notes and outright counterfeits), called colorful names like Yellow Dog, Red Cat, Smooth Monkey, Blue Pup, and Sick Indian. The so-called "paper money disease" was bad timing for the Mormons. The Ohio legislature cracked down on wildcat banks, and refused to incorporate the Kirtland bank. So Joseph came up with a new plan: Overnight, the Kirtland Safety Society Bank became the Kirtland Safety Society *anti*-Banking Company, by taking the existing bank notes and stamping "anti-" and "-ing" around the word "bank."[li]

This worked great. For a few weeks, Kirtland was feeling flush. Everyone's pockets were full of paper money, all the local debts were wiped out and couriers were dispatched back east to pay off the crushing business loans to the church's mercantile firms. Any customer entertaining doubts about the Kirtland bank's stability could plainly see the vault was filled with boxes, each labeled "$1000."

A Kirtland Safety Society Bank three dollar bill. "Anti-" and "-ing" have been stamped around the word "bank" in an attempt to get around Ohio laws against out of control wildcat banks by making an "anti-banking company."

What they didn't know is that except for a top layer of bright, shiny, silver fifty-cent coins, the boxes were filled with "sand, lead, old iron, stone and combustibles." [lii]

Less than a month after the bank's opening, the gig was up. The bank had been operating illegally from day one. A newspaper expressed skepticism about their financial worth, and panic soon followed. Bills came back, out-of-state merchants started refusing their notes, and no bank would touch them. Joseph's secretary and the acting Bank Cashier, Warren Parrish, resigned in disgust, quit the church and began to openly describe the church's shaky banking practices. Joseph swiftly closed up shop to avoid a run on the bank as anyone with Kirtland bank bills in their wallets now desperately tried to get rid of them. [liii]

The creditors returned with a vengeance and swarmed on Joseph, now deeper in debt than ever. Bank President Sidney Rigdon was brought in to court "for making spurious money." [liv] The debacle was so damaging, even Mormons were turning against Joseph. Most had already given all they owned to the United Order, but others lost what modest fortunes they had [lv]. Six of the twelve apostles were openly speaking out against him. Even faithful Apostle Parley Pratt, one of his most passionate missionaries, threatened to outright sue him. Joseph immediately ordered him to stand trial and tried to excommunicate him for it, but the High Council itself was so fiercely divided, the trial fell apart in disorder. [lvi]

Thirteen suits were brought against Joseph. He was arrested seven times in four months. One particularly pugnacious Ohio businessman accused Joseph of sending Mormon assassins to kill him so he could not proceed against the bank, but when it came to trial, the case was dismissed for lack of evidence. All this "persecution" actually had a silver lining—Joseph's flock rallied to his defense and raised over $38,000 to bail him out. [lvii]

Dancing Queen

In mid-July, Joseph left for a five-week missionary tour in

David Fitzgerald

Canada, hoping to lay low until the heat cooled off. He came back to find the meltdown worse than before. Half the church, including all three of his Book of Mormon witnesses, had abandoned him and were following a young girl who claimed she could see the future by peering into a black stone. The new prophetess would dance herself into a frenzy until she finally dropped to the floor in exhaustion and burst forth with revelations—most of them against Joseph. [lviii]

Joseph set to work to reclaim his throne. He silenced the dancing girl prophet (we're not told how) and won back Oliver Cowdery and David Whitmer, at least somewhat. They returned to the fold "half-contrite and half-suspicious"[lix] and soon went to Missouri. Unstable, demented Martin Harris would become so unbearable he was finally kicked out of the church, not to return again until he was an old man. Joseph held a conference and was sustained as the church President by unanimous vote.

But it was a hollow victory. Many bankrupt and resentful Mormons had left the church to start their own because they thought the Kirtland Bank had been nothing more than a moneymaking scheme all along.[lx] The church's mercantile firms were out of business, the Kirtland steam mill was dead in the water, and the church's biggest asset, land values, were sinking to appalling depths. Kirtland was disintegrating.

Soon loyalist Saints were brawling with anti-Smith Saints in the temple. Joseph called for a public trial to punish the rebels. Rigdon took the stand and unleashed a violent tirade against them, including a laundry list of their crimes: lying, stealing, adultery, counterfeiting and swindling. His accusations grew ever more rabid until he reached a fever pitch of obscene language that stunned the congregation. But what had begun as a witch-hunt quickly turned into a battle. The dissenters were just as furious, and had shown up in force, with grievances of their own. Angry charges and counter-charges flew back and forth until Joseph lost all control and the trial collapsed entirely.

The last straw came on January 12, 1838, when a warrant

was issued for Joseph's and Sidney Rigdon's arrests on charges of bank fraud. They fled the state, just ahead of an armed posse riding out to capture them for trial. The remaining faithful Saints went with them to Missouri, to join with the other Mormon settlements on what was then the very western edge of American settlement. Joseph's prize, the glorious temple he had spent years building, was abandoned to the dissenters. The walls that had echoed with songs of praise to Joseph now resounded with denunciations of him from the enemies who hated him the most.

Kirtland would not be the last time the Mormon believers would have the Promised Land dangled before them with angelic signs and wonders; suffer hardships, sacrifice and loss of life to reach it; settle there and build farms, cities and a costly temple; only to have to pack up and uproot all over again for another round of Utopian bait and switch. It would be a recurring theme for fourteen years, as the Saints moved from New York to Ohio, to Missouri, to Illinois, to Utah...

To the Promised Land, Take Two: Return to Eden

Ohio? Forget about Ohio. Joseph had already revealed that Independence, Missouri was not only the site of the Garden of Eden, but would also be the "New Jerusalem," the precise landing point for Jesus at his return (which would be soon— very soon!). Scrappy Mormon colonies had been in the new state of Missouri since 1831, to "build up" the city of Zion in Jackson County. But the reception for Joseph and their fellow Saints left much to be desired. The Missouri Mormons were already embroiled in local problems of their own.

They had never been welcome in Missouri. The local religious denominations despised them and decried them as a false religion. The Saints were tight-knit, clannish and had an armed militia. Everything they did raised the worst fears of their neighbors.

They dominated local economies and undercut local businesses by trading only with each other whenever possible. Missourians feared they would dominate elections, too, since they voted in lockstep according to their Prophet's orders. And their numbers seemed to get bigger every day. Perhaps they never had a chance of peaceful co-existence with the people they referred to as "Gentiles." As any Palestinian could tell you, Chosen People don't make good neighbors—especially if you live on their Promised Land.

When the local LDS newspaper began printing Joseph's new revelations, the prior settlers were alarmed to read that God had promised all the land of Missouri to their Mormon neighbors—who were therefore entitled to secure it, by force if necessary. The church paper reported commandments from God for the Saints to "assemble yourselves together to rejoice upon the land of Missouri, which is the land of your inheritance, which is now the land of your enemies,"[lxi] and that they would "literally tread upon the ashes of the wicked after they are destroyed from off the face of the earth." [lxii]

As tensions mounted, Mormons suffered increasingly worse harassment, mob violence and expulsions. After years of repeatedly losing their homes and property, with no help from petitions or lawsuits, the government finally set aside land for Mormon settlement. For a brief while, it seemed like there might be an end to the animosity between Saints and Gentiles... until the summer of 1838, when Joseph and hundreds of Mormon refugees from Kirtland began to show up. Missourians were freshly outraged, and just like that, the bad days were back again—but even worse than before. Now it would be war.

God's Secret Army

In June, there were rumors of a secret society of Mormon vigilantes. Some called them the Avenging Angels, the Brothers of Gideon, or curiously, the Daughters of Zion, but the name that finally stuck was the Sons of Dan, or for short, the Danites—a shadowy group that would loom large for generations afterwards, both in Mormon folklore and fearful anti-Mormon propaganda.

Sampson Avard was a dangerous man—tough, cunning,

ruthlessly efficient and coldly ambitious. Shortly after Joseph and Sidney Rigdon arrived in Missouri fresh from their narrow escape from the law in Kirtland, Avard brought them his secret plan to defend the faithful: a covert paramilitary band under his command complete with its own secret signs and passwords, its members sworn to secrecy, pledged to rob, pillage, lie or kill if necessary, and bound to one another with severe oaths of dire punishments. Their mission was to defend the Saints from aggression, act as bodyguard for the presidency, and best of all to Sidney Rigdon, they would also serve as secret police for ferreting out dissenters.

Rigdon had become obsessed with hunting down heretics and wasted no time eagerly employing the Danites to root out his enemies within the church; his great success was having once-powerful rivals like Oliver Cowdery and David Whitmer excommunicated. Avard played to the desires of Rigdon and Joseph by ensuring that heresy against the presidency was punished without mercy. He demanded that his men "support the presidency in all their doings, right or wrong," and warned that "If I meet one damning or cursing the presidency, I can curse them too, and if he will drink I can get him a bowl of brandy and after a while take him by the arm, and get him one side in the brush when I will into his guts in a minute, and put him under the sod." [lxiii]

Blinded by such well-calculated displays of loyalty, Joseph gave Avard free reign to do as he saw fit, which included awarding the Danites carte blanche to "waste away the Gentiles by robbing and plundering them of their property." [lxiv] But Joseph and Sidney Rigdon had created a monster they could not control. Soon Joseph would feel the need to distance himself from Avard's ruthlessness and disavow any knowledge of the Danites' raiding and pillaging, at one point even denying that they even existed except as a mere figure of speech! [lxv] He would finally claim he had denounced Avard the minute he discovered how nefarious Avard's activities had became. But the truth is, during the vicious summer and fall of 1838, until November (when he would turn traitor on Joseph and leave the church), Samson

Avard was one of the most powerful and feared men in the church, and for good reason.

The (First) Mormon War

The violence of that summer had been a long time coming. For five long, bitter years the Saints in Missouri had swallowed their rage and meekly submitted to all the insults and indignities heaped on them. Now they had grown sick of turning the other cheek. Encouraged by the knowledge of his new secret army, Sidney Rigdon gave voice to the Saints' seething resentment in a speech given at a Fourth of July celebration, reaching a crescendo with these words:

"But from this day and hour, we will suffer it no more... it shall be between us and them a war of extermination; for we will follow them till the last drop of their blood is spilled, or else they will have to exterminate us; for we will carry the seat of war to their own houses and their own families, and one party or the other shall be utterly destroyed." [lxvi]

In what proved to be not his finest moment of diplomacy, Joseph published copies of the incendiary speech in pamphlets. [lxvii] The enraged Missouri newspapers went ballistic, and an ugly season of brutal skirmishes and raids began. It would come to be known as the 1838 Missouri Mormon War (to distinguish it from later Mormon wars in 1844 and 1857). Wandering bands of Gentile gunmen stalked the land, torching haystacks, granaries and isolated farmhouses; stealing horses and cattle; and beating Mormons when they came upon them. Mormon settlements came under siege.

"Joseph Smith or the Sword!"

On October 14, Joseph gathered his troops in the northwestern Mormon settlement of Far West, and gave a rousing speech, including these fateful lines:

"If the people will let us alone, we will preach the gospel in peace. But if they come on us to molest us, we will establish our religion by the sword. We will trample down our enemies and make it one gore of blood from the Rocky Mountains to the Atlantic Ocean. I will be to this generation a second Mohammed, whose motto in treating for peace was 'the Alcoran or the Sword.' So shall it eventually be with us— 'Joseph Smith or the Sword!'" [lxviii]

News that the Mormons had gone on the offensive with fifteen thousand men spread like wildfire. The folk in the neighboring countryside fled in their wake, and the Mormons plundered the towns of Gallatin, Millport and Grindstone Fork. The population was terrified that all of northern Missouri would be laid to waste; within a week every isolated Mormon cabin was reduced to a pile of ashes. [lxix] Wild reports exaggerated Mormon attacks, like a modest skirmish at Crooked River, into dreadful massacres, poisoning of wells and impending plans to loot and burn even more towns. Express riders carried the news to the Missouri governor Lilburn Boggs.

Extermination

On October 27, the Governor, who had never in five years lifted a finger to stop harassment of the Saints, now issued an executive order declaring that the Mormons must be treated as enemies, to be exterminated or driven from the state. Right on cue, three days later, two hundred militiamen carried out a horrific massacre on the last remaining outlying Mormon settlement, Haun's Mill. They trapped the defenders in the blacksmith shop, shooting them like fish in a barrel. When women tried to flee for the thickets, they were gunned down as well. After shooting every Mormon they could see, they moved in to the blacksmith shop to finish off the wounded. When one old man surrendered his gun, a militiaman proceeded to hack him into pieces with a corn-cutter [lxx]. A nine-year-old boy was caught hiding under the bellows. His younger brother, shot in the hip and playing dead, heard them drag him from his hiding place. When one man said, "Don't shoot, it's just a boy," the other coolly replied, "Nits will make lice," and shot the boy in the head point-blank. Of the thirty-eight men and boys in the settlement, seventeen had been killed and fifteen wounded.

When news of the massacre reached Joseph in Far West, it was joined by new hourly reports from his scouts that the opposing forces had doubled in size—no, tripled. Even with their loot, the Mormons were desperate for food and fuel, and already outnumbered five to one by troops on their way. Within two days, the town would be under siege by ten thousand Missourians. Joseph kept up a bold facade for his men, promising the Lord would send an angel to fight alongside every one of them. [lxxi] But on the inside, he was desperate to forestall their annihilation, and knew that a compromise had to be found, "honorable or dishonorable." [lxxii] He secretly sent out a delegation to find the opposing general "and beg like a dog for peace." [lxxiii] Before the day was out, they had succeeded, but the terms were harsh: all Mormons would immediately leave Missouri, all Mormon property would be confiscated and all arms surrendered, and the Mormon leaders would surrender to be tried for treason.

As they mulled this over, the Missouri troops continued to march on the city. When they were within six hundred yards of the Mormon barricades, Joseph, Sidney Rigdon, Parley Pratt and other leaders came forward under a white flag, setting off a rowdy, jubilant roar of victory from the militia forces. The Mormon War was over.

Joseph and the others spent a miserable night in the open, forced to endure rain and the taunting of their guards. Around midnight, the general appeared to inform them they would be shot the next morning in the public square.

The End—Not

It's interesting to think about how different Mormonism might be today if the firing squad actually had executed Joseph the next morning as planned. Some of the most distinctive LDS doctrines might never have come to light, like polygamy, baptism for the dead or that all Mormon men could become gods themselves. All in all, we would be missing 133 of the divine revelations that he received from 1840 to 1844. Instead, in one of the many unduly incredible events that Joseph seemed to collect throughout his life, he was saved by insubordination. The officer in charge regarded it as cold-blooded murder and refused to carry out the execution, threatening his superior officer with a military tribunal. So Joseph and about sixty other Mormons were turned over to a civil court of inquiry on charges of treason, murder, arson, burglary, robbery, larceny and perjury. The star witness for the prosecution was none other than opportunistic ex-Danite leader Sampson Avard, who threw Joseph under the bus in a self-serving testimony, whitewashing his own role and heaping blame on Joseph and Sidney Rigdon. After the inquiry, all but a handful of the prisoners were released. Joseph and the other leaders wound up being held in jail for four months, awaiting trial for treason against the state, murder, arson, burglary, robbery and larceny. [lxxiv]

When the trial finally came around, Joseph's counsel argued for a change of venue to another county. Since it was nearly impossible to find twelve local men who had not been involved in the Mormon war, the lawyers won their point. But as it happened, there would never be a second trial. In April of 1839, on the way to the new prison, Joseph and his brother Hyrum managed to bribe their guards and escape on horseback, just in time to catch up with the last group of Saints leaving Missouri. Lucky bastard!

Or perhaps it was more than just luck... It may also have been that his imprisonment had become a political embarrassment for the Governor, and a timely escape would have been quite handy [lxxv]... In any case, lucky escapes like this were about to get fewer for Joseph. Even a cat with nine lives runs out eventually.

***

For further reading:

Yet again, Fawn Brodie's *No Man Knows My History* and Jon Krakauer's *Under the Banner of Heaven* are highly recommended (see ch. 1 endnotes)

For more on the Kirtland financial scandal, see Jerald and Sandra Tanner's *The Mormon Kingdom* Vol. 1, (Salt Lake City: Utah Lighthouse Ministries, 1969)

For more on the Mormon War in Missouri, see Todd M. Compton and Leland Homer Gentry's *Fire and Sword: A History of the Latter-day Saints in Northern Missouri, 1836-39* (Draper, UT: Greg Kofford Books, 2010)

Endnotes: Chapter 3

[xlviii] Brodie, p. 95
[xlix] ibid., pp. 178-179
[l] ibid., p.195
[li] ibid., p. 196
[lii] ibid., p.197
[liii] ibid., p.198
[liv] ibid.
[lv] ibid., p.199. The church made several short-lived attempts to institute communism. Brigham Young was able to install United Orders in over 200 Mormon communities, but by his death in 1877, most of them had failed, and by 1900, all the Orders were essentially extinct.

[lvi] ibid., pp. 202-3

[lvii] ibid., p. 201

[lviii] Lucy Smith, *Biographical Sketches*, pp. 211-13; cited in ibid., p. 205

[lix] ibid., p. 205

[lx] Adams, Dale W., "Chartering the Kirtland Bank," *BYU Studies,* 1983, Vol. 23, No. 4, pp. 467–482

[lxi] Krakauer, p. 100

[lxii] ibid.

[lxiii] Reported by Reed Peck, mss. *Correspondence, orders, etc,* pp. 49-50; cited in Brodie, p. 216

[lxiv] *History of the Church*, Vol. III, pp. 180-1; cited in Brodie, p. 215

[lxv] Brodie, pp. 215-6

[lxvi] ibid., p. 223

[lxvii] A copy is still in the Chicago History Society Library. Also reprinted in *Church History*, vol. II pp. 157-65, Lamoni, Iowa

[lxviii] Brodie, pp. 230-31

[lxix] ibid., p. 233

[lxx] ibid., p. 237

[lxxi] Reed Peck mss. cited in Brodie, p. 238

[lxxii] ibid., pp. 108-9, cited in Brodie, p. 239

[lxxiii] ibid., p. 103, cited in Brodie, p. 238

[lxxiv] Bushman RSR, pp. 363–372

[lxxv] ibid., pp. 382–386

Chapter 4

The Blood of the Prophet

To the Promised Land, Take Three: The Beautiful Place

A month later Joseph stood upon a hill, gazing out on a breathtaking spring vista. Before him a broad, glittering bend of the Mississippi lazily swung around a garden of marshes and virgin woodlands below his feet. Across the river lay the peaceful green Iowa hills. Joseph was deeply moved. "It is a beautiful site," he murmured, "and it shall be called Nauvoo, which means in Hebrew a beautiful plantation." It doesn't, actually. Joseph's Smith's proficiency in Hebrew was very limited. There is a poetic Hebrew word not in normal usage, spelled *nun, aleph, vav, hey* - נאוה - but it is pronounced "Naveh" or "Navah," not "Nauvoo."

After languishing for months in dank prison cells, it must have truly seemed like a paradise to Joseph, and no less to his followers who had endured a lean, killing winter and yet another mass migration. Their ordeals in the Mormon war and the Haun's Mill Massacre had made the national news. Illinois was touched by the mistreatment the Saints had suffered in Missouri and welcomed them as refugees. They had found a beautiful region, all but uninhabited, with an owner willing to sell them plentiful acreage on credit. After all their years of misery, it seemed that they had at last reached a place to call their home.

And even though it wouldn't last, those few short years in Nauvoo would be some of the happiest and most productive for the Saints. They would also see a rush of startling new revelations: that their dead loved ones would also be able to be saved, that families would be able to stay together in the afterlife, even that they could become gods themselves!

But they weren't out of the woods just yet. Weakened from their grueling winter travails, the settlers were no match for an outbreak of fever that killed many of them the first year, including Joseph's own father and brother. The survivors set to work draining the malarial swamps, felling the timber and laying out city streets and farmland in a tidy grid, with the cornerstones of an even more magnificent new temple atop the hill as the centerpiece.

Their extensive missionary efforts in England and Wales would begin to pay off, especially among the unemployed workers from the manufacturing districts. Well-to-do Londoners seemed quite unimpressed with their preaching, but for the poor and working classes displaced by the Industrial Revolution, suffering from nationwide economic chaos and crowded into grim, filthy industrial tenements, the missionaries' pitch of a new gospel—and a new life overseas—was an easy sell. "They would rather be slaves in America than starve in this country," Parley Pratt wrote. "I cannot keep them back." Two hundred converts left for Nauvoo in 1840; the next year the number had jumped to 1,200 and then 1,600 the year after that. By 1844, there would be over 8,000 clamoring to escape Britain[lxxvii] and Nauvoo's population would be 12,000 strong, rivaling Chicago. The Mormons' accomplishments were praised in newspapers from as far away as Boston and New York. The Church seemed to be on a roll, and Nauvoo poised to become the headquarters of God's Kingdom on Earth. But in five years, it would be a ghost town.

Trouble in Paradise

It seemed no matter where they fled, they couldn't escape their troubles. Isaac Galland, the kindly man who had sold them their twenty thousand acres in Illinois on credit, been baptized and hand-chosen by Joseph to be his chief land agent, quickly set about to secure them more land in Iowa. But Galland turned out to be a horse thief and counterfeiter who was out to bleed the church dry with fraudulent land deals. When his scams finally came to light in court, his deeds to the Iowa territory turned out to be forged. The 250 families who had been working the land for a year had to return to Nauvoo, most of them penniless. [lxxviii]

Joseph continued to have problems of his own. Despite his escape, he was still considered a fugitive from justice in Missouri, in constant danger of being extradited to stand trial for treason. At least twice, bounty hunters would come after him trying to collect the price on his head. One of these attempts was in May 1841, when a sheriff's posse managed to catch Joseph by surprise outside Nauvoo and arrested him. They came very close to hauling him across the border to stand trial for treason before Joseph managed to slip out of their custody with a writ of habeas corpus. [lxxix] Nauvoo's city charter had a unique (and not strictly legal) provision that could free anyone the municipal council chose to protect—very handy for protecting Saints with a bounty on them, like Joseph.

In retaliation, Joseph angrily (and publicly) prophesied that their old enemy, Missouri ex-Governor Boggs, would "die by violent hands within one year." That was all the encouragement needed, and on May 6, 1842, while Boggs was in his study reading the newspaper, a gunman skulking outside the window fired four shots, hitting him twice in the neck and twice in the head. The assassin's gun was found and traced to a man who had recently arrived from Nauvoo, Orrin Porter Rockwell—a member of Joseph Smith's "Destroying Angels" Danites and one of his most devoted bodyguards and enforcers. Rockwell was an imposing figure: big as an ox with a pit bull's eyes and long, scraggly hair like Sampson; Joseph had prophesied that no blade or bullet could harm him if he kept it uncut. He was also an accomplished horseman and a dead shot with a reputation for having killed as many men as a gunslinger.

Unfortunately for Rockwell's record, Boggs was too stubborn to die. As soon as he recovered from his head wounds, he immediately charged Joseph as an accessory to murder, and sheriffs rode out yet again to arrest Rockwell and his Prophet. Porter Rockwell hightailed it to Philadelphia, and for four months Joseph went underground around Nauvoo, hiding in a secret vault under his cellar steps, or traveling by night up and down the river and lying low on small islands or isolated farms. He wrote Emma tender love letters while on the lam. During the weeks he stayed at the farm of one Edward Sayers, he also persuaded Mrs. Sayers to become one of his new wives.[lxxx]

(below)
Harsh anti-Mormon Missouri Governor
Lilburn W. Boggs

(right)

The man who put four bullets in the back of Gov. Boggs' head. Joseph's toughest and most lyal bodyguard and enforcer, Porter Rockwell.

When he died, his *Salt Lake Tribune* obituary accused him of participation in at least a hundred murders

Joseph finally succeeded in having the case thrown out, but there was still serious trouble at home. Many disgruntled Saints thought he was richly profiting from land speculation and underhanded business deals even while his followers toiled for him like ants and were forced to cram together in ramshackle wooden hovels or calico tents. Discontent was a constant source of anxiety; no one was safe from the threat of excommunication, not even his oldest and most loyal confidants. Privately, some Saints feared he had become a fallen prophet.

Then there were whispers that church leaders secretly kept harems of wives—even taking other men's wives! In print and in public, Joseph vigorously and repeatedly denied the filthy rumors that never seemed to go away. This was largely because they were true (see chapter 5 for more details). Polygamy, as it turned out, was more than just Joseph's dirty little secret; it would actually wind up being the death of him. The end began with the affair of Dr. Bennett.

The Doctor is In

Dr. John Cook Bennett showed up in Nauvoo in 1840, after writing to Joseph to tell him of his desire to join the new church. In hindsight it's clear that the rumors of polygamy were a major enticement for Bennett. He claimed to be a bachelor; in fact he had deserted his wife and three children back in Ohio. Ambitious, urbane and licentious, with extravagant tastes and a pronounced deficit of moral fiber, Bennett wasted no time insinuating himself. He and Joseph were kindred spirits and got along like a house on fire. Emma never liked him; she didn't trust the smooth talker [lxxxi] and had already seen her husband chum around with too many slick scoundrels. Sooner or later, they always stabbed him in the back. In Bennett's case, it would take about a year and a half.

Dr. John Cook Bennett, dressed in his Nauvoo Legion uniform. A rising star in the church, he soon showed his true colors as an oily opportunist, chronic womanizer and

a dangerous backstabber.

At first, Dr. Bennett was a rising star: he treated victims of the malaria and cholera epidemic, supervised the draining of the swamps, helped craft the Nauvoo city charter and was essential in getting its provisions passed by the Illinois legislature. His lobbying efforts even received kudos from a young Whig congressman, Abraham Lincoln. For a year and a half, he was Joseph's closest advisor, and was showered with special favors denied to other loyal followers who had already made great sacrifices. In short order Joseph made him "assistant president" of the church, Counselor in the First Presidency, mayor of Nauvoo, Chancellor of its "university," Secretary of the Nauvoo Masonic Lodge, and leader of their militia, the Nauvoo Legion.

However, behind the scenes, Bennett was also a seducer of untold numbers of women, and most shocking, had promised, and carried out, as many abortions as needed to keep his affairs secret. And that wasn't the worst of it. Too late, Joseph realized that, once again, he had created a monster. Bennett had swiftly gone from trusted confidante and bosom pal to a dangerous, volatile rival. He even suspected Bennett of planning to murder him by staging an "accidental" shooting during Legion target practice. [lxxxii]

But strangely enough, the deal-breaker for their friendship wasn't his suspicion of a murder plot, but rivalry over the same girl, young Nancy Rigdon (more on the Nancy Rigdon affair later). When the scandal broke, Joseph blamed Bennett for the whole incident and wrote up Bennett's excommunication. But getting rid of Dr. Bennett wouldn't be so easy; Bennett had just as much dirt on Joseph. So Joseph was forced to compromise: Bennett would amicably step down from his positions and receive a public vote of thanks for his fine work as Mayor of Nauvoo. Joseph hoped that would be enough to get Bennett to slink out of the picture, but instead, he stuck around.

This put Joseph in an awkward dilemma: if he kicked out Bennett, there was no telling what trouble the unscrupulous doctor could stir up. On the other hand, stories of Bennett's debauchery were spreading all over town now; if he kept Bennett around, it would seem like the Prophet was harboring a known adulterer and abortionist. Joseph picked the second option, and privately cut a deal not to exile him if Bennett would make a public confession. The doctor readily agreed, and delivered an inspired performance at a special session in the Masonic Hall, weeping as he confessed many of his transgressions to the crowd. But when Joseph came through on his end and pleaded on Bennett's behalf for mercy, the Saints were astonished and outraged. Joseph had to spend four weeks on damage control trying to justify his protection of Bennett to his irate flock, but it was no use. It would either be Bennett's neck on the chopping block, or his.

The Doctor is Out

Joseph excommunicated and denounced him in public. Reading between the lines of Joseph's guarded public statements, it's clear that from the beginning Bennett was not only preaching "spiritual wifery," but that he saw the celestial marriage doctrine as a mere charade and simply ignored it whenever he liked. [lxxxiii] Joseph alleged that he had given Bennett a stern rebuke in 1840 for his philandering—and another in 1841. From the vantage of our 20/20 hindsight, Joseph's moral outrage was dubious. He had been informed that Bennett had abandoned his family long before this, and had been perfectly willing to overlook that. And since Joseph had already been encouraging his inner circle to practice celestial marriage in secret, it's patently obvious Bennett had been operating with Joseph's officially unofficial sanction all along.

Joseph's worst fears came true: Bennett retaliated with a vengeance by launching a series of lurid exposés of the Mormons. They were serialized in a Springfield paper for months, picked up by newspapers around the country and finally published as a tell-all book, filled with juicy details of deception, sex orgies and murder. Bennett spun imaginative and elaborate tales outlining for example, how every Mormon woman was a sacred prostitute in one of several orders, with names like the Chambered Sisters of Charity or the Saints of the Black Veil. He also claimed to blow the lid off the secrets of the "Destroying Angels", the crack squad of the most ruthless Danites, trained to be fanatic assassin spies. [lxxxiv] Incidentally, it was Bennett who squealed to Boggs that he had been shot on direct order of the Prophet. Bennett claimed Joseph had issued a five hundred dollar reward to whoever killed the hated ex-governor. [lxxxv] But most damaging of all, he aired Joseph's Smith's dirty laundry, and unlike the bulk of his potboiler "exposé," the details he gave of Joseph's many indiscretions with other men's wives and daughters were all too accurate.

The fallout from Bennett's vicious concoction of outrageous lies and devastating truths was irreversible. Bennett had blown Pandora's box wide open, and try as he might, Joseph would never fully contain the damage. He did luck out that Bennett had so grossly over-exaggerated so much of his tell-all, it made it easy to dismiss; and Bennett was so obviously an opportunistic weasel with an axe to grind he discredited himself. But at home the Saints were shaken to the core. Mormon husbands returned from their far-flung missions only to find their wives called out by name in print as concubines in Joseph Smith's extended harem. One former Apostle came close to suicide from his ensuing depression.

Fallout from the never-ending scandals also killed any chance Joseph had of revealing his plural marriage doctrine more openly. Instead, he had to redouble his efforts to keep it under wraps. This meant painfully ironic displays, such as ever more fervent verbal gymnastics from polygamous church leaders denying its existence, and an affidavit solemnly declaring that nothing but traditional marriage had ever been practiced in Nauvoo, signed by several of Joseph's plural wives. That same year, Joseph printed a tract by a certain Mr. "Udney Hay Jacob" which justified polygamy on Biblical and practical grounds.

But if Joseph—er, that is, Mr. Udney H. Jacob—hoped to stem the tide against plural marriage, it boomeranged on him.

The tract ignited so much furious backlash Joseph was forced to quickly renounce it as an "unmeaning rigmarole of nonsense, folly and trash." [lxxxvi] Once things had cooled down, Joseph made another attempt to sell the Saints on polygamy. He and his closest cronies had been practicing it for several years already; on August 12, 1843, Joseph took the next step by privately revealing it as a new doctrine to the members of the church's High Council. The reception was less than ideal: the meeting immediately erupted into an uproar, and the controversy split the church leadership into pro- and anti-polygamy factions. Apostle William Law led the anti-polygamist minority—with the secret support of Emma, who quietly went around to Mormon women, warning them that they needed to stand fast against the doctrine if they didn't want their husbands taking more wives.

Unknown to most of the rank and file of the church, a secret war had begun between the rival leadership factions, and the rift would never heal. But in the meantime, Joseph had big plans.

The Man Who Would Be King... and President... and High Priest...

Joseph charged into the new year of 1844 like there was no tomorrow.

His dreams and schemes were more grandiose than ever, and he engaged in a dizzying flurry of political activity aimed at leveraging his spiritual authority into political and military power:

- Dissatisfied with the Whig and Democratic frontrunners, on January 29, 1844, Joseph announced his candidacy for President of the United States, and immediately converted hundreds of missionaries across the country into his nationwide campaign supporters.
- On February 20, after considering possible sites for new Mormon colonies including Texas and Mexico, he dispatched scouts to explore likely locations in Oregon

and California.

- On March 11, he hand-selected "princes" for a top-secret theocratic policymaking body, the "Council of Fifty." [lxxxvii] His council would operate as a sort of shadow government off and on into the 1870s. [lxxxviii]
- The council began acting as if Nauvoo was a sovereign city-state, sending ambassadors to England, France, Russia and the Republic of Texas. [lxxxix] The Mormon "minister to Texas" was told to negotiate a treaty and secure a massive tract of land (about three-fifths of modern Texas, the eastern half of New Mexico, the Oklahoma panhandle, a third of Colorado and parts of Kansas and Wyoming). In return, the Mormon nation would help defend the Texans against Mexico.
- Also in March, Joseph petitioned Congress for the power to raise and lead a 100,000 man army, answerable only to him, to patrol the western border from Texas to Oregon (Congress would pass on the offer).
- On April 11, just four days after he publicly announced for the first time that faithful male Saints could eventually become gods, he had the Council anoint him as "King, Priest, and Ruler over Israel on Earth." [xc]

Neighboring counties became increasingly alarmed by the growing theocracy next door. The Mormons had raised a militia of almost four thousand men—at a time when the entire U.S. Army was only 8,500 strong [xci]—and plans for an arsenal and gunpowder works were underway. The prior December, Joseph had prepared a petition for Congress, asking that Nauvoo be made a completely independent federal territory, the Nauvoo Legion be incorporated into the United States Army, and that the mayor of Nauvoo be given power to call out U.S. troops as needed. It was one of Joseph's biggest political blunders. It never had a snowball's chance of getting Congressional approval. All it accomplished was alienating what few friends they still had in Illinois. [xcii]

**General Joseph Smith's Last Address, John Haven, 1888
Joseph's private militia, the Nauvoo Legion, grew to nearly
4,000 strong–almost half the size of the entire U.S. army at
the time.**

Law Breaker

And he was turning friends into enemies in his own church as
well. His trusted second counselor, William Law, a man of
unquestioned integrity, had become the unofficial leader of the
anti-polygamy faction, and had repeatedly pleaded with Joseph
to withdraw the doctrine of plural marriage. The Prophet was
adamant that he could not; it was God's commandment, not
his. The disagreement strained their relationship to the
breaking point; Joseph then shattered it completely by
attempting to seduce Law's wife.

**William Law, Joseph's loyal second counselor – until
Joseph tried to steal his wife.**

Law demanded Joseph make a public confession and
"cease from his abominations."[xciii] Joseph chose to
excommunicate him instead. But Law wouldn't stand for it. He
responded by declaring Joseph a "fallen prophet" and on May
12, 1844, announced a new breakaway sect, the Reformed
Mormon Church. Next, he bought his own printing press and
on June 7, ran off a thousand copies of the premiere edition of
the *Nauvoo Expositor*. The newspaper railed against Joseph's
theocratic contempt for separation of church and state, his
Machiavellian ambitions and shady business dealings, but
primarily aimed at exposing his secret doctrine of polygamy,
or as the lead editorial put it, "to explode the vicious principle
of Joseph Smith, and those who practice the same
abominations and whoredoms."[xciv]

The first issue of the newspaper was also the last. The
Saints burned every copy of the paper they could find. Joseph
proclaimed the paper a public nuisance and dispatched the
Nauvoo Legion to destroy it. On the night of June 10, over two

hundred armed men marched to the *Expositor* offices, sledge-hammered down the door, smashed the printing press, scattered the type, and torched the wreckage to ashes. [xcv] William Law and his fellow dissidents tried to accuse Joseph in court...but Joseph owned the court, along with every other branch of local government. Their backs were against the wall and they feared they would be murdered. So Law and other dissidents fled for their lives, and spread news of the attack. They didn't know it, but they were about to put an end to Joseph Smith.

Joseph had had a good run. He had taken mythmaking, sheer charisma and chutzpah to greater heights than anyone had any right to expect—bolstered by a particularly stalwart personality cult, and spoiled by a string of ridiculous lucky breaks and narrow escapes. But now his years without sufficient reality checks had ended. At long last, Joseph had finally gone too far.

His unchecked political ambitions had turned Illinois into a powder keg, and Joseph had just tossed a match into it. The public was infuriated at the blatant destruction of a man's private property and an attack on a free press by a would-be theocracy. Newspapers howled this outrage was more than unconstitutional—it was treason—and called for war and extermination. All across Illinois, anti-Mormon rage ignited and spread like wildfire; soon there were cries for vigilantes and lynchings, and armed bands were driving isolated Mormon families out of their homes to flee for the safety of Nauvoo. Even Iowans and Missourians were crossing the river in droves, hungry for blood. [xcvi]

Realizing he had unleashed hell and fearing for his life, on June 18, Joseph declared martial law and mobilized the 5,000-man Nauvoo Legion to defend the city. The governor of Illinois, wanting to avoid a civil war, called on the Mormon army to stand down, and for their leader to turn himself in to stand trial. When Joseph, hiding in a secret attic room of his mansion, read the governor's letter on June 22, he was in despair; he knew as soon as he fell into non-Mormon hands he was a dead man. So that night, he and his brother Hyrum crossed the Mississippi in a skiff and fled into the Iowa wilderness to make a break for the Rocky Mountains.

If he had made it into the safety of the West, perhaps that might've even spelled the end of Mormonism. But while they awaited the horses that would take them away, he received an urgent letter from Emma begging him to come back. The Saints thought he was abandoning them out of cowardice. "You always said if the church would stick to you, you would stick to the church; now trouble comes and you are the first to run." [xcvii] Stung by her words, he returned home, perhaps the most decent thing he had done in his entire checkered career. He had no illusions about his chances: "I am going like a lamb to the slaughter."[xcviii]

The Blood of the Prophet

Joseph and eleven others surrendered on June 24, and traveled to Carthage, twenty-five miles away, past gangs of rowdy, drunken militiamen who jeered and heckled and roared for his blood. All but Joseph and Hyrum were freed on bail. They remained in custody in the Carthage jail, guarded from the howling mobs outside by just a single company of militiamen, the Carthage Greys—who were just as eager to lynch Joseph themselves.

Worried for their safety, the jailer allowed Joseph and Hyrum to remain in his own quarters upstairs rather than locking them up in the cells below. They were also permitted visitors, which allowed them to get ahold of two smuggled handguns, a six-shooter pepperbox revolver for Joseph and a single-shot pistol for Hyrum. Joseph may have known he was going to the slaughter, but he wasn't going out like a lamb.

Towards the end of the day on June 27, while two apostles, Willard Richards and John Taylor, were visiting, Joseph sent for some wine, which they all shared except Hyrum. [xcix] As they handed the empty bottle back to the guard and he started down the stairs, there was a noise at the outer door, then shouts to surrender and the sound of gunfire.

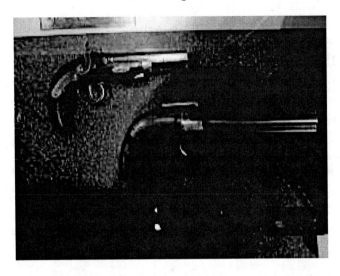

The actual guns used by Joseph and Hyrum at Carthage Jail on
display at the LDS Church Historical Museum, Salt Lake City.
Source: *www.rethinkingmormonism.com*

It was not the Nauvoo Legion staging a gallant rescue, as
Joseph hoped, but 125 or so militiamen of the fiercely anti-
Mormon Warsaw Dragoons, disguised in blackface by rubbing
gunpowder on their faces. Only seven of the Carthage Greys
were on guard outside, and they were in on the plot. They had
loaded their muskets with blanks; after firing one harmless
volley, they stepped aside to let the attackers storm inside,
guns blazing.

The bedroom door had no lock or latch; the four men
scrambled and threw themselves against the door to brace it
shut, but bullets were already tearing through. Hyrum was hit
immediately in the face and exclaimed, "I'm a dead man." He
was struck four more times before his body hit the floor.
Joseph cracked open the door and fired blind, unloading all six
shots into the passageway. Three attackers fell, wounded; the
others rushed the door.

Joseph threw down the empty gun. Richards and Taylor
had no weapons to defend themselves except hickory walking
sticks; they desperately tried to beat away the musket barrels

thrust into the doorway. As the Dragoons forced their way in, a storm of bullets filled the air, both from the attackers thundering into the bedroom and through the windows from the crowd of shooters outside. Taylor tried to escape out the window and was struck twice, in the thigh and chest, slamming him to the floor. There he was hit twice more, one bullet tearing into his forearm and the other "cutting away a piece of flesh from his left hip as large as a man's hand." [c] Richards was inadvertently pinned down between the door and the wall, miraculously unnoticed and unwounded in the charge except for a stray bullet that grazed his throat and earlobe.

Artist's depiction of Joseph Smith's final moments.
Source: www.rethinkingmormonism.com

Joseph also tried to get out through the window; for one terrible instant at the sill he looked out at the sea of upraised musket barrels and gleaming bayonets below, brandished by a howling mob with garish black faces. Some reports said he tried to give the Masonic call of distress ("Oh Lord, my God, is there no help for the widow's son?"), but only got out "Oh Lord, my God" after being shot twice in the back and once in the chest from outside. He plunged forward and dropped twenty feet to the ground. The rabid crowd descended on him;

a second lieutenant in the Carthage Greys reported that as soon as he hit the ground, he was "shot several times and a bayonet run through him."[ci]

Upstairs, lying wounded in a pool of his own blood, John Taylor would survive his wounds, but his watch was broken—permanently stopped at sixteen minutes and twenty-six seconds past five o'clock on June 27, 1844. Mormons have venerated the date and time ever since as the exact moment of the martyrdom of their prophet, Joseph Smith, age thirty-eight.

The Succession Crisis

At dawn the next morning, the faithful were awakened by the terrible sound of doom. A horse thundered up out of the wilderness at full gallop, its rider a howling, wild-haired giant. Porter Rockwell, the prophet's chief bodyguard and relentless enforcer, raged through the streets of Nauvoo shouting "Joseph is killed! They have killed him! Goddamn them! They have killed him!"[cii]

The faithful were staggered by this final disaster. After years of persecution and suffering, the father of the church, God's chosen prophet, the one man who had held everything together was gone forever. There would never be another like him. As ten thousand mourners filed through his mansion to pay their final respects, they wondered how the church would survive this ultimate loss.

Joseph had worn several hats: He was "Prophet, Seer, Revelator, and Translator," "President of the Church," "President of the First Presidency," and "Trustee-in-Trust" of the Church. But he had never spelled out any clear provisions for a successor—instead, he had only hinted at various conflicting criteria for the transfer of power. [ciii] So after his death, no one knew if these roles would be broken out to different men, or just one—or who that successor would be. And several would-be prophets were already scrambling to fill the power vacuum.

Behind the scenes, the church leadership had already split into two warring factions of polygamists and anti-polygamists.

Unbelievable as it seems now, at the time of Joseph's death, the church was still oblivious to the issue that had torn the church leadership in two and directly led to his demise. Apart from his inner circle, 95% of Mormons still had no clue that some of their leaders were taking plural wives or decreeing that celestial marriage was a divinely-mandated requirement for the spiritual exaltation of every Mormon (well, every Mormon male, anyway).

The Apostles like Brigham Young who had secretly taken plural wives already, knew their position was in danger unless they moved swiftly to install one of their own to power. The anti-polygamists like Sidney Rigdon and William Law feared (and not without good reason) that polygamy would destroy the church, and were just as desperate to install a successor who would nip the practice in the bud before it took hold. Emma Smith, who despised polygamy with a long and well-nourished seething hatred, warned that if she didn't approve of the next leader, she would do the church all the injury she could.

The D.O.A. Candidate: Samuel Smith

She and the other anti-polygamists maneuvered frantically to confirm a new prophet from their camp. Joseph's own son, Joseph Smith III, perhaps had the most legitimate claim to the throne, [civ] but he was only eleven years old. So instead they turned to Joseph's younger brother Samuel, whom many already assumed would inherit the mantle of leadership. He was not only one of the eight witnesses to the gold plates, one of the original co-founders and a high councilor of the church, but a few days before his death, Joseph had reportedly named him as his successor.[cv]

Much to the irritation of pro-polygamy Apostle Willard Richards, who argued no leader should be named until the entire Quorum was present,[cvi] their faction rushed to get Samuel confirmed before the rest of the Apostles could return home from their various assignments. Just as it seemed the anti-polygamists had succeeded in handing their man the reins to the church, Samuel suddenly became mysteriously and violently ill. On July 30, 1844, just barely a month after Joseph and Hyrum were killed, Samuel dropped dead at the age of 36. The official cause of death was attributed to a "bilious fever."[cvii]

(Left) Samuel H. Smith, Joseph's brother and next in line to head the church. (Right) Hosea Stout, the man who murdered Samuel on Brigham Young's behalf, according to the Smith family.

But for years, the surviving Smiths would swear it was murder. They accused Willard Richards and his first cousin, Brigham Young, of orchestrating Samuel's death, and even identified the killer: Nauvoo chief of Police Hosea Stout. The chief became Samuel's personal caregiver when he fell ill, and had given him a daily medicine, a 'white powder,' until his death. Samuel died trying to spit out his "medicine," crying out that he had been poisoned (while another family member who had stopped taking the same unidentified powder recovered and survived).[cviii]

Stout was also a Danite with a reputation for violence and a cold-blooded disposition, and already connected with several murders and assaults involving apostates and church critics.[cix]

The Crackpot Candidate: Sidney Rigdon

With Samuel Smith suddenly (and conveniently) out of the picture, rival church leaders saw their own chance at seizing the brass ring. Sidney Rigdon hurried back to Nauvoo from Pittsburgh, announcing to all that he had seen visions of Joseph ascended to heaven on the right hand of God and had received a revelation appointing him "Guardian of the Church." But Willard Richards successfully stalled until a conference could be called to decide the matter. Brigham Young made it back a few days later, two days before the conference.

Sidney Rigdon

A fiery Baptist preacher turned powerful Mormon leader who quickly insinuated himself into Joseph's inner circle. But he was also sickly and emotionally erratic, and suffered from "nervous spasms and swooning." When the church rejected him as its new prophet, he threatened to expose the church's secrets – but Brigham shut him up by threatening to tell Rigdon's secrets...

Rigdon gave a theatrical, overwrought performance for an hour and a half making his case to become the church's new leader. But by now most were fed up with his hysterics and general whininess. When he was soundly rejected, he went from pious hopeful to a diva scorned; he fumed and interestingly enough, swore he would "expose the church," the second time he had made such an intriguing threat. But Brigham Young responded with a mocking, mincing performance of his own:

"Brother Sidney says, 'if we go to opposing him he will tell all of our secrets!' but I would say, oh don't, Brother Sidney! Don't tell our secrets, oh don't!"

He then added a telling counterthreat of his own:

"...if he tells of our secrets, we will tell of his—tit for tat* . . ."
cx

That shut Rigdon up. He backed off, defeated, and was soon excommunicated. Eventually he would gather what followers he could and slink off to Pittsburgh to start a breakaway sect of his own. The LDS congregation voted that the Quorum of the Twelve Apostles would act as the new First Presidency—which meant that the de facto leader of the church was now the president of the Quorum: Brigham Young.

*And wouldn't you just love to know what secrets were behind all these mutual blackmail threats?

Strang Dreams

The drama wasn't over. There were still pretenders to the throne that would have to be dealt with over the six months following the Prophet's death. Plenty of rival church leaders all claimed that Joseph had personally ordained them as his successor when no one else was looking. Of all of the wannabes, none fought for it quite as hard as a new convert,

James J. Strang. He opened with a signed letter from Joseph Smith, appointing him as President of the church. What's more, he testified that an angel appeared to him at the moment of Joseph's death and appointed him President of the church.

James Strang
Would-be successor to Joseph Smith. Strang had his own set of actual ancient plates to back up his claim, but still couldn't convince the flock. He had to settle for being the creepy theocratic king of Beaver Island, Lake Michigan.

But best of all, he had his *own* book of ancient gold plates! Actually, they were made of brass, not gold, and the book had only three tiny pages, each about the size and thickness of a credit card, but they did have one considerable advantage over Joseph's Book of Mormon: they actually existed. You could pick them up and look at them with your physical, actual hands and eyes, not the hands and eyes of faith.

Taking a cue from Joseph, Strang gathered a group of

witnesses to vouch for his new ancient plates, too. They all swore that Strang, following a divine vision, led them to an oak tree on a hill and told then to dig there, for about three feet down they would find the ancient plates. In case anyone was suspecting a hoax, he also had them be sure to carefully examine the ground around the tree; they could find no trace of any tampering. Sure enough, just as Strang said, three feet down, entangled in the roots, they unearthed a case of baked clay containing ancient brass plates. Naturally, Strang also had his own set of Urim and Thummim, and could translate the unknown script on his plates. Strang said that they recorded the final testament of an ancient American king, with the not-at-all-made-up-sounding name of "Rajah Manchou of Vorito."

With all that going for him, Strang was able to rack up an impressive number of supporters, including several prominent church bigwigs: all of the living Book of Mormon witnesses (except Oliver Cowdery, who had gone Methodist); the Prophet's wife Emma and his mother, along with most of Smith's family; and several other prominent members of the early LDS church hierarchy—all accepted Strang's claim to Joseph's mantle of leadership. (Amazingly, Strang even invited the notorious horndog John C. Bennett to join his sect, only to have to kick him out shortly thereafter, for reasons you can probably guess).

Since angels had declared that finding and translating King Rajah Manchou's book would prove he was the new chosen Mormon prophet (Strang had let everyone know in advance), the Saints were to follow him to the new Promised Land, Vorito, also known as Voree, Wisconsin. Brigham Young was less impressed with the evidence of King Rajah Manchou of Vorito, and the Quorum of Twelve promptly excommunicated Strang. But armed with angels, signs and wonders, Strang insisted the excommunication was null and void: the Quorum had no right to sit in judgment of *him*, since after all, *he* was the lawful President of the church.

Perhaps not too surprising, the letter from Joseph Smith was eventually determined to be a forgery. Much later, Strang's former law partner bragged that he and Strang had fashioned the plates out of an old brass teakettle, engraved them with a saw file, and used acid to age them. To bury them, they bored out a long slanting hole deep under the oak tree with an auger. They laid out the earth on a cloth as they dug, and once they had slipped the plates snug among the roots, they tamped the earth back into the hole to leave no trace of their work. [cxi]

Despite such debunking, Strang remained a strong early rival to Brigham Young, poaching many members. At their height, the Strangites had about 12,000 members to Brigham's 50,000. He had to switch his promised land from Voree to Beaver Island in Lake Michigan, when high real estate costs made it tough for his flock to gather there. On the island, he declared himself spiritual king of his own ecclesiastical monarchy (complete with a royal robe, a tin crown, breastplate and wooden scepter). As king he flip-flopped on the polygamy issue, taking on several wives but losing many followers in the process. Strang justified this by yet another ancient book he claimed to have translated, the Plates of Laban. Unlike his Voree plates, this time, except for the obligatory group of witnesses who affirmed they had seen and handled them, no one else seems to have ever seen the new set of plates.

Strang went on to become a successful Michigan state representative, but came to a bad end. He was shot three times from behind and then savagely pistol-whipped by a pair of disgruntled Strangites. His assassination occurred in public, on the Beaver Island dock, in broad daylight, in full view of several officers and men of a Naval vessel docked there, none of whom made any effort to warn Strang beforehand or come to his aid afterward. King Strang lingered for three excruciating weeks before finally dying. To add insult to injury, his killers were never punished. On the contrary, they were given a mock trial, fined $1.25 and released to become the toast of the town. Strang's Voree Plates disappeared around 1900, never to be seen again.

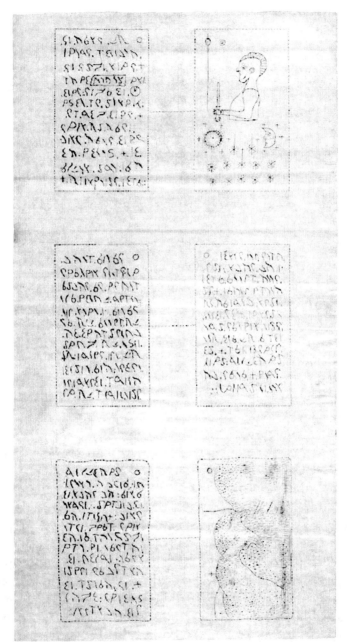

**A facsimile of Stang's three "Voree Plates of Rajah
Manchou of Vorito." (front & back sides)**
Photo: www.strangite.org/Plates.htm

More and more Mormons

The Mormon Church would continue to fragment after Joseph's death. Today the "Strangites" are a few hundred believers with an office near Voree who call themselves "The Original Church of Jesus Christ of Latter Day Saints." Sidney Rigdon's "Rigdonites" would eventually become "Bickertonites," now known as the 15,000-strong Primitive Church of Jesus Christ (Bickertonite).

And there would be still more Mormon splinter groups (and splinters of splinter groups), with names like Cutlerites, Hedrickites, Wrightites, Gladdenites, Godbeites; the Pentecostal Church of Jesus Christ of Latter-day Saints; the True Church of Jesus Christ of Latter Day Saints; the Perfected Church of Jesus Christ of Immaculate Latter-day Saints; the Church of Jesus Christ, the Bride, the Lamb's Wife; the Congregation of Jehovah's Presbytery of Zion; the Church of Christ with the Elijah Message; and the rather J.K. Rowlingsesque Church of the Potter Christ (I'm not kidding you). By some counts there have been more than 130 breakaway sects of Mormonism (others have it at over 200), some extinct and others no larger than a single family; most only of interest to themselves and the more obsessive Wikipedia editors.

The biggest splinter group of them all would be the Missouri-based Reorganized Church of Jesus Christ of Latter Day Saints (RLDS), formed in 1860 when several breakaway Mormon factions finally rallied around Joseph's eldest son, Joseph Smith III. Today they call themselves the Community of Christ and claim a quarter of a million members across 50 countries, who are breaking up into still more splinter groups of their own.

To the Promised Land (This time for sure)

But of course, the majority of the Saints fell under the leadership of Brigham Young. In almost every way he was the opposite of Joseph Smith. Joseph was tall and athletic, handsome with mesmerizing blue eyes and a ready smile. Brigham was a short, squat slab of a man, over 250 lbs. at his heaviest, with cruel, piggy eyes and an unflattering billygoat beard. Joseph was a charming extrovert and an impulsive dreamer; Brigham was tough as nails, earthy, blunt and practical, with his nose to the grindstone and his attention riveted on every last mundane detail. Joseph thrived on attention and was a charismatic, inspiring leader and speaker. Brigham didn't give a damn if people liked him or not, so long as they did what he told them. Only Joseph could have created his religion, and only Brigham could have kept it going.

Joseph was dead, and across the Midwest non-Mormons were eager to see his church gone, too. Illinois became the site of a second "Mormon War", as roaming bands of militia still terrorized Saints where they could find them. Calls to expel the Mormons became more widespread and strident. The state legislature voted overwhelmingly to repeal Nauvoo's problematic city charter, and by default, the church became its own government. By the winter of 1845, it was painfully clear there was never going to be any peaceful co-existence in Illinois—or anywhere else in the United States. The Saints would have to leave the country and head out to find a new home in the wilderness out west.

**The Prophet's successor, Brigham Young.
His eyes say everything you need to know about where he's headed in life.**

The church leaders negotiated a truce that would allow the Saints time to abandon Nauvoo. All winter long they made preparations for a mass exodus, and in early 1846, the Saints began to leave along what would be known as the Mormon Trail. They traveled westward for over a year towards what was then Indian territory and Mexico. Some would be forced to make the trek on foot, pushing handcarts or even carrying all their meager belongings in their arms. Many would never survive the grueling journey, but in July of 1847, the first wagons made it through the mountains and looked out upon the Great Salt Lake valley. On July 24, Brigham, weary and sick with fever, famously declared, "This is the right place." The Saints had finally found their Promised Land... Utah.

And the rest is history.

Today Salt Lake, Tomorrow the World

The Mormon Church—evolution in action: What had by all indications begun as an impulsive hoax had become a moneymaking gamble on a mystical book giving a faux history of Ancient America. But then it made the Darwinian leap to become a fresh and ingenious fringe religious movement. Creative ideas and aggressive marketing (such as reaching out to many poor and disaffected converts in Britain and Europe) increased their numbers. Vicious persecution put the fledgling cult into the crucible; the ordeal burned off the half-hearted, and tempered the faith of the survivors to a fierce new strength. Those hardy souls who made it through the ordeal were more dedicated than ever, bound together unshakably and bolstered enough to survive the long, harsh, crushing exodus to a place where they could set up their own kingdom on earth. Add to that solid business plans, near-ridiculous rates of reproduction, a truly massive pool of volunteer labor operating with complete loyalty to a small central authority, and top it off with tax-free status for their operations, and you have all the makings of a successful world religion. Or even a major multinational corporation.

For further reading:

As with chapters 1, 2 and 3, Fawn Brodie's *No Man Knows My History* and Jon Krakauer's *Under the Banner of Heaven* are highly recommended (see ch. 1 endnotes).

For more of Joseph Smith's rather odd (and failed) prophecies, see Richard Packham's article "Joseph Smith as a Prophet" on the Secular Web at: http://www.infidels.org/library/modern/ richard_ packham/jsmith.html

---

Endnotes: Chapter 4

[lxxvi] Thanks to the Society of Humanistic Judaism for the translation help with these Hebrew words.
[lxxvii] Brodie, p. 265
[lxxviii] ibid., p. 260
[lxxix] Krakauer, p.110
[lxxx] Brodie, p. 327
[lxxxi] Ostling, p.12
[lxxxii] Brodie, p.310
[lxxxiii] ibid.
[lxxxiv] ibid., pp. 314-315
[lxxxv] ibid., p. 324

[lxxxvi] ibid., p. 320
[lxxxvii] ibid., p. 356
[lxxxviii] Ostling, p.13
[lxxxix] ibid.
[xc] ibid.
[xci] ibid., p. 1
[xcii] Brodie, pp. 356 -357
[xciii] Krakauer, p.128
[xciv] ibid., p. 129
[xcv] ibid.
[xcvi] Brodie, p. 378
[xcvii] Krakauer, p. 132
[xcviii] ibid.
[xcix] *History of the Church*, vol. VII, p. 101
[c] Willard Richards, "Two Minutes in Jail" in *Times and Seasons*, Vol.5, No.14, Aug. 1, 1844, pp.598-9
[ci] Krakauer, p.134
[cii] ibid., p. 193
[ciii] ibid., p. 194
[civ] ibid., p. 195
[cv] Smith, George D., ed., *An Intimate Chronicle: The Journals of William Clayton*, p. 138; William Clayton Diary, typescript, 12 July 1844, original in First Presidency's Archives
[cvi] Abanes, p. 207
[cvii] Gaunt & Smith, pp. 44–51
[cviii] Mary B. Smith Norman to Ina Coolbrith, Mar. 27 1908, cited in *Origins* p.153
[cix] Abanes, op. cit.
[cx] Van Wagoner, p. 664
[cxi] *The Saints' Herald*, 35 December 29, 1888, pp. 831–32

David Fitzgerald

Part Two

Mormon-a-Rama: Everything you want to know about the Mormons—and much more...

Introduction

Cherished Mormon Beliefs
(And how they are complete bullshit)

But enough of the history lesson. If you skimmed through the first portion of the book and are still on the fence as to whether Mormonism is the One True Faith™, or if you're a snarky atheist heathen eager to make the next pair of LDS missionaries your chew toy, this section may be more what you're looking for.

Because let's face it: what truly puts the Church of Jesus Christ of Latter-day Saints in a league all their own is their freaky beliefs. Mormons once took perverse pride in being "a peculiar people," but over time they've increasingly yearned for mainstream acceptance. For decades now, they've been desperate to lose the "weird" label, trying to constantly prove "Hey, we're not weird!" Which alone is a sign that they might be a little weird...

Now, don't get me wrong, it's not like the rest of mainstream Christianity is exactly a wellspring of pure reason. But frankly, Mormonism is like steampunk Scientology—chock full of so many wonderful, mondo-bizarro, sweetly racist, crackpot 19th century notions that we could pick any one of them and write a whole book on that alone.

And since the entertainment value of religion is an important facet of this book series, there's one thing you can say about the Mormons on that score: they never disappoint.

Chapter 5

Days of Our Wives: Polygamy

What's the first thing you think of when you consider out-there Mormon beliefs? Yes! Polygamy! Though at first glance it may sound promising—at least to your average straight male—like most things, in real life it isn't so pretty. You only have to skim a gallery of Brigham Young's 55 starkly plain pioneer wives, or observe a flock of present-day FLDS mothers all dressed alike in their Little-House-on-the-Prairie wear and beehive hairdos to quickly see that polygamy as often practiced feels more like a system of cattle-breeding than a 24/7 wild sex romp. In fact, as investigative journalist Andrea Moore-Emmett has made clear in her chilling exposé *God's Brothel*, for far too many women and children brought up in isolated, inbred, fundamentalist compounds, modern polygamy is downright harrowing (keep reading).

It's an interesting paradox: Christians today still love to knock Mormons for their long-abandoned (officially, anyway) doctrine of plural marriage. But there's plenty of polygamy in the Bible, and throughout, God is just fine with it. Nearly all the big-name righteous Old Testament patriarchs, including Abraham, Jacob, Esau, Gideon, Saul, David, Solomon, and still more, all had their share of multiple wives, not to mention also enjoying handmaidens, concubines and the occasional harlot. On the other hand, oddly enough, the Book of Mormon explicitly *condemns* polygamy in several places (Ether 10:5;

Jacob 2:24, 27; 3:5).

Mormon apologists have tried to defend polygamy by claiming it was really a survival necessity, or a nobly-intended blessing, intended primarily for the benefit of the surplus of spinsters too old to be married; the facts show otherwise. In reality, there was a shortage of women on the frontier, not an overabundance. Besides, the overwhelming majority of plural wives were not old maids, but far more often nubile young teenagers, considerably younger than the first wife.

Do You, Joseph, Take These Women?

"Whenever I see a pretty woman, I have to pray for grace," Joseph once remarked to a friend.[cxiii] Polygamy (or as he sometimes called it, "The Blessing of Jacob") may have started as early as 1830. I say "may have" because it's nearly impossible to say when the "the Principle" began. Initially, Joseph didn't tell his wife or friends about it; the only ones in the know were the new spouses. For several years it was kept top secret, taught to no more than a very select few—and actively and emphatically denied, publicly and in print, repeatedly, for years. As early as 1832, he explained to his innermost circle the reason for all the deception was to protect the holy truth, nestled deep inside like the gooey center of a Tootsie Pop: The Lord had vouchsafed that the taking of extra wives was "a true principle, but the time had not yet come for it to be practiced" [cxiv]—or at least, not made public. His first plural wives were just fine with that, since they were already married to other men, several of whom he sent off on far-away and protracted missionary assignments. The wives they left behind were known as "Church Widows." Just as scripture instructs us, Joseph did not forget to take care of the widows.

Due to the problematic circumstances, it's also hard to pin down just how many bonus wives he managed to collect over his short but frisky lifetime. Even today the exact count is still debated by scholars, but most agree it appears close to 50, at least. Mormon historian Todd Compton, author of the exhaustedly researched *In Sacred Loneliness: The Plural*

Wives of Joseph Smith, has come up with thirty-three well-documented wives, eight more likely wives with less certain evidence, and still eight other suspected wives who sealed themselves to Joseph for eternity in posthumous temple weddings shortly after his death (Mormon weddings, or "sealing," can be "for time", meaning just for this life, and/or "for eternity" after death), for an estimated total of at least 49 wives during his life—that we know of.

And Joseph didn't stop accumulating even more wives just because he was dead. Dozens more continued to be sealed to him for years afterwards. Researcher Stanley Ivins reported that Joseph was sealed to 66 or 67 living women, and after his death, another 149 dead women were sealed to him as well. [cxv] Incidentally, sealing themselves to Joseph for eternity would mean that when their *own* husbands arrived in the afterlife, they would be in for a shock: suddenly finding themselves without their wife or children for eternity. How they were supposed to carry out their track to godhood without them is anyone's guess...

Joseph's wives included five pairs of sisters, and one mother/daughter pair. At least twelve were already married to other men. Another ten were under the age of twenty; of these, six originally came into the Smith house to live as wards. His youngest brides were fourteen. One wife, Mary Elizabeth Rollins Lightner, claimed that Smith secretly approached her in 1834—when she was twelve—and let her know "about his great vision concerning me. He said I was the first woman God commanded him to take as a plural wife." [cxvi] It wasn't Joseph's idea; he also informed her an angel with a sword threatened to kill him if he failed to marry her. As it turned out, she wasn't the first, but she did become Smith's ninth wife (at age 24, while married to another man).

The real first appears to have been Fanny Alger, an attractive and popular 17-year-old orphan girl living in the Smith house in Kirtland as a domestic servant in 1833. Contemporaries described her as "comely," and "nice," a "very pretty, pleasing young girl" loved by all. It was well known that she and Emma were extremely fond of one another; less known that Joseph was also fond of her. Fanny and Joseph had an ongoing affair for around two years, until one day sometime in 1835 when Emma spied on them through a crack in the barn planks and "saw the transaction." Enraged, Emma tossed the girl out ^{cxvii}—a pattern that would be played out again and again in the Smith household for the rest of their lives together.

Honestly though, it's a bit much to characterize Joseph and Fanny's special relationship as anything so lofty as a "spiritual marriage." In actuality, Fanny only became a plural wife in hindsight. Decades later, after polygamy had come out of the closet and become respectable, church leaders looked back on Fanny and decided she must have been the first of Joseph's celestial wives and retroactively elevated her from filthy little hussy to first plural wife. By then, Fanny had long since moved away to Indiana, married and raised lots of kids. Whenever questioned about her relationship with the Prophet, she had no comment.

But at the time, it was nothing short of scandal. Book of Mormon secretary and angel eyewitness Oliver Cowdery lost all respect for Joseph after the Fanny Alger affair—or as he put it, the "dirty, nasty, filthy affair." In August 1835, Cowdery issued an official denunciation of polygamy—while Joseph was away. It was later replaced by section 132 of *Doctrine & Covenants*. Cowdery was also replaced, eventually being tried for several church offenses, including "insinuating that the Prophet had been guilty of adultery," and at last excommunicated.

Another early incident nearly ended Joseph's matrimonial career before it began. A disgruntled ex-Mormon (he had left the church because a special revelation given on his behalf had misspelled his name) and a drunken gang came after Joseph by night, smashing their way in and dragging him out of bed out onto the frozen ground. They stripped him naked and after a savage beating, tarred and feathered him. One of them demanded Joseph also be castrated; he had been too intimate with the man's sister, Nancy Marinda Johnson. They had even brought a doctor with them to carry out the procedure, but at the last moment, the doctor couldn't bring himself to go through with it. Nancy Marinda later became one of Joseph's first plural wives. [cxviii] He continued to take more wives throughout the 1830s in Ohio and Missouri, ramping up his spousehunting into high gear in Nauvoo around 1842-43. He did whatever was necessary, including bald-faced lying, to conceal it from everyone except a very carefully select few of his inner circle. [cxix]

It's easy to dismiss his doctrine of polygamy as nothing more than a remarkably convenient sanction for an unchecked libido. And though there is ample evidence that his "plural marriages" were often motivated by restlessness in his pants rather than divine coercion by sword-wielding angels, he also used polygamy to serve non-sexual, albeit still somewhat twisted, purposes. Historians like Compton and Lawrence Foster have noted that Joseph often asked his close friends for their wives and daughters. In 1842, he approached Apostle Heber C. Kimball and asked for his wife. After three agonizing days, Kimball, "with a broken and bleeding heart," [cxx] led his wife to the prophet and handed her over. But—psych! Joseph didn't really want her. He told the gobsmacked couple the whole ordeal had only been a loyalty test. However, a year later, Kimball offered up his young daughter Helen to become another of Joseph's wives, and this time the prophet accepted.

Besides demanding wives and daughters as a test of his followers' devotion, plural marriages served a political goal for the Prophet as well. Joseph pressured Church leaders to be polygamous, a policy that bound him and his closest lieutenants together in an extensive, interlocked dynasty. D. Michael Quinn's meticulously researched history *The Mormon Hierarchy: Extensions of Power,* uncovered just how incestuous church leadership became. During the Church's first hundred years, fully half of the 123 men in the LDS hierarchy were relatives of one or more of the existing General Authorities.

The *Encyclopedia of Mormonism* estimates that during the 19th century, only 20 to 25 percent of adult Mormons were involved in polygamous families. The typical Mormon polygamist had two wives; three was uncommon. More than that was rare except for church authorities, who were strongly encouraged to practice plural marriage and sire large families. *cxxii* Joseph Smith and Brigham Young, of course, each topped the charts with nearly fifty documented spouses for Joseph (or more), and at least fifty-five for Brigham.

Picking Up Girls—The Jo Smith Way

Just how *did* Joseph Smith manage to compel so many young women to spiritually shack up with him, especially before polygamy became officially announced? Largely with strong-arm tactics: Joseph pressured girls with tight deadlines, big promises and heavy spiritual blackmail. Helen Kimball (daughter of apostle Heber C. Kimball, see above) gave a revealing glimpse into his playbook in her memoirs: When her father first told her about Joseph's plans for her, she was shocked; she had never heard of polygamy or plural marriage, and besides, she was only a fifteen-year-old girl, and already in love with a boy closer to her age. Joseph gave her a 24-hour deadline to make up her mind, and told her "if you take this step, it will ensure your eternal salvation and exaltation and that of your father's household and all of your kindred." *cxxiii* Helen succumbed to Joseph's matrimonial extortion to become his (probably) twenty-sixth wife. In her later years she wrote spirited defenses of polygamy, though oddly never mentioning her marriage to Joseph. During her tenure as his wife, though, she wrote tormented poetry confessing her loathing and temptation to rebel, at one point writing "I hated polygamy in my heart."*cxxiv* Fortunately, after Joseph's death, she was able to enjoy the rest of her teenage years and even marry her childhood sweetheart after all.

Just prior to Helen, Joseph had set his eyes on Lucy Walker. In her memoir she described her "courtship" with great detail. After her mother died of malaria, Joseph sent her father away on a mission and broke up the children among other families, taking sixteen-year-old Lucy into his house to work for Emma. One day Joseph called for her and informed her that God had commanded him to take her as another wife.

He explained the secret, new doctrine of plural marriage and afterwards asked her what she had to say. "Nothing," she replied, thinking, *"How could I speak? What would I say?"* She wrote of feeling "tempted and tortured beyond endurance" and wanting to die right there to be with her mother. [cxxv]

Joseph ended with an ultimatum, telling the speechless girl, "I have no flattering words to offer. It is a command of God to you. I will give you until tomorrow to decide this matter. If you reject this message the gate will be closed forever against you." [cxxvi] She wrote, "this aroused every drop of Scotch in my veins," and for a few tense moments stood fearlessly staring him in the eye without a word. "I felt at this moment that I was called to place myself upon the alter a living sacrifice..." [cxxvii]

When she spoke, she said Prophet of God or no, she could not take such a big step without a sign from God; she would rather die. He came up to her, beaming, and assured her she would have one, "a joy and peace that you never knew." And after a sleepless night earnestly praying for guidance, just before dawn her requisite sign came to her and she gave in.

"It was not a love matter," she wrote, "...but simply the giving up of myself as a sacrifice to establish that grand and glorious principle that God had revealed to the world." [cxxviii] On May 1, 1843, just after turning seventeen, she was hurriedly wed to Joseph in a secret ceremony while Emma was away on a shopping trip to St. Louis. Lucy admitted in court in 1892 that Emma never knew of the marriage.[cxxix]

The Nancy Rigdon Incident

But not all succumbed to his charms; we know of at least five prospective brides who spurned him.[cxxx] One of these rejections blew up in his face so spectacularly it cost him two of his closest lieutenants.

One day in 1842, Joseph invited nineteen-year-old Nancy Rigdon to the home of another Nancy: Mrs. Nancy Marinda Hyde, wife of apostle Orson Hyde, whom Joseph had sent off on an extended missionary assignment to Palestine. Mrs. Hyde, in the meantime, had become another of Joseph's plural wives. Joseph greeted the girl, ushered her into a private room and locked the door behind them.

After swearing her to secrecy, he told her how he had liked her for several years, and that he wished that she would be his. He hastened to assure her the Lord was well pleased with the idea, and that "there was no sin in it whatever." [cxxxi] The shocked girl went ballistic. She had already been warned about Joseph's designs for her by the notorious John C. Bennett (who also had his eye on her; she snubbed his advances, too), so not only did the feisty girl not fall for his standard God-has-commanded-me-to-take-you-as-another-wife proposal, she immediately turned on him, raging away with hot tears.

Flustered, Joseph called Mrs. Hyde into the room to help win Nancy over. The young wife tried to tell her that she had been surprised herself when she first learned about celestial marriage, but promised it was true, and that "great exaltation would come to those who received and embraced it." But Nancy countered that "if she ever got married, she would marry a single man or not at all." [cxxxii] Then she threatened to scream her head off until the entire town came running unless Joseph let her go at once. The rattled Prophet did just that.

The next day he tried again, this time via personal letter to Nancy. (Incidentally, you can read it for yourself: the text is still available today, published in the *History of the Church*, vol. V, pp. 134-6. It is presented as "an essay on happiness", with an editorial note innocently declaring, "It is not positively known what occasioned the writing of this essay.") The letter is not a pleasant read. Really, it's little more than a sanctimonious verbal thumbscrew that includes this gem: "That which is wrong under one circumstance, may be, and often is, right under another... Whatever God requires is right, no matter what it is, although we may not see the reason thereof till long after the events transpire."

It goes on from there, switching back and forth between carrot and stick, promising joy and peace in obedience, but darkly warning that "blessings offered, but rejected, are no longer blessings." A few lines of attempted verse follow, including "Be wise today; 'tis madness to defer: Next day the fatal precedent may plead." He informs her that God is more liberal in his views than we are ready to believe, but at the same time, is more awful in the executions of his punishments than we suppose him to be...

Not smart. His touching words didn't just fail to win over the heart of young Nancy—they bit him on the ass. She promptly ran to her father with the letter. Never terribly stable at the best of times, Sidney Rigdon sent for him at once. Joseph arrived to find Rigdon wild-eyed with fury, demanding an explanation for his behavior. At first, Joseph stonewalled and denied everything. But when the girl's father shoved the letter in his face, he broke down and admitted the truth, although not before attempting to get himself off the hook by claiming he was only testing Nancy's virtue. [cxxxiii] Sidney Rigdon didn't buy it, and things deteriorated between them after that.

Soon everyone in town knew about Joseph's botched romance of Nancy. Joseph blamed John Bennett for the whole disaster, and their relationship soon crashed and burned. When Bennett turned against Joseph, one of the damning pieces of evidence brought to light against Joseph was his letter to Nancy.

Emma's Sister Wives

Sometime in early 1843, Joseph somehow managed to convince Emma that polygamy was inevitable. She threatened to take a second husband [cxxxiv] or to leave Joseph altogether [cxxxv], but in the end, like many Mormon wives after her, she resigned herself and reluctantly agreed to let her husband take on more wives, so long as she could pick them. [cxxxvi] Luckily enough, prospective wives were already right under their own roof. Two pairs of young sisters were living with them at the time, four young female wards under Joseph's guardianship: Eliza and Emily Partridge, and Sarah and Maria Lawrence. After long and bitter deliberation, Emma at last selected Emily and Eliza (aged 19 and 23, respectively), and they were sealed to Joseph on May 11, 1843. Unknown to her, both girls had been already secretly married to her husband two months earlier.*cxxxvii*

Emma Smith, Joseph's first wife, bitterly opposed polygamy. She was unaware of most of his other wives, and made life hell for the ones she did know about. After Joseph's death, she did everything she could to stamp it out in the church.

Emma consented to Joseph marrying the fatherless Lawrence girls as well. The fact that both sets of sisters had inherited thousands of dollars may have eased her mind somewhat. It certainly appealed to Joseph, who dipped into all their estate funds. He helped himself to ten thousand dollars from the Partridge estate, [cxxxviii] and eight thousand dollars in English gold from the fatherless Lawrence sisters, which ultimately resulted in a lawsuit filed against him. [cxxxix] According to Joseph's private journal, on the same day he married the Partridge girls, he also bought a fine new carriage for Emma. But the lavish present didn't console her very much; she adamantly refused to allow any more wives, and she seems to have immediately regretted her decision, nagging at him doggedly to be done with plural marriages and making life hell for the sisters until she eventually ran them out of the house (she wanted them out of town, too). Unfortunately for her, the Lawrence girls were not Joseph's third and fourth new wives; actually, they were his 27th and 28th, and he was nowhere near finished accumulating more.

Besides the two pairs of sisters, another wife who actually lived in the Mansion House with Joseph and Emma was Eliza Snow. Eliza was Emma's age, and the two were close confidants. Emma even employed Eliza to spy on Joseph for her, which she did up until Joseph secretly took her as his 15th wife in 1842. In the Mansion House, the Prophet's Nauvoo residence, Emma's bedroom was to the right of his, and Eliza's was on the left. According to a persistent tradition, one February morning in 1843, Emma caught Joseph and Eliza embracing in the hall. Enraged, she seized a broomstick and began beating her. Eliza tripped while trying to escape and tumbled down a full flight of stairs. The whole house was awakened by the racket. While her terrified children cried for her to stop hurting "Aunt Eliza," Emma drove Eliza, still in her nightdress, out of the house into the winter cold. Joseph finally managed to calm Emma and get Eliza back inside. But Eliza, who was pregnant with Joseph's unborn child, miscarried the baby. [cxl]

A New Revelation

Fueled by hard-to-ignore incidents like this, rumors of Mormon polygamy began to become public, enough to be routinely and earnestly denied in newspapers, in Mormon publications and Mormon scripture. Finally, in 1843, Smith (currently on wife no. 34), announced the revelation of celestial marriage to stunned church leaders. Like Muhammad, Smith received remarkably convenient divine revelations at short notice, especially—also like Muhammad—when he met a new girl and wanted to take her as another wife.

His brother Hyrum, who had several wives of his own (but apparently not the same problems with the first wife as Joseph), knew Emma was unhappy and offered to break the news of the new revelation to her. "I believe I can convince her of its truth," he assured Joseph, "and you will hereafter have peace." But Hyrum returned from his mission to Emma with his tail between his legs, and said in all his life, he had never been so abused by a woman. Joseph told him, "I told you, you didn't know Emma as well as I did."[cxli]

After it was written, Joseph and his brother presented the revelation to his wife Emma, who said she did not believe a word of it and "appeared very rebellious"—even though it mentions her, by name, repeatedly. According to the revelation (still proudly reprinted in every edition of D & C—see doctrine 132), Christ commanded the practice of polygamy as a "new and an everlasting covenant" and declared that anyone who rejects the new practices will suffer damnation and will not "be permitted to enter into my glory." Jesus also said that the first wife's consent should be sought before a man married another wife, but if she did not consent to the plural marriage, that Christ would "destroy" the first wife, and that the husband would then be exempt from asking his wife's consent in the future.

The polygamy issue tore apart the church with one schism after another and ultimately was the cause of Joseph's downfall. But even after his death it remained a secret, at least officially (they weren't really fooling anybody). It would stay an open secret until 1852, when Apostle Orson Pratt (Parley's brother) outed it as church doctrine in a public speech, finally ending over twenty years of adamant denials from church authorities that there was any such thing going on.

To Brigham's dismay, letting the cat out of the bag was an utter fiasco. The unexpected about-face added to the church's political problems, and was a huge embarrassment for LDS leaders now caught with their pants not just down, but on fire. Overseas, new converts in France and England were shocked and appalled by the unexpected news. The flood of European converts and cash fueling Utah's growth trickled down to a drop in the bucket. An unhappy missionary in Britain reported that 1,776 new Saints had quit the church in disgust.[cxlii] And worse, now that the secret was out, the general public could now see the cracks in the facade.

Problems with Polygamy

Polygamy, it seemed, wasn't exactly conducive to domestic tranquility. One reason was simple economics: after adding a plural wife, or two, or more, Mormon men often found they were unable to support the multiple families adequately. [cxliii] The addition of a new wife often resulted in matrimonial warfare, [cxliv] especially when she was considerably younger than the first. The friction ran both ways. Senior wives feared being replaced by younger wives; younger wives were intimidated by the power politics of the senior wives and often found themselves treated like servants.

Complaints from the women of the church didn't faze Brigham Young, who flat-out told them, "You sisters may say that plural marriage is very hard for you to bear. It is no such thing." [cxiv] He added if it was the duty of a husband to take a wife, it was the duty of the woman to submit cheerfully. During another sermon, he gave Mormon women an ultimatum: "My wives have got to do one of two things, either round up their shoulders to endure the afflictions of this world and live the religion, or they may leave, for I will not have them about me."[cxlvi]

Seeing as he had at least 55 wives of his own, he apparently didn't have to worry much about losing a few himself. In 1856, Brigham Young grew so tired of having to resolve the continual squabbles in polygamous households, he vowed to provide any unhappy wife with a divorce and free ticket for passage out of the Utah territory—but he was forced to eat his words when so many women rushed to take him up on the offer he had to modify his promise.[cxlvii]

The End (but not really) of Polygamy

Nevertheless, for nearly four decades, open, official polygamy was the rule, and Mormons bred like rabbits while the rest of the country clucked their tongues in disapproval, and continued to block Utah from joining the U.S. as long as they continued the "barbaric" practice. They could have polygamy, or they could have statehood for Utah, but they couldn't have both. Pick one. Surprise! A timely new revelation reversed the "new and everlasting covenant," and the official end of polygamy fell on Oct 6, 1890. The church's "Manifesto," added to the *Doctrine and Covenants*, said nothing to suggest the revelation on polygamy was being revoked or—heaven forbid!—was in error; it simply announced that the church was no longer teaching plural marriage, or permitting its practice. And though plural marriage was an essential component of the doctrine of celestial exaltation, the doctrine was swiftly revamped to make do without it (Don't worry, in the afterlife, men will still be allowed to have more wives).

However, despite their tough new official stance, for over a decade, the Church leadership continued to secretly authorize plural marriages, and add wives of their own.[cxlviii] More than 250 polygamous marriages took place with the full authorization of the First Presidency between 1890 and 1904. (Official church position today blames any plural marriages during this period on two rogue apostles, scapegoats John W. Taylor and Matthias E. Crowley [cxlix]) In 1904, Church president Joseph F. Smith, nephew of the prophet and with five wives of his own, issued a "Second Manifesto" against polygamy and assured the apostles and the public no more polygamous marriages were being performed—while he continued to personally authorize them.

Polygamy Today

Today, polygamy is alive and well. At present there are about a dozen major Mormon and Christian fundamentalist "polyg" groups scattered throughout the United States, Mexico and Canada, primarily in the west, but even as far afield as New England and Florida. But of course the majority of all polygamists live in Utah.

Nothing annoys the LDS church more than the Mormon fundamentalists, and vice versa. Both sides point the finger at each other and say, "They're not real Mormons!" And whose fault is that? The official church continues to distance itself from the fundie polygamists, but they can't come down too hard on them; in their hearts of hearts, they know it's the polygamists who have Mormon scripture on their side. After all, Joseph did call it "the most important doctrine ever revealed to man on earth," and that without it, no man could ever reach the fullness of exaltation in the Celestial heaven. They tell each other that eventually, all of them *will* be polygamists, if not now, at least in the afterlife.

Meanwhile, the breakaway sects say they are the only ones really practicing the religion and denounce the official church, convinced that it was corrupted by the Manifesto. They also continue to poach new members from the mainstream LDS faithful. The fundamentalists remember when the third LDS president John Taylor was holed up in 1886, hiding out from federal officers hunting polygamists, and asked God if plural marriage should be abandoned. That night, Jesus and Joseph Smith appeared in an eerie light, bearing this bit of polite personal correspondence from God almighty:

"My son John, you have asked me concerning the New and Everlasting Covenant how far it is binding upon my people.

Thus saith the Lord: All commandments that I give must be obeyed by those calling themselves by my name unless they are revoked by me or by my authority, and how can I revoke an everlasting covenant, for I the Lord am everlasting and my everlasting covenants cannot be abrogated nor done away with, but they stand forever.

Have I not given my word in great plainness on this subject? Yet have not great numbers of my people been negligent in the observance of my law and the keeping of my commandments, and yet have I borne with them these many years; and this because of their weakness—because of the perilous times, and furthermore, it is more pleasing to me that men should use their free agency in regard to these matters. Nevertheless, I the Lord do not change and my word and my covenants and my law do not, and as I have heretofore said by my servant Joseph: All those who would enter into my glory must and shall obey my law. And have I not commanded men that if they were Abraham's seed and would enter into my glory, they must do the works of Abraham. I have not revoked this law, nor will I, for it is everlasting, and those who will enter into my glory must obey the conditions thereof; even so, Amen."

As the Lord points out, how can a new and everlasting covenant be revoked? But despite God giving his word in great plainness on the subject, just four years later the church did just that, and put an official end to polygamy—while continuing to practice it secretly. With mixed messages like this, it's no wonder fundamentalists continues to draw new members from the LDS church.

The Untouchables

So things have been at a stalemate for over a century. The Utah constitution talks tough on polygamy: it is "forever prohibited." But these days very few polygamists ever see a courthouse, let alone a jail cell. Polygamists have learned to avoid a paper trail by legally marrying just one wife. The others are wed in purely religious ceremonies without any marriage license. There are laws against cohabitation, but they are vague and hard to enforce, and prosecution for polygamy or bigamy hinges on one of the wives testifying against the husband, making cases hard to prosecute and convictions virtually impossible.

And in reality, Utah and neighboring states couldn't arrest the thousands of polygamists within their borders even if they wanted to devote the money, time and manpower attempting to investigate, try and incarcerate them. There simply aren't enough jail cells to hold them all. The numbers of Utah polygamists are difficult to determine; estimates range from 30,000 to 100,000, and growing. [cli]

One reason it's difficult to get a more precise count is that the largest group of polygamists are independent families unaffiliated with any group. These include mainstream Mormons who are closet polygamists, keeping their status so secret that even their neighbors don't realize what's going on next door, much less the state or the mainstream LDS church, who would excommunicate them. In the major polyg groups, many mothers give birth every year, and often children are born without a birth certificate. Fundamentalist groups also regularly suffer schisms and splinter off into rival sects, often violently. And new groups continue to pop up from the ranks of mainstream Mormons who want to return to the bedrock principles of their faith.

Religious Persecution?

There are less obvious factors at work that also hinder prosecution. In 1953, a crackdown on the polygamist enclave of Short Creek, Arizona turned into a massive PR disaster for the government. Images of crying children being torn from their mothers' arms and fathers taken away in handcuffs generated tremendous outside sympathy for the polygamists and ultimately accomplished nothing. And though church leadership officially condemns fundamentalists and refuses to recognize any connection with them, many Mormons today are descendants of polygamists, and harbor at least a grudging respect for those living the principle as the Prophet taught.

Polygamy has gained recent public exposure through HBO's *Big Love* (2006-2011), a series attempting to present a non-judgmental view of the practice. Today, suburban families like the Dargers and their blog, *Love Times Three*, or the Browns on TLC's reality TV show *Sister Wives*, all make wonderful poster children for polygamy. And for what it's worth, they all appear to be educated, productive, consensual adults who chose the lifestyle of their own free will, making informed decisions, supporting one another and working together to raise their loving families in the modern world. So if they can work out the jealousy issues and be happy, fair play to them.

Because multiple soccer moms more or less happily cohabitating in suburbia are not the problem—the dark side of polygamy is the truly horrifying opposite of such cozy arrangements. Most people, including the happy suburban polygamists, would be deeply disturbed by the conditions women and children brought up in starkly theocratic fundamentalist clans are forced to endure.

"Polygamists say they are being attacked because of their religion, but where in the Constitution does it say it's okay to molest and impregnate young girls?" [clii] said one survivor, who ran away at age 14 to escape becoming the fifth wife of a 48-year-old man. Under the Bill of Rights, everyone is free to worship as they see fit and parents are entitled to bring their children up in their own religion. But parents are not allowed to make martyrs of their children. [cliii]

One hundred and fifty scholars of the Fundamentalism Project, a five-year study of religious movements across five continents, have seen that there is a single profile all across fundamentalism. All are patriarchal, anti-feminist, anti-pluralist, and anti-liberal, with a belief that God is male, the man in the family is the ultimate authority, and freedom only makes sense in the context of what is sacred. [cliv] Mormon fundamentalism has taken all these attitudes to unthinkable limits.

In 2002, 14-year-old Mormon Elizabeth Smart was taken

from her Salt Lake City bedroom at knifepoint. Nine months later, she was found, freely wandering the streets of nearby Sandy, Utah, with a homeless former SLC temple worker and his wife, a former organist for the Mormon Tabernacle. The man was unshaven with an unkempt beard, styling himself after an Old Testament prophet. The trio dressed in seedy white robes and sandals, with a burqa-like veil for Elizabeth, who had become the second wife. When the police finally made the connection and took them into custody, the girl was evasive and uncooperative to her rescuers. She finally gave in after being grilled for almost an hour by detectives asking if she was Elizabeth Smart, echoing Jesus' response to Pilate: "thou sayest." She had come completely under the spell of her kidnapper and rapist.

Fundamentalist polygamist groups are continually splintering off into bloody schisms. On the afternoon of May 10, 1977, Rulon Allred, prophet of the Apostolic United Brethren, was shot dead in broad daylight. A chiropractor, Allred was treating patients in his office in a Salt Lake City suburb when two young women walked in, pulled out pistols, gunned him down and calmly strode out again. His killers turned out to be from the LeBaron polygamist group, operating on orders from Evril LeBaron, *their* prophet.

LeBaron was eventually convicted of orchestrating at least seventeen other murders and attempted murders, all according to his "Book of New Covenants," a hit list of people he felt deserved blood atonement, which included his brother, daughter, son-in-law and stepson. Polygamist killings aren't always driven by schismatic politics; sometimes God just tells them to do it. Jon Krakauer documented the brutal, ritualistic 1984 double murder of Brenda Lafferty and her infant daughter by her fundamentalist brothers-in-law, Ron and Dan Lafferty, in his gripping *Under the Banner of Heaven*.

The Utah Attorney General and Utah County Attorney's Office have officially pulled back from prosecuting consenting adult polygamists under state bigamy laws except in cases of fraud, abuse or violence. [clv] But there have been enough horror stories coming out of secluded compounds in the southwest to bring down the law on their self-styled patriarchs.

Scary Polygamy: Life Inside a Polygamist Cult

The Fundamentalist Church of Jesus Christ of Latter-day Saints, or FLDS, is primarily located in the former Short Creek area, now known as Hildale, UT, and Colorado City, AZ, twin cities straddling the Utah/Arizona border. The FLDS has about 10,000-15,000 members there; they also have known settlements in Canada, Mexico and Texas. Today, the FDLS is probably the best known and most notorious polygamist sect since its leader, Warren Jeffs, made the FBI's Ten Most-Wanted List. He was wanted for so many sexual felony offenses it's difficult to keep track of them all, but they included accomplice to rape for arranging marriages between minors and adults, sexual conduct with a minor, incest, aggravated sexual assault for intercourse with a 15-year-old and a 12-year-old, as well as the ongoing rape of his nephew and niece, which began when they were 5 years old and 7 years old, respectively.

Laura Chapman was born and raised in the FLDS, in a household of 36 people, including four wives and 31 children; she was the 25th child born. Today, in her 40s, she's an anti-polygamy activist and an articulate spokeswoman on behalf of those who have managed to escape polygamist cults. She told her story to investigative journalist Andrea Moore-Emmett for *God's Brothel*, one of 18 women profiled in the book (the majority of information in this section comes directly from their own stories in *God's Brothel*). Laura jokes that she's related to nearly everyone in Utah who has anything to do with polygamy. Her family tree has eight generations of Mormon polygamists and reaches into several different FLDS splinter groups. The murdered polygamist leader Rulon Allred was her great-uncle. Her aunt married into the LeBaron group that killed him.

She herself was born into the Kingston clan, a secretive branch of the FLDS that owns a network of assorted businesses and land holdings across the west (including, among many others, a law office, a coal mine, a pawn shop, a bar, and a casino) worth upwards of $200 million. But despite all their money, the majority of the group is on welfare and lives in severe poverty. Most polygamist groups rely heavily on food stamps, Medicaid, economic development funds, and other government services to support their enormous families. Welfare fraud is a given; many plural wives are on welfare as "single mothers."[clvi] Communities like Hildale/Colorado City put a serious crunch on state welfare systems. In one year (July 2002-July 2003), the FLDS families in one community took in more than $3 million in food stamps and cash assistance. [clvii] Ironically, though polygamists consider themselves above the law, they are proud of their dependence on government aid. They call working the system this way "bleeding the beast," an intentional effort to bring down the U.S. government. [clviii]

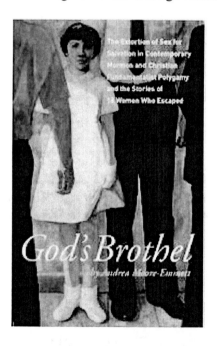

Investigative journalist and former Mormon Andrea Emmett-Moore interviewed 18 women who escaped from abusive polygamous cults in her book, *God's Brothel*. Their stories are harrowing.

In the Kingston group, the men do little or nothing to support their families. Women and children are worked for as many as sixty hours a week for near-minimum wage in the Kingston businesses. Instead of receiving paychecks, their wages are deposited in a Kingston bank account (rent, debts and a mandatory 10% tithe are automatically deducted) and they are paid in scrip that can only be spent in Kingston-owned stores. [clix] They are also made to understand that if the church requires their money, they will pull it from their bank accounts. They are deprived of having any real experience with money. "We were told to sacrifice everything for the kingdom," said one former member, "to the point that if we found a penny in the street we were to turn it in." [clx] And each year, members must sign a form reaffirming their loyalty to the group and firm belief in the religion, and that when they die, everything they own will go to the church. [clxi]

Slave Girls and Lost Boys

Even before they enter the working world this way, Kingston girls are born into a life of servitude. Their childhoods don't include play; there's no time for anything but work. "By age ten, I was baking a dozen loaves of bread at a time," Laura recalled. "By 13, I was cooking meals for our entire family (of 36 people) and sewing clothes." Boys' treatment depends on their family connections and ability to conform. Since there are not enough girls to go around, the older men tend to regard them as their competition and many are driven away to fend for themselves.

With little education, sometimes not even a birth certificate or a social security number, or even a real surname, these "Lost Boys" bounce from one low-end job to another to survive, or eke out a hand-to-mouth living on the street. Other low-status males stay in the community, but only to become worker bees for the group. [clxii] Still others just die suddenly, or disappear without explanation. People might be told this troublesome boy or that drowned in the creek... boys who knew how to swim. "They told us one boy suffocated from car exhaust after pulling over to the side of the road for a nap," a former member reported. "Another one was supposed to been hit by a semi truck while crossing the highway because he didn't see it coming." Strangers caught snooping around the community are dealt with swiftly. In the LeBaron group, one new member was shocked to hear rumors of violence and learn of previous murders committed by the group; she was also given a gun and instructed, "If anyone ever comes around, shoot 'em first and drag 'em inside." *clxiii* In the Hildale/Colorado community, everyone is a member of the sect, including the mayor, the judge and the police. Suspicious deaths are never questioned, much less investigated. *clxiv*

Though the leadership controls the money and lives quite comfortably, the rank and file members are conditioned to believe an impoverished life is a blessing for their benefit to "refine their souls" and make them more "perfected." *clxv* They are not allowed to hang pictures on the walls; at one point, the leaders even ordered all the wallpaper torn down. Another time, all personal possessions were taken from everyone and only given back one by one when the Prophet deemed they had been earned. *clxvi* Members are told if they sacrifice now, they will all have their pick of rich people's homes when Christ returns and destroys the unbelievers. *clxvii*

So they live their lives in overcrowded conditions, in horrid squalor, in out-of-the-way desert enclaves. Many children are filthy and smell terrible because they can only bathe once a week to save on water. *clxviii* The Utah desert basically has two seasons—scorching hot and freezing cold. Some mothers have to make do for the children without heat, electricity or running water. One woman reported her husband regarded furniture as a worldly vanity, so they slept on the floor. *clxix* Keeping everyone fed is a constant challenge. Some gather pig weed from the desert to supplement their diet; many engage in dumpster diving—raiding the trash from behind grocery stores at night for produce. Even rotting produce is taken; the men insist that nothing be wasted. *clxx*

The sect leaders tend to be paranoid of doctors. They fear doctors will encourage their women to stop having more children, so they avoid any medical care except in extreme emergencies, preferring to heal with prayer and the priesthood blessing of the laying-on of hands. Women get no pre-natal care; the men deliver the babies. The group has to constantly cope with communicable diseases from not inoculating their children. Whooping cough has become an annual calamity.

Dying From the Inside Out

The psychological environment is every bit as toxic. In the group, children don't get educated, they get indoctrinated. As one leader told Andrea Moore-Emmett: "We don't teach them the things of Babylon. They only need spelling, Hebrew, English, and some computer skills so they can transcribe scripture." [clxxi] Like all cults, obedience is the highest virtue. All members are given "memory gems" to memorize. These are phrases members are required to repeat aloud twice a day at the exact same time, all together, no matter where they are or what they are doing. [clxxii]

Women are commanded to be happy. If they fail in their duty to put on a convincing appearance of happiness, they are punished. This is because if they are unhappy, it means they allowed Satan into their lives. [clxxiii] "Not a single woman I've ever known is happy, even though they all say they are," said one FLDS survivor. "And believe me, a lot of them confided in me." [clxxiv] One survivor said she had to escape polygamy because it felt like she was dying from the inside out. [clxxv]

Members are strictly forbidden to mix with "outside" children, those in "Babylon." Boys are allowed to finish high school and go on to college, but the Prophet chooses their career paths. Most girls get pulled from public school around age 14, about the time they are to be married as plural wives. Part of the sect's teaching is that no one can reach heaven unless one of his daughters is married to a Kingston leader. [clxxvi]

It gets worse.

The Kingston Bloodline

Incest is endemic in fundamentalist polyg enclaves, but inbreeding is particularly rampant among the Kingstons. The leaders claim that the Kingston family line traces all the way back to Jesus Christ, and therefore, they have holy blood. [clxxvii] Girls are routinely married to close male relatives to "purify the bloodline" and are told it's okay to marry their cousins or uncles or nephews because "God will change the blood." [clxxviii] You can imagine the genetic nightmare that results: Kingston mothers have given birth to blobs of protoplasm, or gone through eight or nine pregnancies without ever giving birth to a live baby. [clxxix] Some newborns are so deformed, they become "poofers," the community slang for any infant—or rebellious child—that mysteriously disappears, "gone in a poof." [clxxx]

It is disturbingly easy to spot members of the Kingston clan; severe inbreeding has turned them into a circus sideshow. Congenital defects are rife: some babies are born with fused limbs, or with no fingernails; many suffer from dwarfism, spina bifida, Tourette's Syndrome or various mental illnesses. [clxxxi] Some of their children have microcephaly, which means their head is abnormally small, turning them into "pinheads." The condition causes a host of problems like shortened lifespan, retardation, seizures, and impaired motor function ranging from clumsiness to full-blown spastic quadriplegia.

Mutations like Down Syndrome are also common, but it's not unusual for Kingston mothers to stroke their bellies and wish for "a Down's." As they see it, Down Syndrome children are compliant, and best of all, bring in $500 per month in government assistance. [clxxxii] But aside from that blessing, sect leaders say birth defects are a punishment for mothers who are not sufficiently submissive to their husbands or faithful to the church. [clxxxiii]

And still, it gets worse...

Laura's Story

What could be worse than virtual slavery, an environment of squalor and disease, incest and severe inbreeding? Add a pervasive culture of pedophilia. Add coercion, enforced by brutal, constant battering and abuse. Now top it off with forcing its victims to revere their abusers. Let's return to Laura Chapman's story. [clxxxiv]

People in the Kingston group are fond of saying Laura Chapman's father is one of the most Christ-like men they've ever met.

Her own earliest memories are of being molested and raped by him when her mother was away. He would enter her room at night and she would wake up to him forcing himself on her. After he left, she would tremble in fear for hours. "That lasted until I was 13."

When she was four, one of her stepbrothers tied her to a bedpost and tried to rape her. "Afterward I was crying. My father told me he would slap me until I stopped crying, which he proceeded to do. My mother made herself busy in the kitchen so she wouldn't have to watch." Beatings by her father or one of his four wives were common. "No mother can protect her child from the other mothers." The community preaches, "You can all but kill a child for disobedience."

Laura remembers being suicidal as far back as the age of six, but not knowing how to do it. Most of the women and children who have escaped the cult have reported having to wrestle with suicidal impulses. "I'd lie on my bed and will my heart to stop beating or to stop my breath."

Between the ages of 13 and 15, some of her brothers routinely fondled her. When she told her mother, the two of them went to her father. "He told my mom he wanted to talk to her alone; when she came out, she said, 'Your father says we have to let (the brothers) be who they're going to be.'" At age 15, she tried unsuccessfully to run away from the community after a beating from one of the other mothers, her own mother's sister.

On the night of her 16th birthday, her father took her for a ride in his Cadillac. Driving down the highway at 60 m.p.h., he informed her it was time for her "Sexuality Lesson," a tradition for all his daughters. Now she was to think of herself as a sister-wife to her mothers, he told her, and warned her not to tell her mother about the lesson she was about to receive; sister-wives don't tell each other about intimacies. While her father was telling her all this, her hand was on the door handle. She debated whether or not to pull it and jump to her death. Instead, she stayed in the speeding car. She lived to survive that awful night and many others.

Marriage and Family

Laura was soon married off to a boy from another FLDS branch, the Barlow group. Like all polyg girls, she was expected to start having children and continue having a new baby every year for the rest of her life; the Barlows preach that "women are vessels to be worn out in childbirth." During her time with the new group, she also saw the same abuses she had experienced in her own Kingston group, and seen in the Allred group where her mother's people lived, and in the LeBaron group where her cousins lived, and in the independent polyg enclaves she knew through her grandfather.

Living with her new in-laws, "I could hear my father-in-law's second wife beating the children," she remembers. She had told Laura how her husband had thrown her down the stairs when she was pregnant. The unfortunate woman soon contracted genital herpes on her rectum... and the small grandchildren became infected with genital herpes in and on the mouth. As the disease is only spread by genital contact, the only reasonable conclusion is child sexual abuse by the grandfather.

Over the years Laura's husband was chronically unemployed. They could never make ends meet and were continually moving in and out of his parents' house. After giving birth to five children, she told her husband she wanted to do right by them and stop having more. The Barlows believe birth control is murder; he told her if she used birth control, he wouldn't have anything more to do with her.

Later, she confided to him about the sexual abuse she had suffered from her father and brothers. Instead of being outraged, he told her how, at the age of 19, he had molested his 11-year-old sister. After that she knew she couldn't trust him with their daughters and began planning her escape and slipping off to the local library to learn how to talk to her children about sexual abuse.

Escape and Revenge

The clincher came on their tenth anniversary, when her husband presented her with a ring—and then told her he had to take another wife so that he could go to the Celestial Kingdom and be exalted to godhood. They had never been legally married; she quickly talked him into having a legal ceremony. She didn't tell him the real reason she wanted the legal marriage: so that she could demand child support when she escaped. A month later, she did escape, and moved out with her children. Her husband immediately took a second wife, a 16-year-old.

Laura rebuilt a new life for herself, her four daughters and a son with special needs. Working part-time, she earned a high school equivalency and then a bachelor's degree in sociology and human development with a minor in psychology. She has also personally helped other mothers and girls escape from polygamy themselves, and has often goaded government agencies to do their job and press charges when accusations of incest and abuse come to light.

Laura has seriously hurt the polygamists. In return, they've threatened her life, and that of her family. When her sister escaped her own polygamous husband, she was kidnapped while working a paper route. The men took her back to her husband and threatened to kill her in blood atonement. The police looked the other way, saying, "You can't be abducted in your own home."

Today, Laura Chapman doesn't shy away from the fight, but continues to help victims of polygamy escape and adjust to life in the real world, and to be a strong anti-polygamy activist. In March 2002, she addressed a women's conference at the United Nations on human rights violations in polygamy. As for those who abused her, she puts it simply: "My best revenge is to live a healthy life."

***

For further reading:

On early polygamy: Todd Compton's *In Sacred Loneliness: The Plural Wives of Joseph Smith* (Salt Lake City: Signature Books, 1997)

For personal accounts from women who have escaped from modern fundamentalist polygamist circumstances, see Andrea Emmett-Moore's harrowing *God's Brothel* (San Francisco: Pince Nez, 2004)

Assassinated cult leader Rulon Allred's daughter Dorothy Allred Solomon has written several books on her experiences: *In My Father's House* (Franklin Watts, 1984); *Predators, Prey, and Other Kinfolk: Growing Up in Polygamy* (W.W. Norton, 2003); *Daughter of the Saints: Growing Up In Polygamy* (W.W. Norton, 2003); *The Sisterhood: Inside the Lives of Mormon Women* (Palgrave Macmillan, 2007)

Endnotes: Chapter 5

[cxii] Ostling, p. 59
[cxiii] Wyl, p. 55
[cxiv] Ostling, p.121
[cxv] Brodie, p.488
[cxvi] Newell & Avery, p. 65
[cxvii] Ostling, p. 60
[cxviii] Brodie, pp. 118-119
[cxix] Krakauer, pp. 120-21

^{cxx} Ostling, p. 62

^{cxxi}Quinn, *MH:EoP* pp.163-197, 731-745

^{cxxii} Ostling, p. 67-68; 69-70

^{cxxiii} ibid. p. 62

^{cxxiv} *Representative Women of Deseret*, p. 112—cited in Brodie, p. 480

^{cxxv} Compton, pp. 463-465

^{cxxvi} Brodie, p. 478

^{cxxvii} ibid.

^{cxxviii} Ostling, p. 63

^{cxxix} Temple Lot Case: *United States Circuit Court 8th Circuit...The Reorganized Church of Jesus Christ of Latter Day Saints, Complainant, vs. the Church of Christ at Independence, Missouri... Complainant's abstract of pleading and evidence.* Lamoni, Iowa, 1893, pp. 371-5 , cited in Brodie, p. 479

^{cxxx} Ostling, p. 65

^{cxxxi} Van Wagoner, p. 295

^{cxxxii} ibid.

^{cxxxiii} Brodie, pp. 310-11

^{cxxxiv} Krakauer, p. 126

^{cxxxv} Brodie, p. 342

^{cxxxvi} ibid., p. 339

^{cxxxvii} Brodie, p. 339; Ostling, p. 68

^{cxxxviii} Brodie, ibid.

^{cxxxix} Ostling, p. 64

^{cxl} Brodie, pp. 345-46

^{cxli} ibid., p. 341

^{cxlii} Krakauer, p. 205

^{cxliii} Compton, p. 199

^{cxliv} Bagley, p. 40

^{cxlv} Young, *Journal of Discourses*, 17:159

^{cxlvi} ibid., 4:55

^{cxlvii} ibid., September 21,1856, *Journal of Discourses*, 4: 55-56; Kenney, ed., *Wilford Woodruff's Journal*, October 6,1856, 4:464

^{cxlviii} Ostling, p. 73

^{cxlix} D. Michael Quinn, "On Being a Mormon Historian and Its

Aftermath" 1981 speech reprinted in: Smith, ed., *Faithful History*, p.87

[cl] *Historical Record* 6:226

[cli] Moore-Emmett, p. 25

[clii] Krakauer, p. 27

[cliii] Moore-Emmett, p. 45

[cliv] ibid., p. 47

[clv] "'Sister Wives' Lawsuit Opens Window on Modern Polygamy," Peg McEntee, *Salt Lake City Tribune*, Jun 1, 2012

[clvi] Moore-Emmett, p. 144

[clvii] ibid., p. 38

[clviii] Ibid., p. 93

[clix] Krakauer, p. 18

[clx] Moore-Emmett, p. 68

[clxi] ibid., p. 88

[clxii] ibid., pp. 50-51

[clxiii] ibid., p. 119

[clxiv] ibid., p. 181

[clxv] ibid., p. 50

[clxvi] ibid., p. 66

[clxvii] ibid., p. 144

[clxviii] ibid., p. 172

[clxix] ibid., p. 60

[clxx] ibid., p. 144

[clxxix] ibid., p. 50

[clxxii] ibid., p. 66

[clxxiii] ibid., p. 41

[clxxiv] ibid., p. 128

[clxxv] ibid., p. 41

[clxxvi] ibid., pp. 85-86

[clxxvii] ibid., p. 67

[clxxviii] ibid., p. 93

[clxxix] Krakauer, p.19

[clxxx] Moore-Emmett, p. 173

[clxxxi] ibid., p. 67

[clxxxii] ibid., p. 173

[clxxxiii] ibid., p. 67

[clxxxiv] Laura's story here is taken from ibid., pp. 90-100

Chapter 6

White or Wrong: Racist Dogma

One tip-off of the Book of Mormon's 19th-century origins is its blatantly racist attitudes towards dark-skinned ethnic groups, and Africans in particular. For nearly 150 years, blacks were not allowed into the priesthood; which in Mormon terms, meant they were locked out of heaven, and could forget about becoming a god. But in 1978, the church finally bowed to public criticism—or if you prefer, president and prophet Spencer W. Kimball received a divine revelation that "all worthy male members of the church" would be "eligible for priesthood and temple blessings."

Why couldn't they join the priesthood before then? Because Africans were cursed with black skin before they were born, when they were pre-existent spirit children in heaven. Brigham Young had declared in 1854 that the curse would only be lifted after all the other children of Adam received their resurrection from the dead. The church has yet to come up for a good explanation why the ban on black priesthood was rescinded ahead of schedule.

Given no good reason for the change of policy, the news came as a shock to the flock, and not all the Saints were willing to accept it. Just as they had when the church abruptly flip-flopped on polygamy, the staunchest believers left the church in disgust and joined fundamentalist Mormon breakaway sects.

Their divinely sanctioned prejudice wasn't reserved just

for Africans. They also believed Native Americans were originally "white and delightsome" Israelites before they were also cursed with a "skin of blackness" for their filthy wickedness—but don't take my word for it:

*"After they had dwindled in unbelief **they became a dark, and loathsome, and a filthy people**, full of idleness and all manner of abominations."*

(1 Nephi 12:23)

*"And he had caused the cursing to come upon them, yea, even a sore cursing, because of their iniquity. For behold, they had hardened their hearts against him, that they had become like unto a flint; **wherefore, as they were white, and exceedingly fair and delightsome, that they might not be enticing unto my people the Lord God did cause a skin of blackness to come upon them**. And thus saith the Lord God: I will cause that they shall be loathsome unto thy people, save they shall repent of their iniquities. **And cursed shall be the seed of him that mixeth with their seed; for they shall be cursed even with the same cursing**. And the Lord spake it, and it was done. And because of their cursing which was upon them they did become an idle people, full of mischief and subtlety, and did seek in the wilderness for beasts of prey."*

(2 Nephi 5:21-24)

*"It came to pass that those Lamanites who had united with the Nephites were numbered among the Nephites; And **their curse was taken from them, and their skin became white like unto the Nephites**; And their young men and their daughters became exceedingly fair, and they were numbered among the Nephites, and were called Nephites. And thus ended the thirteenth year."*

(3 Nephi 2:14-16)

*"Behold, the Lamanites your brethren, whom ye hate **because of their filthiness and the cursing which hath come upon their skins**, are more righteous than you; for they have not*

129

forgotten the commandment of the Lord, which was given unto our father -- that they should have save it were one wife, and concubines they should have none, and there should not be whoredoms committed among them...

*"O my brethren, **I fear that unless ye shall repent of your sins that their skins will be whiter than yours**, when ye shall be brought with them before the throne of God...*
*"Wherefore, a commandment I give unto you, which is the word of God, that ye revile no more against them **because of the darkness of their skins**; neither shall ye revile against them because of their filthiness; but ye shall remember your own filthiness, and **remember that their filthiness came because of their fathers.**"*

(Jacob 3:5, 8-9)

And the skins of the Lamanites were dark, according to the mark which was set upon their fathers, which was a curse upon them because of their transgression and their rebellion against their brethren, *who consisted of Nephi, Jacob, and Joseph, and Sam, who were just and holy men. And their brethren sought to destroy them,* **therefore they were cursed; and the Lord God set a mark upon them,** *yea, upon Laman and <u>Lemuel</u>, and also the sons of Ishmael, and Ishmaelitish women. And this was done that their seed might be distinguished from the seed of their brethren, that thereby the Lord God might preserve his people, that they might not mix and believe in incorrect traditions which would prove their destruction.* **And it came to pass that whosoever did mingle his seed with that of the Lamanites did bring the same curse upon his seed.**

(Alma 3:6-9)

Despite that ominous threat from the Lord in Alma 3:9, Joseph Smith seemed to forget and prophesied that the Red Man would become "white, delightsome and just" in just a few generations, and encouraged his followers to take Indian wives.

Brigham Young wasn't nearly so charitable towards blacks. He legalized slavery in Utah and pronounced the mark of Cain was "the flat nose and black skin." His descendants were "black, uncouth, uncomely, disagreeable and low in their habits, wild, and seemingly deprived of nearly all the blessings of the intelligence that is generally bestowed on mankind."[clxxxv] Miscegenation was an abomination. Brigham insisted, "If the white man who belongs to the chosen seed mixes his blood with the seed of Cain, the penalty, under the law of God, is death on the spot. This will always be so." [clxxxvi]

This attitude continued into the 20th century, only the rougher edges were smoothed out. Modern church leaders didn't rail against those low, uncouth blacks; they gently explained why Negroes deserved second-class treatment. Turns out it's all their fault:

"There is a reason why one man is born black and with other disadvantages, while another is born white with great advantages. The reason is that we once had an estate before we came here, and were obedient, more or less, to the laws that were given us there. Those who were faithful in all things there received greater blessings here, and those who were not faithful received less...There were no neutrals in the war in heaven. All took sides either with Christ or with Satan. Every man had his agency there, and men receive rewards here based upon their actions there, just as they will receive rewards hereafter for deeds done in the body. The Negro, evidently, is receiving the reward he merits."

Joseph F. Smith, *Doctrines of Salvation*, 1954; 1:61, 65-66

"...Negroes are not equal with other races where the receipt of certain spiritual blessings are concerned, particularly the priesthood and the temple blessings that flow therefrom, but this inequality is not of man's origin. It is the Lord's doing, is based on his eternal laws of justice, and grows out of the lack of Spiritual valiance of those concerned in their first estate."

Bruce McConkie, *Mormon Doctrine*, 1966 edition, pp. 527-528

If you're wondering if such blatant racism made foreign missionary work difficult, you're right. But they found work-arounds for the problem. For instance, in Brazil, where nearly everyone you meet is a spectacular mélange of different races, LDS missionaries limited their missionary efforts for years to white immigrants from Germany, up until World War II. [clxxxvii]

To make matters even more confused, during Mormon President David McKay's tenure (1951-1970), it was quietly decided that skin color and black features weren't marks of Cain/Ham after all, only African heritage. This doctrinal twist didn't exactly jibe with early church doctrine (or make sense), but it did have the advantage of opening up the priesthood to the ripe mission field of dark-skinned Pacific islanders: Fijians, Philippine Negritos, New Guineans, Samoans, Tongans Tahitians, et al. Polynesia has gone on to become the church's biggest foreign success. [clxxxviii]

Since 1978, LDS apologists have wrestled with a way to rationalize the ban on black priesthood. Though McConkie sheepishly told church members to "forget everything I have ever said" in defense of the ban [clxxxix], no official explanation has ever been offered. Armand L. Mauss, Mormon author of *All Abraham's Children* (2003), detailed his church's problematic teachings on blacks, Jews and Native Americans, and admitted that Mormon racial theology could be of "strictly human origin." After all, "prophets are not perfect and don't claim to be; nor do they always act as prophets in what they say or do." [cxc] Just how followers are expected to know when their prophets are speaking for God—and when they aren't—remains a mystery.

***

For further reading:

Nobody Knows: The Untold Story of Black Mormons (2009) is an award-winning documentary about African American Latter-day Saints.

Endnotes: Chapter 6

clxxv Ostling, p. 101
clxxvi ibid., p.102
clxxvii ibid., p.96
clxxviii ibid., p.108
clxxix ibid., p.104
cxc cited in ibid., p.107

Chapter 7

Things to do in Mormonism When You're Dead: The Mormon Afterlife

Mormon theology has it all over its fellow western religions when it comes to the afterlife. You want a heaven? Bam! Here're three of them! Muslims may get 72 nubile and ever-willing virgins, but Mormons get as many wives as they can collect—plus all their children, too. And not only that, but worthy Mormons—well, worthy Mormon *men*—have the potential to become exalted to godhood themselves (and as of 1978, that now includes worthy black Mormon men, too).

Eternal Progression

In the Mormon version of our universe, God has a physical body just like ours, because he is an exalted man. As the famous Mormon saying goes: "As Man is, God once was; and as God is, Man may become." The journey to godhood begins on Kolob. Depending on which Mormon you ask, Kolob is the name of the planet where God, whose name is really Elohim, lives; or the star closest to heaven; or is just a metaphorical symbol of Jesus; or no one really knows. I've gotten all these responses to the question from different Mormons, which might indicate that Saints aren't entirely comfortable about outsiders asking too much about Kolob...

But good authority has it Kolob is where God our Heavenly Father lives with his wives and spirit children, including his sons Jesus and Lucifer and all of us before we were born. But hold on a minute—you say you don't remember anything about having a premortal life as a spirit baby on Kolob? Not to worry, there's a perfectly logical explanation.

You see, when a spirit child comes down to Earth from Kolob to be born, there's a slight problem. The baby's physical body, or the "earthly tabernacle," is unfortunately just a smidge too small to fit the incoming spirit child. Apparently, spirit bodies take up a surprising amount of real estate in the physical realm, and sadly, this divine design flaw makes it necessary for the spirit body to shed some spiritual weight before incarnation can take place (how a spirit can have weight remains a divine mystery). So what has to go are all the memories of your amazing life in heavenly pre-existence on Kolob with God and all the other teeming millions waiting for their chance to be born. Which is the reason you can't remember anything about your life before your birth.

That pre-life life is also known as the First Estate. The life you're living at the moment is the Second Estate; it's just the staging area for your eternal life, the Third Estate—the quality of which will range from meh to pretty sweet to unbelievably fabulous, depending on how Mormon-ly you live your life.

When you become a god, assuming you are a worthy white Mormon male (or a worthy black Mormon male after 1978) who kept all the commandments faithfully and took at least one wife, you'll create your own universe to rule with your family. This is part of the reason Mormons take family so seriously: families will be united eternally, unless, of course, your sons want to go create their own universes.

Confused? Here's a simple chart to let you know how eternal progression works...

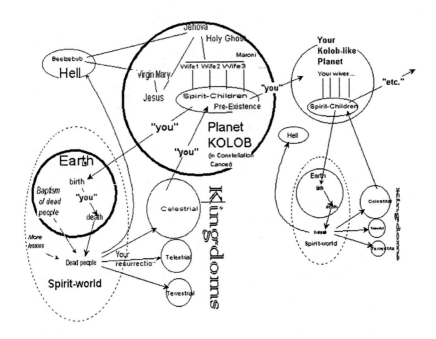

chart courtesy of nowscape.com

Still confused? Just remember that Mormon heaven comes in three levels, or "degrees of glory." They are, in ascending order of coolness:

The Telestial kingdom

The telestial kingdom is the bottommost heaven. You could say it's either a low-rent heaven or an upscale hell—your pick. *Doctrine and Covenants* section 76, taking a note from Revelation 22:15, says this level is full of "liars, and sorcerers, and adulterers, and whoremongers, and whosoever loves and makes a lie." It also includes those heathens who never got the news about the gospel. Since they didn't accept Jesus as their Savior, they first get sentenced to a thousand years in Spirit Prison (see below), and then upon release are resurrected to pick up an immortal physical body and get assigned to the telestial kingdom.

The Terrestrial kingdom

Next highest is the terrestrial kingdom. It's just okay. Respectable folks who "were blinded by the craftiness of men" (*D&C* 76) and thus rejected the fullness of the gospel during their mortal lives wind up here; in other words, this is where all the non-Mormon religious people go. It's also where half-assed Mormons who "are not valiant in the testimony of Jesus" go if they aren't careful. Unlike most other forms of Christianity, which insist you have to accept Jesus before you die or the offer expires, Mormons teach that you can accept Jesus after death, and still make it as far as this middle-class heaven.

Ultimately, in LDS theology, it's God's call if you can achieve the highest level of heaven or have to settle for the terrestrial kingdom. For instance, according to *Doctrine and Covenants* section 137, God judges all those who died before Mormonism came along—retroactively. Using his all-knowing discernment, he knows everyone who *would* have chosen Mormonism with all their hearts, based upon their works and the "desire of their hearts" (*D&C* 137). The same for those who died without ever hearing about Mormonism, which seems to contradict D&C 76, which says they have to spend a thousand years in Spirit Prison first. And from a strictly Complete Heretic point of view, if God can just go back and save everyone without Mormonism, then why bother with the whole convoluted scheme in first place? And if this Mormonism biz is so necessary after all, why did he have to wait so long to bring it about?

The Celestial kingdom

Those good Mormons who don't ask questions like those get to go to the swanky heaven, the celestial kingdom, along with innocent children under the age of eight, and those who died without hearing of Mormonism, but would have received and accepted it if they had ever been given the chance. There they will live with God and Jesus Christ and Joseph Smith. It doesn't get any better than that. The gate to celestial heaven is like "circling flames of fire," God and Jesus sit on a blazing throne, and the streets of the kingdom? You guessed it: paved with gold. Pretty sweet.

Even though it's the best heaven, it's further divided up into three levels, too. To get to the best part of the best heaven, there are a number of hoops to jump through. One of them is being eternally married, or "sealed." Spouses are joined for eternity ("sealed") in a simple five-minute rite conducted by a "sealer." The great Salt Lake City Temple has fourteen sealing rooms and ten sealers on staff; its all-time wedding record was 167 in one day. [cxci] For temple weddings, both bride and groom must be temple-worthy church members in good standing, with a temple recommend from their bishop. Proxy sealings can also be performed for deceased persons; dozens of women sealed themselves to Joseph Smith after his death. Those Mormons who have done everything right and have been eternally sealed in a temple live in the highest degree of glory, together with their families forever.

Besides the three layers of Heaven, there's also **Spirit World**, which is the waiting area for dead spirits until the final day of resurrection. Good Mormon spirits wait it out in **Paradise**, while everybody else is stuck in **Spirit Prison**, though they can learn about and accept Mormonism there. Not much else to do there, really. While there's no fire-and-brimstone hell per se in Mormon theology, the wicked do their weeping and gnashing of teeth in Spirit Prison, which is also sometimes referred to as **Outer Darkness**. Somewhat confusingly, Mormon damnation occurs in degrees. There's the temporary damnation of Spirit Prison, but the worst sinners remain in Outer Darkness for eternity. This includes Lucifer/Satan and his angels, and the "Sons of Perdition"— those who have committed the unpardonable sin. What is the unpardonable sin? Among a few other things, it's blasphemy against the Holy Spirit, which in LDS theology means Mormons who have turned their back on the church.

Baptism for the Dead

Hey, wait a minute, what about all those people who died before Joseph Smith started Mormonism? Do they really all have to spend a thousand years of wailing and gnashing of teeth in outer darkness? Of course not; the Mormons have it covered. That's the reason they've assembled their gigantic genealogical database in a massive underground vault in Utah, and have been busy filling it with the names of everyone on earth whose births, marriages, and deaths have been tabulated since records began. Currently the LDS Family History Library has collected over 2 billion names—the equivalent of 7 million 300-page books on microfiche—and it expands by 5,000 microfilm rolls a month. [cxcii]

Every week, a certain quota of these names are distributed to teenaged LDS boys and girls, who have the honor of being baptized in their place; often being baptized on behalf of a dozen or more deceased individuals in a row.

Baptism of the Dead (beside being the most awesome George Romero movie title ever) does not "save" the deceased—it merely gives them the opportunity of choice in the afterlife to accept or reject Mormonism. Which prompts some questions: Presumably, no one in Spirit Prison who hears the Mormon gospel rejects it, so everyone but the most degenerate sinners goes to at least the default heaven, the telestial kingdom. So why such a complicated clunky procedure just to provide a choice for each and every single individual who ever lived? Wouldn't it make more sense for God to give *everybody* the choice? And as admirable as it is for them to assemble a massive database, let's think about this: does anyone really think they're going to be able to track down *every* person in the entirety of human history? What about all the rest of those poor bastards? If they're out of luck, God's a bit of a bastard himself—but if he can save them in his infinite mercy, why make us go through all these soteriological gymnastics in the first place?

Like some of the other tenets of Mormon theology,

baptism for the dead appears to stem from Joseph Smith latching on to obscure biblical verses and running with them. The apostle Paul mentions baptism for the dead in 1 Corinthians 15:29: "Else what shall they do which are baptized for the dead, if the dead rise not at all? Why are they then baptized for the dead?" Christians today don't really know what to make of this statement of Paul's, and apologists insist that he's just talking about something that those bad pagans did. But ironically, the Mormons could be right, and it might have been an early Christian practice that did not survive. Church heresy-hunters like Tertullian claimed that the practice came from the heretical Marcionites, early rivals to orthodox Christianity.

Saints normally concentrate on proxy-baptizing their own ancestors, but of course once you start, you want to get them all... even if they might currently be in some other religion's heaven. Catholics in particular have been angered to learn many Catholic saints have been spiritually poached by Mormons—not to mention their own sainted mothers and other ancestors, who are tirelessly and meticulously harvested by volunteers in the church's "name extraction" program from public records. Officially the Catholic Church just ignores the matter.

The American Jewish Committee took it less calmly when they discovered Mormons had acquired the records of the Nazi "final solution," and were industriously baptizing the murdered Jews of WWII. After the news came to light, the LDS church signed an agreement with Jewish organizations in 1995 promising to put a stop to baptizing deceased Jews—but ten years later, genealogical researcher Helen Radkey caught the church *still* at it, despite denials by church authorities! Unsurprisingly, Christopher Hitchens said it best: "Whether this was cultish or sectarian it was certainly extremely tactless: a crass attempt at mass identity theft from the deceased." [cxciii] If it weren't meaningless nonsense it might be offensive. Oh and by the way, speaking of tactless and offensive, Adolph Hitler has also been baptized for the dead. See you all in Heaven!

Incidentally, though Hitler made the cut, rest assured they

wouldn't let just *anybody* in to the Mormon afterlife. In 1926, and again in 1966, the First Presidency officially reaffirmed the church policy which forbade all temple ordinances to any "people who had any Negro blood in their veins." The church's genealogical department flagged the names of "those of known Negro blood" to prevent them from being accidentally allowed in heaven. But in 1974, when the twin threats of a NAACP lawsuit and a Congressional investigation of racially discriminatory use of U.S. Census records loomed, the church quickly and quietly changed their policy. [cxciv]

The doctrine still is a source of both irritation and amusement to nonbelievers. When Mormon Presidential hopeful Mitt Romney gave his atheist father-in-law a posthumous baptism in 2012, TV host Bill Maher promptly held an "unbaptizing" ceremony on *Real Time With Bill Maher*:

"In case you didn't hear, it was discovered last week that Edward Davies, Ann Romney's father—an enthusiastically anti-religious scientist who called organized faith 'hogwash,' was posthumously baptized in the Mormon tradition 14 months after he died. They tried to do it sooner, but he wouldn't stop spinning in his grave."

Maher then donned a pointy sorcerer's hat and waved a magic wand over a photograph of Davies. "By the power granted in me by the Blair Witch," he pronounced, "I call upon the Mormon spirits to leave your body the fuck alone."

One website, angry that the Mormon Church insists being gay is a choice but doesn't think people should have a choice about being posthumously baptized, decided to do something about it—by letting people choose homosexuality for dead Mormons. At AllDeadMormonsAreNowGay.com, you can enter the name of a deceased Mormon (or the site can find one for you) and—presto! The dead Mormon is now gay in the afterlife. Silly? Sure, but no more silly than Baptism for the Dead in the first place.

Blood Atonement

Back in the day, condemned men in Utah could pick their fate: either death by hanging or by firing squad, the only state to offer such a choice. Utah was one of the only states in the country to execute people by firing squad; the only others were Mormon-heavy Nevada and Idaho, and Oklahoma. And though it was never used, Utah has the distinction of being the only state that also had beheading on the books (from 1851 to 1888) as a legal method of execution. Why did these states favor such sanguinary capital punishment?

It's because of the old Mormon doctrine that sin cannot be forgiven without the shedding of blood. And where does that gruesome idea come from? From the New Testament—particularly in verses like Hebrews 9:22, which explicitly says just that. In mainstream Christian theology, the necessary blood comes from Jesus, whose blood can redeem even the vilest of transgressions. In Mormonism, Jesus blood is powerful stuff indeed, but there are some sins that are just too much even for him. The only hope of salvation for sinners who commit murder or break their covenants with God is by the shedding their own blood.

The church tends to waffle on the subject of blood atonement. In general, the doctrine is one of several has-been Mormon beliefs that can be traced back to Brigham Young—and which quickly fell out of favor after his death (see also the Adam-God doctrine, the Deseret alphabet, the inhabitants of the Moon and Sun, etc.). Today some embarrassed modern LDS apologists insist blood atonement was just a rhetorical device, and that when early Mormon church fathers made scary-sounding pronouncements during the Mormon Reformation (see ch.11), like "Saints had a right to kill a sinner to save him," [cxcv]—well, that was all just a figure of speech.

But depending on which church leader is talking to you and when you ask him, blood atonement is either a crucial doctrine with a long and honored practice, or never really existed, or both. As one commentator in the Mormon journal *Dialogue* put it:

"In his writings, Joseph Smith only hinted at the doctrine, Brigham Young successively denied and asserted it, Joseph F. Smith ardently defended it, and in more recent years, Hugh B. Brown repudiated it and Joseph Fielding Smith and Bruce R. McConkie both have vigorously defended it in principle while staunchly denying that the Church has ever put it into actual practice, whereas most other General Authorities have prudently preferred to remain silent on the subject." [cxcvi]

Things to do in Mormonism Before You're Alive

Mormons have to have lots of children; not because the persecuted fledgling religion desperately needed to increase its numbers as quickly as possible in the early years—actually, that's precisely why. But theologically speaking, God needs Mormons to have lots of babies in order to provide "mortal bodies" for all his "spirit children" who are still waiting to be born on earth (One of the benefits of being God is that you get to have loads of sex with your wives and make billions of spirit babies).

These days, the church has finally toned down its hard-line stance against family planning, allowing that sex can be for more than just procreation, and the number of children a couple has should be left up to them and the Lord. This is quite a step up from the terse directives of past presidents like Ezra Taft Benson, who said: "Do not curtail the number of children for personal or selfish reasons." Before that somewhat dour pronouncement in 1987, we had more colorful discourse from Pres. David O. McKay, who thought couples practicing birth control were no better than "the panderer and the courtesan" who "befoul the pure fountains of life with the slime of indulgence and sensuality." [cxcvii] And as we've already seen, charming mottos like "the woman is a vessel to be worn out in childbirth" are still heard in the Talibanlike knots of desert dwelling polygamists.

Singles are out of luck, since exaltation is only available to family units; though President Spencer W. Kimball promised (without going into specifics) that no unmarried souls would be deprived of eternal blessings on account of anything they couldn't help. Nevertheless, he urged lovelorn saints to keep themselves well-dressed, well-groomed and as attractive as they could manage. [cxcviii]

The divine repercussions make divorce among Saints very thorny... Utah has always had a high divorce rate overall, but temple marriages rarely end in divorce. The church does not forbid it, but divorce does tend to gum up the works of the exaltation process. A couple can apply to have their sealings "for time" and/or "for eternity" broken, but it quickly gets messy when kids are involved. Adopted children are sealed to their adoptive parents. Church leaders are instructed to discourage adopted children from looking for their birth parents. [cxcix] Children born to a sealed couple are automatically sealed to them, even after a divorce. Church handbook regulations stipulate that children cannot be sealed to one parent only, but particularly sticky cases are appealed all the way to the First Presidency and decided on a case-by-case basis. In cases of unwed mothers, the official position states every effort should be made "to establish an eternal family relationship," but if a marriage just isn't in the cards, the backup plan is adoption. [cc]

***

For further reading:

"Is Mormonism a Cult? Who Cares? It's Their Weird and Sinister Beliefs We Should be Worried About." *Slate*, Oct. 17, 2011

That site again: AllDeadMormonsAreNowGay.com

Endnotes: Chapter 7

[cxci] Ostling, pp.194-5

[cxcii] ibid.

[cxciii] "Is Mormonism a Cult? Who Cares? It's Their Weird and Sinister Beliefs We Should be Worried About." *Slate*, Oct. 17, 2011

[cxciv] Quinn, *MH:EoP*, pp. 819, 854-855

[cxcv] Bagley, pp. 51-53

[cxcvi] *Dialogue: A Journal of Mormon Thought*, v. 15, no. 3, p. 93

[cxcvii] Ostling, pp.172-73 see also notes on p. 421

[cxcviii] *Doctrine and Covenants: Student Manual*, Religion 324-325, Salt Lake City: Church Educational System, The Church of Jesus Christ of Latter-day Saints, 1981, p. 328

[cxcix] Ostling, p. 173

[cc] ibid., pp.172-3

Chapter 8

A Peculiar People:
More Mormon Weirdness

Mormons in Space

Joseph Smith was not afraid to go where no man had gone before, describing the stars and planets (which he seemed to think are the same thing) closest to Heaven. Unfortunately, while science fiction authors can make fine religious founders (I think you know who I mean), religious founders don't always make great science fiction writers.

Strange Old Worlds: Kolob, Oliblish and Enish-go-on-dosh

Case in point: Taking the *Book of Abraham* seriously is hard enough once you know anything about its origins (see ch. 12)—but reading Joseph's "explanation" of Facsimile No.2 in *The Book of Abraham* (pp.34-35; or turn to the next page) takes the cake for pontificating, outer spacey theologobabble (and runner-up prize goes to the LDS apologists who spend long, windbaggy pages trying to make sense of Joseph's incoherent notes).

For example, according to his note for Fig. 1, Kolob is the first creation, nearest to the residence of God. One day in Kolob is equal to a thousand of our earth-years. Oh, and the ancient Egyptians apparently call our earth "Jah-oh-eh." That's about all that makes sense in this paragraph, though we're also told Kolob is:

"First in government, the last pertaining to the measurement of time. The measurement according to celestial time, which celestial time signifies one day to a cubit."

I recognize all these words, but together they make no sense. Perhaps they are only coherent according to celestial grammar...

Fig. 2. tells us that next to Kolob is Oliblish, the "next grand governing creation." Oliblish (as the Egyptians called it) holds the key of power pertaining to other planets—whatever that means. According to Fig. 3, the bird-headed figure in a boat is God on his throne, and also "the grand key-words of the holy priesthood." Fig. 4 gives us more details on Oliblish, or as Joseph puts it:

"Answers to the Hebrew word Raukeeyang, signifying expanse, or the firmament of the heavens; also a numerical figure, in Egyptian signifying one thousand; answering to the measuring of the time of Oliblish, which is equal with Kolob in its revolution and in its measuring of time."

***Book of Abraham* facsimile no. 2**
Egyptologists identify this as the hypocephalus of an individual named Sheshonk. A hypocephalus is a magical *Book of the Dead* funerary text placed under the head of the deceased. Joseph took Sheshonk's hypocephalus and

filled in the missing pieces with parts of text copied from the other fragments in his possession to complete the picture. See ch. 7 of Kevin Mathie's "Examining the Book of Abraham" website (www.bookofabraham.com) for a breakdown of the details.

Fig. 5 says—well, again, maybe better to just let Joseph speak for himself:

"Is called in Egyptian Enish-go-on-dosh; this is one of the governing planets also, and is said by the Egyptians to be the Sun, and to borrow its light from Kolob through the medium of Kae-e-vanrash, which is the grand Key, or, in other words, the governing power, which governs fifteen other fixed planets or stars, as also Floeese or the Moon, the Earth and the Sun in their annual revolutions. This planet receives its power through the medium of Kli-flos-is-es, or Hah-ko-kau-beam, the stars represented by numbers 22 and 23, receiving light from the revolutions of Kolob."

Got all that? It's really quite simple: Enish-go-on-dosh is the Sun, which is also one of the governing planets, and gets its light from Kolob through the medium of Kae-e-vanrash, which is, as you know, the grand key or governing power over fifteen other fixed planets or stars (planets and stars being pretty much the same thing, after all), as well as annual rotations of the Earth, Moon and Sun. Oh, and the moon is also called Floeese. Our planet (assuming that's what he meant by "this planet") receives its power through the medium of Kli-flos-is-es, or Hah-ko-kau-beam (not to be confused with the medium of Kae-e-vanrash) and the stars represented by numbers 22 and 23, receive light from the revolutions of Kolob, because that's where starlight comes from, revolutions of some other planet—or is Kolob supposed to be a star? Joseph's explanatory notes need their own explanatory notes.

Life on the Moon & Sun

An article in an 1892 issue of the *The Young Woman's Journal*, published by the LDS Young Ladies' Mutual Improvement Associations of Zion, assures us that "Nearly all the great discoveries of men in the last half century have, in one way or another, either directly or indirectly, contributed to prove Joseph Smith to be a Prophet," and provides some little known astronomy facts from Joseph Smith to prove the point:

"Astronomers and philosophers have, from time almost immemorial until very recently, asserted the moon was uninhabited, that it had no atmosphere, etc. But recent discoveries, through the means of powerful telescopes, have given scientists a doubt or two upon the old theory. [cci]

"As far back as 1837, I know that (Joseph Smith) said the moon was inhabited by men and women the same as this earth, and that they lived to a greater age than we do—that they live generally to near the age of 1000 years. He described the men as averaging near six feet in height, and dressing quite uniformly in something near the Quaker style. In my Patriarchal blessing, given by the father of Joseph the Prophet, in Kirtland, 1837, I was told that I should preach the gospel before I was 21 years of age; that I should preach the gospel to the inhabitants upon the islands of the sea, and to the inhabitants of the moon, even the planet you can now behold with your eyes." [ccii]

Brigham Young didn't stop at the moon. In a sermon delivered in the Tabernacle in Salt Lake City he asked:

"We are called ignorant; so we are: but what of it? Are not all ignorant? I rather think so. Who can tell us of the inhabitants of this little planet that shines of an evening, called the moon? ...when you inquire about the inhabitants of that sphere you find that the most learned are as ignorant in regard to them as the ignorant of their fellows. So it is in regard to the inhabitants of the sun. Do you think it is inhabited? I rather think it is. Do you think there is any life there? No question of it; it was not made in vain.

"It was made to give light to those who dwell upon it, and to other planets; and so will this earth when it is celestialized. Every planet in its first rude, organic state receives not the glory of God upon it, but is opaque; but when celestialized, every planet that God brings into existence is a body of light, but not until then." [cciii]

So there you have it: stars like our sun are not gigantic thermonuclear balls of hydrogen, but simply planets (possibly inhabited by tall, long-lived people in Quaker garb) that have received the glory of God. That should give scientists a doubt or two upon the old theory.

Incidentally, what do Mormon apologists say in defense of such wonderfully counterfactual nonsense, still available in every copy of the LDS *Journal of Discourses*? This does not bother them at all, since their prophets were only stating their personal opinions, *not* speaking in their official role as a prophet, apparently forgetting that Joseph and Brigham had a direct line to God and like all Mormon presidents, were gifted with the "key of discernment."

Besides, almost no one but heretics read the *Journal of Discourses* these days. The *Journal*, a massive 26-volume collection of nearly every public sermon by Mormon leaders in the early decades of the church, has fallen out of favor. For many years, no Mormon home was complete without a copy, but after putting up with much embarrassment from its contents, Church authorities decided maybe it *wasn't* such necessary reading after all. [cciv] Today members are gently discouraged from reading the books, although Mormon fundamentalists rely heavily upon it.

Battlestar SaltLaketica

Mormon science fiction improved somewhat in the 20th

century. Before Sci Fi Channel's edgy, sophisticated military science fiction franchise *Battlestar Galactica* was cool, it was the considerably less-edgy, less-sophisticated 1978 TV series *Battlestar Galactica*. The series creator, Mormon Glen Larson, had set out in the late 1960s to do a science fiction series. His original pitch was a show called "Adam's Ark," which was to feature a retelling of different Bible stories set in a futuristic space opera.

The unlikely mashup languished in development hell until *Star Wars'* blockbuster success caught television executives' attention, and sure enough, when the newly renamed *Battlestar Galactica* debuted, it was hailed as "*Star Wars* for TV." It was a wildly popular hit, but high production costs killed it after seventeen episodes (it made an attempt at a comeback with the unfortunate *Galactica 1980*, but that thankfully died after only six episodes). The opening narration, spoken by *The Avengers'* Patrick Macnee, gave the set-up:

"There are those who believe that life *here* began *out there*, far across the Universe; with tribes of humans who may have been the forefathers of the Egyptians, or the Toltecs, or the Mayans...that they may have been the architects of the Great Pyramids, or the lost civilizations of Lemuria...or Atlantis. Some believe that there may yet be brothers of man, who even now fight to survive—somewhere beyond the heavens!"

The story begins in a galaxy far, far away—so to speak. Colonies have been settled on twelve worlds by descendants of the Lords of Kobol, the homeworld and fabled birthplace of humanity, where the gods live. Humans have been fighting a thousand-year war with a race of killer robots called the Cylons. Just as peace seemed at hand, a traitor betrays humanity and a Cylon sneak attack decimates the Twelve Colonies. Mankind's only hope is its last remaining warship, the *Battlestar Galactica*. The ship's commander, Adama, shepherds a "rag-tag fugitive fleet" of spaceships fleeing the Cylons "on a lonely quest" to find the legendary lost thirteenth tribe, who settled on "a shining planet known ... as *Earth*."

Unbeknownst to most viewers, Larson's Mormonism gave the show several of its underlying themes and motifs. The Twelve Colonies, like the Twelve Tribes of Israel, ultimately stem from the planet Kobol, an anagram for Kolob. Like the prophet Lehi, who foresees the destruction of Jerusalem in the *Book of Mormon* and escapes with his people to the new world, Cmdr. Adam, er, Adama, escapes the destruction of Caprica and leads his people to a new world. Both the human colonies and the LDS church are ruled by a President and a Quorum of Twelve. Egyptian motifs pop up frequently in BSG and the BOM; one of the most notable examples is the "viper" fighter pilots' helmets, which look like the royal headgear of the pharaohs.

In Colonial theology, the gods of Kobol are humans who have progressed to a more advanced state. In one episode ("War of the Gods") an "angel" tells the heroes, "As you are now, we once were; as we are now, you may become," echoing LDS President Lorenzo Snow's famous tenet, "As man is now, God once was; as God now is, man may become." And like Mormons, instead of getting married, the BSG colonists are "sealed," "not only for now, but for all the eternities" (from "Lost Planet of Ancient Gods"). LDS Temple sealings are "not only for time," i.e., during this life, "but for all eternity." Even Mormon genealogists have a parallel in the "sacred work" of Colonial "genetic tracers."

There are other philosophical parallels on topics such as Free Will, Original Sin, Angels and more, but it's more fun to find the parallels in the names of characters and places. In addition to classic Greek names like Apollo, Athena and Cassiopeia, and the zodiac-inspired names of the twelve Colonies (Caprica, Gemini, Piscera, Sagitara, Scorpia, Taura, Virgon, etc.), there are Biblical/BOM names like Cmdr. Adama/Adam and Cmdr. Cain.

On the bad guy side, BSG's Judas is Baltar (a variant of the wicked Babylonian King Balthazar in the Old Testament). His Cylon aide-de-camp is named, appropriately enough, Lucifer. The Cylon capital is Gamoray, not be confused with Gomorrah, the city of evildoers God destroyed with a rain of fire and brimstone in Genesis. Another BSG baddie is Count Iblis, a powerful and charismatic alien who tries to tempt the fleet into making him their leader, but in the end turns out to be a member of an angelic race who was cast out for rebellion. He only has power over those who freely choose to give him power over them. Sound familiar? It's no wonder that Iblis is one of the names for the Devil in Islam.

Some of the names may be tongue-in-cheek or even unconscious. In BSG, Boxey is a boy with a faithful robot dog, or in Galactica-speak, a daggit. As it turns out, Box Elder and Daggett are both counties in Utah.

Mormon TV That Never Was: John the Revelator and the Three Nephites

Glen Larson missed a real chance for more good Mormon television by not coming up with a pilot involving the Three Nephites. Who are they? In the Book of Mormon (3 Nephi 28: 4-40), they were three of Jesus' faithful New World followers who were granted immortality. That alone would have been pretty sweet, but wait—not only would they remain alive until Jesus returned, they were also given *super powers and secret identities*. Their new mission was to wander all over the world like earthbound angels, traveling incognito, like Jesus' own secret agents. The prophet Mormon was about to reveal their names in the BOM, but the Lord forbade him. They would help people in every nation, speaking all languages, doing great and marvelous work, and suffering neither pain or sadness. Satan would have no power over them: no prison or pit could hold them; when cast into furnaces or thrown in to arenas filled with wild man-eating beasts, they would emerge without a scratch.

See the series potential? The script writes itself. And for generations, Saints have been doing just that: telling stories of bumping into a trio of kindly old men who show up to help the faithful get out of jams. When they've saved the day, the three mysterious strangers then disappear and are never seen again, off to rescue another Mormon in peril. There are hundreds of stories of the three guiding pioneer trains to water holes, offering sage advice or timely warnings, saving ranchers or motorists from blizzards, plowing a farmer's field so that he could attend to Church duties, curing illnesses with herbal remedies, delivering food to starving missionaries, stopping by to fix a widow's furnace, pulling people from flaming freeway crashes or saving drowning youths after canoe accidents, thwarting serial killers, even defending outnumbered Israeli soldiers from Arab forces.

Mormons also tell of a mysterious stranger who appeared at the Continental Congress on July 4, 1776, and delivered a heartfelt speech in favor of revolution, just in time to persuade the reluctant Founding Fathers to sign the Declaration of Independence. Was it one of the Three Nephites? Maybe—or it could have been the angel Moroni, or even Jesus' disciple John. Mormons believe that the Apostle John, or John the Revalator, was also made immortal by Jesus. This is curious, since the Bible passage they cite to justify this idea, John 21:21-23, actually goes out of its way to debunk any such notion:

When Peter saw (John), he said to Jesus, "Lord, what about him?" Jesus said to him, "If it is my will that he remain until I come, what is that to you? Follow me!" So the rumor spread in the community that this disciple would not die. Yet Jesus did not say to him that he would not die, but, "If it is my will that he remain until I come, what is that to you?"

Temple Rituals & Sacred Underwear
From Masons to Mormons

When the Mormons erected their first temple in Kirtland, Ohio, their sacred rites were simple affairs involving washing and anointing. But by spring of 1842, the rituals had evolved into a complicated and secret initiation ceremony full of costumes, symbols, and secret handshakes. A considerable amount was freely stolen from Masonic tradition: a creation drama, bestowing of a secret name, special garments, secret handshakes and tokens, promises to fulfill moral obligations, penalty oaths to protect secrecy, progression through three degrees towards perfection, special temple robes and aprons, and more. [ccv] Masonic symbols have been co-opted by Mormons on everything from temples to gravestones to logos—the beehive, the square and compass, two triangles forming a six-pointed star, the all-seeing eye, sun, moon, and stars, and ritualistic hand grips. [ccvi]

Early Mormons weren't bothered by the parallels. Everyone knew the Freemasons traced their origins all the way back to the ancient builders of King Solomon's temple, so the blatant similarities wouldn't have seemed like plagiarism. Any similarities to Masonic rites were naturally only because Joseph was re-introducing the "original" temple rituals to the world, so of course they would *have* to resemble the Masons' "corrupted" rituals—even though in reality, Masonic rites only go back to around the 16th or 17th century, from a mishmash of Jewish kabala, Rosicrucianism, the Bible, alchemy, astrology and other esoteric occult influences.

Joseph loved the Masonic mysteries and ritual. His progress through Masonic ranks was remarkable. He formally installed a lodge in Nauvoo and became a first-degree Mason the same night. The next night he rose to the sublime degree of a Master Mason. [ccvii] Mormon elders eagerly followed his lead and within six months the number of candidates soared to 286. Soon there were five Mormon lodges. The rapid growth shocked and alarmed the non-Mormon Freemasons; at the time there were only 227 Masons in all of Illinois. [ccviii] Worse still, Joseph refused to send lodge records to the Grand Lodge in Springfield for their inspection and rumor had it the rituals and strict membership rules had been corrupted. [ccix] The infuriated Masons eventually revoked the dispensations and declared all the Mormon lodges were unofficial "clandestine" ones. [ccx] Just six weeks after the installation of his first lodge, Joseph unveiled what he called the principles and order of the priesthood, which included "washings, anointing, endowments and keys"—and sacred underwear.

Mormon Underwear

The original "temple garments" were a kind of collared white shirt, closed with strings, worn only during the ceremony and then kept hidden away. But these quickly became standardized as an unfortunate suit of long underwear, which the initiate was instructed to wear always under their clothing (including bras for women), "both night and day," [ccxi] as an "outward expression of an inward covenant."

This led to a widespread conviction among Saints that one should contrive to never be entirely naked, even when changing clothes. Many Mormons have family stories of their never-nude ancestors who wouldn't dare fully remove their sacred undergarments, not even in the bathtub, carefully washing themselves in stages instead. Even as recently as 1968, church officials had to rein in temple workers who were instructing couples to keep their garments on during sex. [ccxii]

The Evolution of the Temple Garment

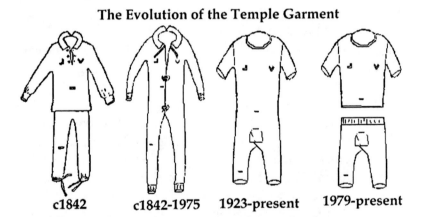

c1842   c1842-1975   1923-present   1979-present

chart courtesy of nowscape.com

Nowadays both temple garments and the rules for wearing them are more relaxed. Over the years, they have evolved into skimpier two-piece white underclothes, available in a variety of ten different fabrics (there is also a military-approved shade of brown for Saints in the armed forces). The design is basically a t-shirt and knee-length boxer briefs, with lower neckline and shorter sleeves for women. There are also customized garments available for those with special needs, e.g. garments designed like a hospital gown for the bedridden.[ccxiii]

Saints are allowed to remove their garments briefly for activities like swimming or sports, but not just for lounging around the house or working in the yard. Since they are ostensibly intended "to cover your nakedness," garments are not to be exposed to the view of others. This has the effect of creating a de facto dress code, since it means having to wear clothing that will keep the garment out of sight, a standard of modesty that has spread even to the church members who don't wear temple endowments.

Receiving the garment is a rite of passage to Mormon adulthood. Upon receiving their endowments in the temple ceremony, initiates are told their sacred undergarments "will be a shield and a protection to you against the power of the destroyer" and "temptation and evil." Mormon folklore abounds with stories of temple garments miraculously stopping bullets, withstanding fire, etc. Mormon hotel magnate Willard Marriott told *60 Minutes'* Mike Wallace his garment saved him in a boat fire that consumed his pants, but left him unscathed above the knee, where his garment covered him. [ccxiv] After Joseph Smith's death, Mormons reasoned that Willard Richards survived the attack at Catharge Jail unscathed because of his garments, and bemoaned that Joseph Smith, Hyrum Smith, and John Taylor had removed theirs on account of the hot weather. [ccxv]

Four sacred symbols (Masonic symbols, incidentally) are sewn into the garment: A reverse L, the mark of the square, appears over the right breast and the V-shaped mark of the compass over the left. The mark of the square stands for exactness and honor in keeping the covenants, and the mark of the compass is a "constant reminder" to keep one's passions within the bounds set by the Lord, hence the "protection from temptation" promised to initiates. Young Mormons are raised on stories of Saints who are saved at the last moment from giving in to their sinful, sexual urges by the sight of the symbols on their sacred garments. *ccxvi*

The navel mark is a ¾" horizontal slash across the abdomen, representing disemboweling—the fate of anyone who dared divulge the secrets of the temple. The knee mark is the same length, placed just above the hem of the right leg. Initially the four marks were cut into the garment during the temple initiation—so deep they would leave scars. This was abandoned after too many protests from Mormon women; *ccxvii* now they come with the marks already stitched in. When the underwear gets worn out, the symbols must be cut off and ritually disposed of. Once they are removed, the garment is to be cut into pieces so that it cannot be recognized; after that the pieces are considered no more than ordinary rags. *ccxviii*

Mormons regard their garments with an almost superstitious awe. They are extremely sensitive about exposing the sacred underwear, especially to gentile eyes. Mormon athletes in the locker room and soldiers in open barracks are advised to be as discreet as possible, treat questions as a teaching opportunity, and to endure ridicule with patience. Public displays of the garment by non-Mormons are deeply offensive, such as when closeted gay Mormon characters were shown wearing the garment in Tony Kushner's controversial play *Angels in America*. In 2003 an anti-Mormon demonstrator at a general conference blew his nose into a temple garment he was wearing around his neck. An onlooker was arrested for battery for trying to wrest the garment away from him. Mormon urban legends tell of irreverent laundromat owners who dare to hang temple garments in the window to make fun of them, only to have vengeful God destroy their business, usually by fire. *cxix*

Top Sacred

Saints defend their Temple Vestments with greater secrecy than even their sacred underwear. This is the costume worn only in the temple. Initiates enter temple dressed all in white: women wear white dresses; men white pants, shirt and tie. Everyone wears slippers in the temple instead of shoes, following the example of Moses who removed his shoes on holy ground. Then the temple vestments are put on over their street clothes: a robe, an apron, and a sash. Men also get a hat that is supposed to resemble a turban, but looks more like something a French pastry chef would wear. Women get a veil instead, used to cover their faces during prayer. All are white and unembroidered except for the apron, which is made to resemble nine green fig leaves stitched together. All these are meant to recall the High Priest's garb of the Old Testament Hebrews, who wore a robe, a sort of breastplate called the ephod, a girdle, and a miter for headgear.

Initiates buy both their undergarments and temple vestments from a church-owned clothing company (though some of the bigger temples have laundry facilities and will rent temples vestments at a low cost). Saints who die in good standing are usually buried in their temple vestments and undergarments. Since 2004, no one is allowed to buy either without a temple recommend from their Bishop, possibly to prevent them being desecrated by heathen jokers or sold on eBay to kinky fetishists.

But fortunately for those same heathen smart-alecs and kinksters who are dying to get their Mormon on, the good folks of Mormon's Secret (mormonssecret.com) have the answer to your prayers. Founded by an ex-Mormon soccer mom familiar with the fabric buying operations and garment construction of LDS Temple Clothing, they happily sell real Mormon underwear to anyone, regardless of their religious affiliation. They follow the authentic Mormon patterns and use heirloom stitching techniques to hand-sew traditional Masonic symbols on each garment.

By the way, you may want to resist the urge to call their temple garments "magic underwear" to their face. Trust me, they've heard that one already.

Your Name in Heaven

Another important aspect of the temple endowment ceremony,

after taking the oaths (and until recently, learning all the ways God may take your life if you reveal the secrets of the temple, like throat slitting and disembowelment), is being anointed with oil and the bestowing of a secret, sacred, spirit name, the new name you'll go by for eternity. Everyone who gets their temple endowment on the same day turns out to have the same name (that is, all women get the same female name of the day and all men get the male name of the day—or an alternate name, if the new name is too close to their old name). On a personal note, I was disappointed to learn that everyone doesn't get a new name handpicked especially for them, and even more let down to find that the names aren't cool spacey monikers like, say, Kolobia or Oliblishus. No, they get saddled for eternity with mundane ones from the Bible or Book of Mormon or other old fogey names better suited for your grandma or grandpa, like Martha, Caroline, Ethel, Frederick, Mark, Delbert, Jethro, etc.

Your secret name comes into play during the temple wedding ceremony. The bride must tell the groom what her secret temple name is. He, however, does not tell her *his* secret name under any circumstances. After the Second Estate (i.e., this life), the man will speak the secret name of his wife to call her forth in the first resurrection and take her with him into the Celestial Kingdom (i.e., the good heaven—faithful Mormons only). Of course, this means the wife better be faithful and obedient and please her husband, because she's completely at his mercy; if he doesn't feel like calling her forth for any reason, she just gets left behind.

Incidentally, what about the unfortunate unmarried Mormon women who don't have a husband to call them up into the afterlife? According to *Doctrine and Covenants* 132:16, singles are relegated to becoming "Ministering Angels." These second-class citizens of God's Kingdom aren't allowed the full benefits of married Saints, but become "ministering servants, to minister for those who are worthy of a far more, and an exceeding, and an eternal weight of glory."

All this spirit name business doesn't apply just to us; it's the same for prophets, Jesus and even God himself. According to Mormon doctrine, while God's name here is "God," it was "Elohim" in the pre-existence and will be again in the hereafter. Jesus' spirit name is Jehovah, just as his brother Satan was known by his spirit name, Lucifer. There are a few linguistic problems with taking all this at face value, however. *Elohim* is indeed the Hebrew name for God in the Old Testament; however it was originally a Northwestern Semitic word for "the gods."

Jehovah and Lucifer are both problematic names as well, since neither word developed until the Middle Ages. "Jehovah" is a word created by attempting to translate the proper name of the God of Israel in the Hebrew Bible into Latin. In vowel-free ancient Hebrew, that name is יהוה, or YHWH, also known as the Tetragrammaton. No one knows how the word should be pronounced, since in the second or third century B.C.E., Jews stopped speaking the word aloud, but it has generally been transcribed as "Yehowah" or "Yahweh." Medieval monks turned the Hebrew letters YHWH into the Latin letters JHVH, which made Yehowah into "Jehovah." [ccxx]

Likewise, "Lucifer" is the Latin translation of another ancient Hebrew word, הֵילֵל, *hêlēl* or *heylel*. The word only appears once in the Hebrew Bible, in Isaiah 14:12, where it satirically refers to the King of Babylon as the "Day Star, Son of Dawn," who has fallen from heaven. The translators of the King James Bible rendered *hêlēl/heylel* as "Lucifer," Latin for "light-bearer," a name for Venus, the morning star. In Luke (10:18) Jesus says he saw Satan fall from heaven. In the Middle Ages, the two passages came to be linked, and "Lucifer" became synonymous with "Satan."

So even though spirit names are supposed to be in the "Adamic tongue," the language of God used before the dawn of time, the spirit names for Jesus and Satan are medieval Latin words invented in the Middle Ages, and God's sprit name comes from a mistranslation from a pagan Mesopotamian word that was originally plural. Very strange...

Bonus Weirdness:
God is Not a Good Investment Advisor

"It never ceases to amaze me how gullible some of our Church members are," one Mormon leader remarked in *Ensign* magazine. [ccxxi] The *Wall Street Journal* agrees; it has called Utah the "Fraud Capital of the World." [ccxxii] And in Provo's Utah County, the real Mormon heart of the state, no place has more white-collar crime: according to FBI agent Jim Malpede, at any given moment the FBI is investigating con artist scams there totaling $50 million to $100 million. Author Jon Krakauer has pointed out that "the uncommonly high incidence of fraud is a direct consequence of the uncommonly high percentage of Utah County residents who are Mormons. When Saints are invited to invest in dubious schemes by other Saints, they tend to be overly trusting." [ccxxiii] In the *Deseret News*, Michael Hines, director of enforcement for the Utah Securities Division, reported that in Utah County, it is common for scammers to ensnare their victims by asking them to evaluate the proposed investment through prayer. Hines warned, "People need to realize that God is not a good investment advisor." [ccxxiv]

The really astounding thing about Utah's high incidence of fraud is how much of it is perpetrated by Mormons on their fellow Mormons. The Saints are a close-knit, insular group to begin with, under great social pressure to conform. Trust of and obedience to their spiritual leaders are well-entrenched virtues; members make sacred covenants in the temple to not speak evil of their church leaders. And despite having to pay upwards of 10% (or more) of their gross income to the church in tithes and other offerings, not to mention the pressure to have and support large families, they are also expected to be financially successful, and conspicuously so, as proof that the Lord is blessing them. Together, all these factors contribute to an environment tailor-made for financial fraud (and for bankruptcy: Utah also frequently leads the US in number of bankruptcy filings). [ccxxv]

In March of 2012, a federal grand jury in Bridgeport,

Connecticut, indicted **Mormon bishop Julius C. Blackwelder**, 59, of Utah, on nine counts of money laundering and mail and wire fraud in connection with an alleged investor fraud scheme. Since 2005, Bishop Blackwelder had allegedly persuaded members of his congregation and other victims to invest their money with his investment pool, the "Friend's Investment Group"—then sold them fake promissory notes, backing them up with equally fake memoranda and account updates which he'd fabricated. All total, he bilked members of his congregation and other victims out of more than $400,000. If convicted, Blackwelder could easily spend the rest of his life in prison; he faces a maximum term of 20 years on each count of mail and wire fraud, and 10 years on each count of money laundering. *ccxxvi*

True confession: while researching the details on Bishop Blackwelder's Ponzi scam, I completely stumbled upon all these *other* cases of Mormon-on-Mormon fraud that I had no idea about previously:

Val Southwick of Ogden, Utah, painted himself to investors as a respectable LDS gentleman, more concerned about the consequences in the afterlife than in this life if he lied to investors. One victim recalled Southwick telling him they didn't need a contract at all; they could just go to the temple together and shake hands on the deal there. But according to investigators, Southwick swindled more than 800 people out of $142 million in one of the largest fraud operations in Utah—a Ponzi scheme that went on for 17 years. Southwick created 150 companies collectively dubbed "VesCor," raising $180 million from investors for property developments. Most of that money has disappeared. After his arrest, Southwick was sentenced to nine consecutive one-to-15 year terms in prison for securities fraud. At his parole hearing, a crowd of his victims came out to tell their stories. "Butch Cassidy couldn't hold a candle to Val Southwick," said one. For his part, he pleaded for his release, tearfully telling the board that if he were freed, he could work to repay those he defrauded. The LDS church agreed to return the $202,761.74 in tithe that Southwick paid between 2001 and 2006. *ccxxvii*

The second-largest financial fraud in Utah history after Southwick was run by Mormon elder and Boy Scout scoutmaster **Travis L. Wright** of Waterford Funding, Waterford Loan Fund and related companies. Authorities alleged Wright operated a Ponzi scheme which took in $167 million from investors in Utah and other states, including a Salt Lake City nurse who lost her life savings. *ccxxviii*

Shawn Merriman, nicknamed "**The Mormon Madoff**," investment firm head and a Mormon bishop, was sentenced to twelve and a half years in prison for scamming more than $21 million from his friends, family, and fellow church members— even his own mother. *ccxxix*

R. Dean Udy was an LDS Stake President and a church Regional Representative in Box Elder County ... and in 2010 was sentenced to 1-to-15 years in state prison on securities fraud charges after pleading guilty to a Ponzi scheme that ran for 12 years or more. Udy first entered into a Consent Order with the Division of Securities in 2002, but that didn't slow him down. He was formally charged in 2005 and pled guilty to two felony criminal counts in 2007. However, he was given a break; the sentence was held in abeyance for 3 years when he agreed to pay full restitution to his investors and to provide accurate information to the State about those investors. But Udy still didn't follow through on his end of the bargain, and after several years of this, the judge finally lost patience and threw him in jail. In June 2010, a federal grand jury indicted him and his son, Cameron, on charges alleging they ran an $11.4 million bank fraud in Las Vegas as well.

Most Utah newspapers wouldn't touch the story, but according to the *Ogden Standard Examiner*, Udy's scammed some 1,500 victims, with an estimated loss of $20 million. "People felt Brother Udy would never do anything wrong." Utah Securities Fraud warned that when money meets faith, bring skepticism: "So what is the lesson here? If anyone uses their church position (explicitly or not) to gain your trust in connection with an investment pitch — run for the hills. Don't trust anyone just because they are a church leader or even a church member. Do your homework and check out the investment opportunity with the Utah Division of Securities." *ccxxx*

Mormon **Anthony Vassallo**, 29, allegedly ran an investment scam that bilked about 150 investors, many of whom he met through his church, out of $40 million. According to the SEC, Vassallo told investors he had developed a software program allowing him to buy and sell options at profits of 3.5 percent a month with little risk.

When Australian appliance company **Kleenmaid** collapsed in April 2009 with over $100 million in debts, it left thousands of angry customers who paid for Kleenmaid products that were never delivered. The company had kept taking customers' money on orders they had no intention of filling. They had even launched a "Customer Loyalty" program where for a fee of $299 customers were promised big savings at numerous major retailers, and a "free luxury holiday valued at $1400" if the customer joined right away—a great deal, except that two weeks later they announced the company's financial trouble, namely, that they owed creditors $82 million. This caused their liquidators to announce that they would be investigating possible criminal charges against Kleenmaid for trading for two years while insolvent. Since Kleenmaid's directors **Andrew Young** and **Brad Young** were high-profile Mormons who had cultivated their image as clean-cut, upstanding ethical pillars of the community, the LDS church moved quickly to deny any ties with the disgraced corporation or the Young Brothers. *ccxxxi*

Five Mormon "men of status and stature" were indicted by a federal grand jury in 2007 on charges they conspired to create a multimillion dollar mortgage fraud scheme thought to total $18 million in fraudulent loans. U.S. District Judge Ted Stewart sentenced **Bradley Grant Kitchen** of Provo, **David R. Bolick** of Sandy, **Steve Wells Cloward** of Orem, **Ron K. Clarke** of Provo, and **Jeffery David Garrett** of Provo to prison terms varying from 12 to 51 months during a series of back-to-back hearings. Stewart said "stealing is stealing, plain and simple," and there is essentially no difference between ripping off a mortgage company or going into a bank and pointing a gun at a teller. "These were men of status and stature," the judge said. "Why they undertook the enterprise they did is a mystery to this court." *ccxxxii*

Mormon **Ted James Johnson Jr.**, and his partner, **Frank Graham Farrier Jr.**, were indicted in 2008 on 42 charges tied to securities fraud targeting fellow Mormons, teachers, university professors and small businessmen. It was not the financial loss, but the deceit that bothered him, Johnson's victim Charles Wayne Gentry said gently from the witness stand in federal court in Roanoke. Gentry, who lost his life savings, said he had never pressed Johnson for details because he thought he knew him. He worshipped with Johnson at The Church of Jesus Christ of Latter-day Saints. It was their work together as Mormons, along with anecdotes he heard from others in the community about lucrative investments made with Johnson, that convinced Gentry he was safe trusting his retirement money to Johnson. He'd gathered his savings, sold his house and store and counseled his wife and brother-in-law to put in their inheritance—$724,000 in all—only to see the money disappear in the collapse of two businesses run by Johnson and Farrier. Gentry had no idea his money was being used to pay the personal expenses of Johnson and Farrier, who pleaded guilty to fraud charges and testified about how he and Johnson had put little of their clients' money in the market.

Instead, Johnson and Farrier ran a Ponzi scheme. The spiraling scam eventually collapsed and cost investors millions of dollars, prosecutors said. "I felt if ever there was a righteous man, it was Teddy Johnson," Gentry said in court. "It's hard to understand the trust I had, my wife and I both had, in Teddy Johnson... I'm very, very disappointed in what I've heard and learned. That hurts me." *ccxxxiii*

Leticia Avila used her LDS Church connections and the promise of cooperation from a high-ranking immigration official to con tens of thousands of dollars from undocumented immigrant church members in Utah trying to find a way to legally remain in the United States, according to more than two dozen affidavits from victims. Many of the alleged victims said what was most upsetting is that they were betrayed by someone who preyed on their religious faith. They trusted Avila because she was a fellow member of The Church of Jesus Christ of Latter-day Saints' Spanish-speaking branch in Millcreek. In some cases, it was a local church leader who suggested they talk with Avila about attempting to get legal visas. Richard Lemos and wife, Nancy Hernandez, two of 28 undocumented immigrants in Utah, testified against Leticia Avila, but after four years of cooperating with law enforcement, the work visas allegedly promised Lemos and his wife never materialized, the case against Avila was dropped and her 28 alleged victims were ordered deported. *ccxxxiv*

Mormons **Wendell A. Jacobson** and **Allen R. Jacobson** were charged by the SEC with securities fraud in 2011. The SEC says the father and son team solicited investors by using their memberships in the Church of Jesus Christ of Latter-day Saints to make connections and win over the trust of prospective investors. The two raised $220 million from investors who thought they were investing in apartment complexes. Instead, they were paying into, you guessed it, a Ponzi scheme, according to the SEC. *ccxxxv*

Utah investment guru **Rick Koerber**, who identifies himself as "Capitalist, Mormon, Dad" on his web site, is currently awaiting trial for allegedly defrauding investors in a multimillion dollar real estate scheme. Koerber collected more than $100 million from investors but spent much of it on expensive cars, restaurants, movie making and his own housing. Federal prosecutors said the number of victims, most of whom live in Utah, could be in the hundreds. But investigators have yet to determine which of Koerber's investors are "purely victims" and who may have "facilitated the crime," he said. Koerber was originally indicted on three counts in May 2009, but 19 additional charges were added in a previous superseding indictment in November of that year, making a 22-count indictment alleging fraud, money laundering and tax evasion. *ccxxxvi*

Daren Palmer seemed to be the picture of Mormon success. Even though he was a multimillionaire, he was quick to carry furniture when someone in his congregation was moving, he volunteered at the church farm, got down on his knees to clean the church sanctuary. By all appearances, he was a successful but humble hometown investor with seemingly flawless instincts who promised returns of up to 20 percent for his clients, many of whom he worshiped with or whose sons he coached in football. He traded in trust. "A lot of people who invested are active members of the L.D.S. church," said Wayne Klein, a court-appointed receiver working to settle claims. "They knew that Palmer was, and that gave them comfort." That was, until Palmer, 42, agreed to plead guilty to federal criminal charges that he ran a $78 million Ponzi scheme. The agreement also says Mr. Palmer spent more than $110,000 from a company account on jewelry "for his personal use." Friends say he and his wife, from whom he is now divorced, flew private jets to New York to shop. The Justice Department has prosecuted dozens of similar so-called affinity fraud cases across the country in recent years. Yet here in Idaho, Mr. Palmer's deception was remarkable for its scale, and its intimacy. His investors included his father, his brother-in-law, his neighbors, a car dealer, a builder whose son he coached in football, and others. Prosecutors say investors lost more than $20 million. He faces up to 30 years in prison though he's expected to receive far less [ccxxxvii].

When real estate investment company AFCO Enterprises collapsed in 1982, around 650 investors, most of them Mormon, lost an estimated $20 million, and AFCO's Mormon owner, **Grant C. Affleck**, was indicted for mail fraud, securities fraud and bankruptcy fraud. Affleck "repeatedly and flagrantly lied to investors," the judge said as he passed sentence, such as telling investors there was no risk to them when he knew very well that was untrue. Court documents showed Affleck persuaded his fellow church members to take out second mortgages on their homes and give AFCO their equity capital, putting themselves at risk of losing their homes. Which they did. Affleck was convicted on 8 of 21 fraud-related counts, and sentenced to 45 years in prison (reduced to 10). [ccxxxviii]

Lying For the Lord

Although he was never indicted for any crime, the reputation of one of AFCO's former directors, Paul H. Dunn, suffered because of the Grant Affleck scandal (see above). Dunn was as high profile a Mormon as they get: a long time LDS General authority, one of the seven Presidents of the First Quorum of the Seventy, a prolific author and popular public speaker; he was even named Utah's Father of the Year. The *Wall Street Journal* reported that despite Elder Dunn's 1978 resignation, civil suit records showed that he continued to have ties with AFCO until it entered bankruptcy proceedings in 1982 and gave advice to directors after he resigned. A few days before the company entered bankruptcy proceedings, Dunn wrote a disgruntled investor a letter assuring him that the soon-to-be incarcerated Mr. Affleck was "fair and Christlike." [ccxxxix]

Dunn survived that little fib being exposed, but his reputation really went to pieces after reporters and critics began to look into his long history of public speaking. For more than 25 years, he had told countless inspirational stories about his life, like how hard work, perseverance and Mormon values enabled him to play major-league baseball for four or five years with the St. Louis Cardinals. Or how God had protected him throughout World War II, one of only six in his 1,000-man combat team who survived, and the only one of the six who wasn't wounded. [ccxl]

For instance, one night his squad was caught behind enemy lines and were forced to leave their refuge in a shell hole and flee through enemy machine gun fire:

"Well, the zero minute came, and we shook hands, and you never saw 11 men scamper like that before.... Three or four of the others didn't get above the surface of the ground; they were cut down with machine guns. One of my good friends was almost cut in two with a burst.... I could tell I had a sniper with a machine gun right on me because the dirt and the mud behind me would just kick right up, move right around me and then I'd move this way and then he'd pick me up again and move back. I was going with all I had.

"By then it was everybody for himself, and as I scampered within 50 yards of our hole, the sniper got a direct beam on me, and the first burst caught me in the right heel. It took my combat boot right off, just made me barefooted that quick without touching me physically, and it spun me around, and I went down on my knee. As I went down another machine gun burst came across my back and ripped the belt and the canteen and the ammunition pouch right off my back without touching me.

"As I got up to run, another burst hit me right in the back of the helmet, and it hit in the steel part, ricocheted enough to where it came up over my head, and split the helmet in two, but it didn't touch me. Then I lunged forward again, and another burst caught me in the loose part of the shoulders where I could take off both my shirt sleeves without removing my coat, and then one more lunge and I fell over the line... I was the only one of the 11 who had even made it the first 100 yards..."

(*New Era*, August 1975, page 7)

In another wartime tale from his audio memoir, *World War II Experiences*, Dunn told the moving story of the death of his army buddy, Harold Brown, in Okinawa. On the night of May 11, 1945, Brown was wounded when a shell struck his foxhole. The next morning, Dunn made his way to Brown's side:

"I scampered over to the hole where he was, and it had almost filled up from the rain and... it's all he could do to hold his head out of the water to stay alive.... Well, I pulled him out of that muddy hole and got him up on seemingly dry ground, and took off his helmet, loosened the bandoleers around his neck... to give him what comfort you can under those conditions and I took a clean canteen of water and washed his face. It was caked with mud and blood. How in the world he lived that night I don't know. I counted, after his death, 67 shrapnel wounds in him, some large enough to where you could put your whole hand in. And yet, somehow, he had held on, but I found out why. As he lay there, his head limp back in my lap, he said, 'Paul, I know this is the end,' and I'd say, 'Harold, it isn't. Just hold on. I'll get you out of this....' 'No, this is the end.'... He said, 'I've held on as long as I could, cause I want you to do two things for me if you would.' 'Why, I says, you just name it. It'll be done...'

"He said, 'If you ever live through this terrible ordeal, will you somehow get word to my mother... Will you assure her that I was faithful to the end in the principles she taught me... Will you do it, Paul?' Gosh, would I do it! How thrilled I am to report to you that the very day I got back in this country, before going to my own home, I took a plane back to Missouri and reported to that dedicated family...

"And he said... 'If you ever have an opportunity... to talk to the young people of America, will you tell them for me that it's a privilege to lay down my life for them.' Now, with that testimony on his lips, he died, as did thousands like him in order that we could come and be like we are tonight. And do you know what we placed over the 77th division cemetery on Okinawa... This is the inscription we put for the Harold Browns and the thousands like him: 'WE GAVE OUR... TODAYS IN ORDER THAT YOU MIGHT HAVE YOUR TOMORROWS.' And he did."

(World War II Experience, a tape by Paul H. Dunn)

Gripping stories like these made Dunn a sought-after speaker... until some discrepancies in his accounts came to light. [ccxli] As it turns out, Dunn never played for the Cardinals or any major league baseball team. As for his war record, Dunn later admitted that only 30 soldiers in his unit died during the entire war, but that the exaggeration of the numbers wasn't important.

His story of running the gauntlet of withering machinegun fire that stripped away his boot, belt, canteen, ammo pouch (and shirt sleeves?) and split his steel helmet in two, but didn't injure him at all... also turns out to be an exaggeration—in fact, only his boot heel ever caught a bullet.

And there's only one problem with the story of his best friend Harold Brown dying in his arms while imploring Dunn to teach the youth of America about patriotism. Reporter Richard Robertson discovered that Dunn's army buddy Harold Brown *didn't die* on Okinawa. In fact, *he hadn't died at all.*

"Maybe he got me mixed up with someone else," a baffled Harold Brown told Richardson when the reporter found him, still living in Missouri. Brown was perplexed to hear about Dunn's story, a story he had never heard about before— especially since he and Dunn had stayed in contact since the war, even visiting each other occasionally!

Richardson had more troubling news to report: he was not the only one investigating Dunn's credibility gap. And when Dunn's little inconsistencies threatened to come to light, the LDS church leadership's first reaction was with threats—not to Dunn, but to the reporter. The church pressured Salt Lake City freelance writer and BYU instructor Lynn Packer, a Mormon (and nephew to Apostle Boyd K. Packer), not to publish stories about Dunn's fabrications. Packer received a memo from Gordon Whiting, then chairman of the BYU communications department, warning him that "publication of the Paul Dunn article will damage the church, will damage the university, will damage the department and will damage you."

He wasn't kidding. When Packer's teaching contract at BYU wasn't renewed for the 1990-91 school year, Whiting acknowledged that the decision was in part because Packer was violating church and university policies that prohibit public criticism of church leaders—even if the criticism is true. But the termination backfired; after the church let Packer go for pursuing the story, he took the information he had collected over the past four years to *The Arizona Republic*.

Meanwhile, the church also expressed their displeasure with Dunn himself. When he was confronted with evidence that his bestselling tapes and books had demonstrable falsehoods, he made several creative attempts to defend himself. "My motives are pure and innocent," Dunn said during an interview in Salt Lake City. He acknowledged that those stories and others were untrue, but he defended the fabrications as a necessary means to illustrate his theological and moral points, to better convey a message and capture an audience's interest. He compared his stories to the parables told by Jesus.

His fellow church authorities didn't find the analogy convincing, apparently; within two weeks of investigating allegations that his war and sports stories were fabricated, they quietly placed Dunn, 66, on emeritus status, 'for health reasons.' In October 1991, he was given permission to write an open letter to the church apologizing for having "not always been accurate in my public talks and writings." Despite his involuntary 'retirement,' and chastisement, Dunn remained the most prolific author among current and former church leaders, continuing to do public appearances and sell books. Up till his death, he received royalties from 23 inspirational cassette tapes and 28 books, which were among the more popular items in LDS bookstores. And all his lies about his major-league baseball career and his miraculous escape under fire can still be found on the church website today.

Jesus Returns . . . to Missouri

At first glance, the corner of River Blvd. and Walnut St. in Independence, Missouri, doesn't seem particularly daunting. Driving up, you pass gentle, tree-lined streets with well-manicured lawns. Then, through the trees on the northwest corner, you spot rows of flags of all nations, and beyond them, a chunky building of grey stone sporting an enormous 195-ft corkscrew spiraling skyward. It's the futuristic-looking headquarters of the Community of Christ, better known as the Reorganized Church of Jesus Christ of Latter Day Saints (RLDS). Just cattycorner to it is another imposing building, the domed Community of Christ auditorium and Children's Peace Pavilion. Across the street, on the southeast corner, stands a third building with tall, teethlike white columns and a boxy upper story with two dark windows, which almost gives the building the appearance of a gigantic carnivorous robot. It's the LDS Visitor's Center.

The last quadrant of this corner seems strangely empty by contrast. Apart from a strip of parking and a modest little building, the lot is taken up by a large grassy field in need of a good watering. And yet according to Mormon doctrine, this patch of ground is one of the most significant sites on the planet: it is ground zero for the Second Coming, the very spot where Jesus will touch down at his return.

Joseph consecrated the site in 1832, and announced a revelation that a "temple shall be reared in this generation. For verily this generation shall not pass away until an house shall be built unto the Lord, and a cloud shall rest upon it..." (*Doctrine & Covenants* 84:4-5) One hundred and eighty years and multiple generations later, clouds still have nowhere to rest upon the empty lot. In fact, to their great embarrassment, the Mormon church does not even own the land; instead it is the property of yet another Mormon splinter group, the "Hedrickites," officially known as the "Church of Christ (Temple Lot)," whose only real claim to fame is scooping up the choice piece of real estate. The LDS and RLDS churches had to be content with buying up all the acreage they could around the sacred site.

Unlike Tim Lahaye's readers and other evangelicals, Mormons don't believe in the Rapture; that bit of Christian sci-fi never quite took hold in their doctrine. Instead, Joseph claimed in 1835 that the Second Coming would take place in just 56 years (*History of the Church* 2:182), on or before 1891. Not to pile on more weirdness, but members of the Persian Baha'i faith declare that Joseph was a true prophet, because he was *actually* prophesying the coming of *their* founder Baha'u'llah—who announced he was the messiah in 1891. Meanwhile, Mormons continue to believe that when Jesus finally does return (they no longer try to pin down the date), he will descend from heaven, and Zion, the holy city of Enoch, will return to the earth from heaven with him. Jesus will personally reign on the earth from the corner of River Blvd. and Walnut St. for a thousand years of peace and righteousness.

Adam and Eve in America

Residents of bigger, cooler states may wonder just how does crummy old Missouri rate to be the millennial throne of King Jesus? Sorry, non-Missourians. Mormons know the Show Me state is not just Jesus' landing strip; it's also . . . *the Garden of Eden.* Yes, you heard that right. According to Joseph Smith, the empty lot on the corner of River and Walnut was the original site of the Garden of Eden at the dawn of time, five thousand years ago.

On a trip through northern Missouri in 1838, a member of the party climbed a high bluff overlooking the Grand River, and discovered what appeared to be the ruins of an altar. The man ran and got Joseph, who examined the stones in silence before declaring that it was the altar of Adam himself, and the valley below them was where Adam and Eve dwelt after their expulsion from Eden. Here they would build a holy city to be named Adam-ondi-Ahman, where Adam would return again to visit his people, seated on a throne of fiery flame (as predicted by the prophet Daniel), "with thousand thousands ministering unto him and ten thousand times ten thousand standing before him."(*History of the Church*, vol. III, p. 35; D&C 117:8, John Corrill, *Brief History of the Church*, p. 28)

Incidentally, the evocative and romantic name "Adam-ondi-Ahman" means . . . well, no one seems to know. Apostle Orson Pratt hazarded the translation "Valley of God, where Adam dwelt," and Second Counselor John Corrill, "the valley of God in which Adam blessed his children." Other guesses have included "Adam with God" or simply, "Adam's grave." The reason for all the uncertainty is that "Adam-ondi-Ahman" is not ancient Hebrew, but comes, of course, from the Adamic language, the pure and undefiled language of God and Adam spoken before God became miffed at humanity for building the Tower of Babel and confused their languages. In other words it's completely made up. Other "Adamic" words include *Deseret*, a word found throughout Utah, which according to Ether 2:3 in the BOM means "honeybee." Also the phrase "*Pay Lay Ale*" ("Oh God, hear the words of my mouth"), which used to be spoken in the Temple endowment ceremony, but now seems to be used only by mischievous ex-Mormon beermakers.

Not a Dr. Seuss character, but Mormon Apostle Orson Pratt, who seems to have thought he could translate the "Adamic" language.

There's more Old Testament archeology to be found in Missouri. Joseph also said that Far West, the temporary Mormon headquarters after their expulsion from Ohio, was "probably the exact site where Cain killed Abel."[ccxlii] You may be wondering, if all these biblical sites were in Midwest America, why does the Bible say that they were at the headwaters of the Tigris and Euphrates in ancient Babylon? And you would be asking a good question, especially since Joseph must have forgotten that seven years earlier, his revelation in the *Pearl of Great Price* (Moses 3:10, 13-14) *also* said that Eden was in ancient Babylon...

You might also wonder how everyone made it back to the Old World from ancient America in time to start civilization, but Joseph thought of that. In a Mormon magazine, *The Juvenile Instructor* (Nov. 15, 1895, pp. 700-701), Oliver B. Huntington filled in the details:

" ...according to the words of the Prophet Joseph, mankind in that age continued to emigrate eastwardly until they reached the country on or near the Atlantic coast; and *that in or near*

Carolina Noah built his remarkable ship, in which he, his family, and all kinds of animals lived a few days over one year without coming out of it."

So in the Mormon view of history, the ancient Hebrews began in Missouri, sailed to Mesopotamia, sailed back after the Tower of Babel and then again centuries later. The evidence for this? Well, there's this rock in Missouri, see...

Cain versus Bigfoot

Speaking of Adam and Eve, longstanding Mormon folklore claims that David W. Patten, one of the twelve original Mormon Apostles, had a mysterious and spooky encounter with their problem child. As the late LDS President Spencer W. Kimball relates in his book *The Miracle of Forgiveness* (Salt Lake City, 1969, pp. 127–128), Apostle Patten claimed he encountered a very tall, hairy, dark-skinned man in Paris, Tennessee, "a very remarkable person who had represented himself as being Cain." As the Apostle Patten told the story:
"As I was riding along the road on my mule I suddenly noticed a very strange person walking beside me... His head was about even with my shoulders as I sat in my saddle. He wore no clothing, but was covered with hair. His skin was very dark. I asked him where he dwelt and he replied that he had no home; that he was a wanderer in the earth and traveled to and fro. He said he was a very miserable creature, that he had earnestly sought death during his sojourn upon the earth, but that he could not die, and his mission was to destroy the souls of men. About the time he expressed himself thus, I rebuked him in the name of the Lord Jesus Christ and by virtue of the Holy Priesthood, and commanded him to go hence, and he immediately departed out of my sight..."

Patten's chilling and plausible tale is made even more fun by Mormons who speculate that Cain is the actual source behind the legends of ...wait for it ... Bigfoot. Yes. Bigfoot. Never ones to dismiss good scientific evidence, in the 1980s some Mormons fingered Cain as the real culprit in a series of Bigfoot sightings in South Weber, Utah.

Boy, Scouts...

Isn't it weird that Boy Scouts are required to believe in God (any god, really) and can't be gay, when Girl Scouts seem to get along just fine without the bigotry towards either atheists or homosexuals? Why is that?

Maybe it's because the Mormons are the largest chartering organization of the Boy Scouts of America. Eagle Scout Dan Hay reports that Boy Scouts are predominantly (68.4%) sponsored by churches, with the LDS church taking the lion's share, sponsoring fully a third of all scouting units (scout troops, cub packs and venture crews). According to MSNBC, Boy Scouts are the church's official boys' youth group; more than one in nine Scouts is Mormon. Brigham Young University even offers a major in Scouting.

The only religious groups that even come close to the Mormons' numbers are the Methodist (9.8 %) and Catholic (7.6%) churches. [ccxliii] But it's the LDS church that exerts disproportionate influence on the Boy Scouts, thanks to both their numbers on the national advisory council and vigorous fund-raising. The Mormon headlock on the BSA became glaringly apparent during the Supreme Court case *Boy Scouts of America et al. v. Dale* (2000), when the LDS church officially declared if the Boy Scouts admitted gay scouts or scoutmasters, they would immediately pull all of their support, taking more than 400,000 scouts and 30,000 scout troops with them. [ccxliv]

Though the first tenet of the Boy Scout Law states that a Scout tells the truth, scouts who don't believe in a god can find their troops pressuring them to hide their atheism and not make waves. But not all scouts agree with the discrimination being practiced by their leadership. Steven Cozza, a 12-year-old Life Scout (now an Eagle Scout), wrote a letter to his local newspaper arguing that the BSA violates its own Scout Law when they discriminate against gays (and atheists, and girls).

In 1998, Steven launched a national petition drive to call on the BSA to rescind its exclusionary policies, which led to the creation of Scouting For All (www.scoutingforall.org), a non-profit group dedicated to opening Boy Scouts to all people, regardless of their religious beliefs, gender, or sexual orientation.

Supporters of BSA reform will have an uphill battle as long as religious groups like the Mormons keep their tight grip on the reins of BSA leadership and the BSA purse strings. As of this writing (in summer of 2012) the fight continues, but the Scouts remain linked to the Saints. Or should I say yoked?

Stephenie Meyer's Twilight Zone

Twi-hard fans probably already know that Stephenie Meyer, the author of Bella and Edward's vamp love book and movie series 'Twilight', is a Mormon. Those anti-fans who aren't on Team Edward OR Jacob and thought the Twilight franchise was heinous enough already may be irked further to learn how Mormon motifs and themes permeate the series. This is according to UCLA Film & Religion Prof. Angela Aleiss, who did a point-by-point comparison [ccxlv] of how Mormon beliefs and culture, influence and imagery run deep through 'Twilight,' right down to how much housekeeping the heroine Bella is always doing.

Stephenie Meyer herself says she didn't deliberately set out to insert Mormon subtext into her books. "I think people make up all these Mormon references just so they can publish 'Twilight' articles in respectable publications like *The New York Times*," series star and sparkly vampire Robert Pattinson told Entertainment Weekly. "Even Stephenie said it doesn't mean any of that."

For what it's worth, I believe Meyer when she says she never set out to weave Mormon imagery into the 'Twilight' background. And to be fair, she freely admits that her faith informs her life, so it's natural that her religious worldview would color her writing. But intentional or no, the Mormon subtext is hard to ignore once Prof. Aleiss points them out:

Of course, one of the threads running through the heart of the book is a theme of abstinence. In 'Twilight', sex = danger, and Edward and Bella's relationship has been compared to a love affair between a man and a delicious jelly donut. Bella also shuns coffee, tea, alcohol and tobacco and advises her father to "cut back on steak," all perfectly in keeping with the LDS dietary restrictions, the "Word of Wisdom," which forbids all of the former and directs members to eat meat and poultry "sparingly." Bella's frequent cooking and cleaning have raised some eyebrows among feminists, who see her devotion to household chores as a reflection of the strong Mormon work ethic and traditional roles assigned to women.

In Mormonism, angels are resurrected humans on their way to becoming gods themselves. Joseph Smith described the angel Moroni as radiating light and "glorious beyond description." Similarly, the Cullens, Meyer's vampire family, were once human but now live in a resurrected condition; their immortality is a kind of probationary period for eternal life. Meyer describes the Cullens, particularly Edward, as "godlike" and "inhumanly beautiful." Bella even describes Edward, whose skin sparkles in the sunlight, as an angel whom she can't imagine "any more glorious". And like Moroni's appearance to Joseph Smith, he visits Bella's bedroom at night. The 'Twilight' film plays with the idea of Edward-as-angel, too. When Edward sits in the science lab with Bella, the outstretched wings of a stuffed white owl peek out just over his shoulders.

Prof. Aleiss notes that, just as Mormons are not married "until death do you part," but for eternity, so Bella describes her relationship with Edward as "forever." Their marriage, and her quick pregnancy, underscore the Mormon emphasis on the family and having children. When Bella's half human/vampire fetus nearly destroys her, her distraught husband suggests an abortion and artificial insemination. Mormons permit abortions if the mother's life is in danger, and artificial insemination is an option for married couples.

Bella quickly vetoes both abortion and artificial insemination, reinforcing the essential Mormon teaching of individual choice, or "agency." Meyer has said that the apple on the cover of the first 'Twilight' novel represents Eve's choice in the Garden of Eden. The poster for 'Eclipse' includes the line: "It all begins ... with a choice." The patriarch of the vampire family, Carlisle Cullen, supports Bella when he explains, "It wouldn't be right to make such a choice for her, to force her."

In the series, Bella also runs into a band of shape-shifting Quileute Indians, who are also, for all practical purposes, werewolves. Quileutes are a real northwest Native American tribe, which of course in Mormon mythology means they are descended from the Lamanites and ultimately, from ancient Israel. Accordingly, Meyer gives all her Quileute characters distinctly Hebrew names. Besides Jacob Black (in the BOM Lamanites are marked by their "skin of blackness"), there is Ephraim, Jared, Joshua, Levi, Rachel, Rebecca, Sam and Seth.

It's interesting to see the Vampire genre, so traditionally packed with Catholic symbols like crucifixes, holy water and Communion wafers, become revamped (no pun intended) for a new generation with the religious associations of a completely different new faith.

Mormons you didn't know were Mormon

Everybody in the 1970s knew TV singer-siblings Donny and Marie Osmond were Mormon, just as 'Twilight' author Stephanie Meyer is one of the most famous Mormons today—with the exception of Mitt Romney. But here are some more celebrities you may not have even realized were Latter-day Saints...

Singers

Move over, Donny and Marie! The Osmonds aren't the only musicians with Mormon roots. There's also, ehrm, **Alice Cooper**. The heavy metal shock rocker (real name: Vincent Furnier) may be better known for his onstage mock executions with guillotines and electric chairs, but before he ran around with boa constrictors, fake blood, and decapitated baby dolls, he was active during his boyhood in the Bickertonite church, one of the Mormon splinter sects founded by Sidney Rigdon. Alice's father (whose middle name is Moroni) was a preacher in the church, and his grandfather was an apostle. They must be proud.

Motown legend **Gladys Knight** (of "and the Pips" fame) was raised Baptist, but in 1997 she followed her son and daughter in being baptized as a Mormon. She admitted to a few initial reservations about the LDS church's track record on black people, but was pleased when told they were "a perfect church run by imperfect people." *Desert Saints* Magazine (Sept. 2006) reported she used to tease the late LDS president Hinckley that Mormons needed to inject some "pep" into their music—which she provided by creating a Mormon choir, Saints Unified Voices, which performs at LDS church firesides. Gladys has sung with the Mormon Tabernacle Choir on several occasions.

In 2011, *American Idol* runner-up **David Archuleta** announced a hiatus from his hugely successful music career to serve his two-years as an LDS missionary. Rocker **Brandon Flowers** of the Killers is from an active Mormon family, and ostensibly remains a practicing Saint today. At least, he's claimed to be a practicing Mormon in several interviews, although he admits rock and roll and Mormonism don't play well together. He's also admitted to having had alcohol and smoked on occasion, although he tries not to... Lead singer and front man for Las Vegas-based emo-pop rock band Panic! At the Disco, **Brendon Urie** was raised in the church, but fell away after high school. His bandmate Ryan Ross has said that Urie is no longer "the good Mormon boy we once knew."

Movie and Television Stars

Hollywood and television have their share of Saints, too. Former child actor and *NYPD Blue* star **Rick Schroder** joined the church eight years after marrying a nice Mormon girl. Nearly everyone involved in the cult hit film **Napoleon**

Dynamite has Mormon ties. **Jon Heder**, the actor who plays the eponymous Napoleon Dynamite is a proud Saint and BYU alum. **Aaron Ruell**, who play's Napoleon's dorktastic brother "Kip," is also Mormon, as are **Jared and Jerusha Hess**, the husband and wife team who co-wrote and directed the film, executive producer and editor **Jeremy Coon**, and 95% of the crew, who came from BYU's film school. So no matter what you think of Joseph Smith, you can at least thank him for an awesome indie cult classic.

Gruff but lovable and walrus-like Quaker Oats pusher **Wilford Brimley** (*Cocoon, The Thing*) is a native Mormon from Salt Lake City and has appeared in LDS productions like the 2001 murder mystery film, *Brigham City*. Beloved pop-eyed 3' 9" tall character actor **Billy Barty** was perhaps the most recognizable little person in the 20th century, with a 70-year career spanning vaudeville, TV, commercials, stage and screen. Less known was the fact that he was a Mormon.

Other stars had Mormon childhoods, but have since given up the church: **Amy Adams** (*Enchanted, Catch Me if You Can*); **Eliza Dushku** ("Faith" on *Buffy the Vampire Slayer, Dollhouse*), **Aaron Eckhart** (*The Dark Knight, Thank You for Smoking*), **Ryan Gosling** (*The Notebook, Lars and the Real Girl*), *Grey's Anatomy* star **Katherine Heigl**, and **Matthew Modine** (*Full Metal Jacket, The Dark Knight Rises*) were all born into LDS families but no longer consider themselves Saints.

Before he was on TV doing extreme close-ups of his tear-filled eyes, mapping out connect-the-dot conspiracies on the chalkboard and filling the remainders table at Costco with unsold copies of his books, conservative pundit **Glenn Beck** says God saved him from being an unknown, friendless loser enslaved to drugs and booze (thanks, God!). An LDS convert, some commentators have contended that his paranoid conspiracy schtick and weepy tendency for on-air waterworks are both informed by his Mormonism.

Hard to believe irreverent, abrasive, raspy-voiced, TV and comedy heavyweight **Roseanne Barr** was ever Mormon, but it's true. Born to a Jewish family in Salt Lake City, she told how she became Mormon in her autobiography *Roseanne: My Life as a Woman*. When she was a 6-year old girl, she took a fall and her face became partially paralyzed, as if from a stroke. The next day, her mother called their rabbi, who said a prayer for her to be healed, without success. So the day after that, her mother tried the Mormons, who came over and gave her a blessing. Miraculously enough, the next day her face was better, and from then on the family were zealous members of the LDS church. Roseanne even became president of her Young Women's class. Then when she was 16, she picked up a medical journal and read about what had caused her facial paralysis. She learned it was Bell's Palsy—which usually only lasts 48 hours. She was so disgusted over her debunked Mormon healing, she immediately went out, drank a beer and smoked two cigarettes.

Sports

Perhaps the most famous Mormon athlete is Super Bowl champion, Hall-of-Famer and San Francisco 49er quarterback **Steve Young**. Not just Mormon, he's Mormon royalty: a great-great-grandson of Brigham Young himself. Other professional athlete stars sporting sacred underwear under their uniforms include basketball players like the Boston Celtics' **Danny Ainge**, the Phoenix Suns' **Tom Chambers** and **Thurl "Big T" Bailey** of the Utah Jazz, who converted after marrying a local Mormon girl.

Politicians

The 2012 presidential race was notable for having not one, but two Mormon candidates battling for the Republican nomination: **Mitt Romney** and **Jon Huntsman, Jr**. Mormon politicians aren't restricted to the Republican party, though perhaps you could be forgiven for thinking so. Democratic senate majority leader **Harry Reid** is a Latter-day Saint, too.

Infamous Mormons

What's the diametric opposite of your average Mormon? How about the leader of the Black Panther Party? In the 1960s, **Eldridge Cleaver** was the scariest mo-fo around to mainstream white America, a self-confessed criminal and serial rapist turned best-selling author and political philosopher, a Black Nationalist, a Marxist and a radical revolutionary working overtime to overthrow the country. At their height, the Panthers were 10,000 strong and terrifying J. Edgar Hoover, who threw every dirty trick he had at them to destroy the organization.

After a shootout with the Oakland police in 1969, Cleaver fled to Algeria, then Cuba, where he quickly became disillusioned with Communism. He became a born-again Christian and returned to the U.S. in 1975, to the delight of evangelicals who welcomed their prodigal son with open arms and tempted him with multimillion dollar contracts to start a Christian television ministry. He resisted, preferring to minister to young black men in prison instead.

Unsurprisingly, he became disillusioned with glitzy, money-hungry mainstream Christianity as well, and in 1982 began looking into alternative religion. Former FBI agent Cleon Skousen, a well-known Mormon author, introduced Cleaver and his wife to the LDS church, and in 1984 he became an on-again/off-again Mormon, until his death in 1998.

Butch Cassidy, the notorious wild west robber immortalized by Paul Newman, was the oldest of 13 children of a Mormon family in Utah. His religious instruction didn't take, apparently, as he went on to become the leader of the Wild Bunch, the most successful train-robbing gang in history.

Though it's not widely advertised, **Ted Bundy**, one of the world's most infamous serial killers, was a member of the LDS Church, although to be fair, he wasn't a very good Mormon. Bundy moved to Salt Lake City in 1974 to attend law school and during the year he lived in Utah became a convert to the LDS Church. Reports say he tended to ignore most of the church's rules and restrictions, and wasn't active in services,

David Fitzgerald

perhaps because he was too busy being a horrific necrophiliac murderer. Four of his victims were young Utah girls; a fifth escaped from his car and escaped with her life. It would be churlish and grossly unfair to put undue emphasis on Bundy's nominal Mormonism, which was surely just one more tool he used to camouflage his sociopathy—but it *is* reasonable to ask, if Mormon authorities really *are* gifted with a divine gift of "discernment," why was no one in the church able to discern that one of the most notorious killers in history was lurking in their flock?

Letters from Brigham:

The Deseret Alphabet

𐐘𐑆𐐏𐑊 𐐢𐐹𐐯𐐱𐑊

Having trouble reading the line above? It's not Martian writing; it's Mormon. One of Brigham Young's less successful plans was the creation of a completely new writing system for the LDS church, the Deseret Alphabet (see below for help deciphering it). Why the hell would the Saints need to have their own *alphabet*? Officially, the reason was to reform standard English spelling, and create a more logical, more phonetic system that would help the influx of new non-English-speaking Mormon converts from overseas learn to read and write. But one can't help but notice that an alphabet of their own would have other advantages as well: It would distinguish Mormon culture from Gentiles, help shield Mormon writings from the prying eyes of outsiders, and control what young church members could read—all very useful for a blossoming theocracy...

So Brigham had George D. Watt, a shorthand expert and the church's first English convert, create a set of thirty-eight

186

characters, one for each of the basic sounds in the English language, and in 1854 the University of Deseret officially announced the Deseret Alphabet. Brigham spent nearly two decades, and over twenty thousand dollars (an enormous amount of money in those days) pushing the new alphabet. But few were very interested in scrapping the English language and starting over with the strange new system.

And typesetting proved an extremely costly endeavor. The University of Deseret's board of regents voted $10,000 to print text books in the alphabet for students in classrooms across the territory, but soon realized it wouldn't be enough; by some estimates the cost of printing a regular library would be over one million dollars.[ccxlvi] Few books were transcribed apart from the Bible, *Doctrine and Covenants* and an English-Hopi dictionary, and only four books were ever published. The first were two elementary school primers. [ccxlvii] Ten thousand copies of each volume were printed in New York and shipped to Salt Lake City. Then a 3-part Book of Mormon was planned. Eight thousand copies of part one were published; the second two parts were never printed. Instead, a complete Book of Mormon was published in 1869, but only about five hundred copies were printed.

See if you can decipher the text on the next page; if you run into trouble, go to the end of the chapter:
Source:
http://www.utlm.org/onlineresources/deseretalphabet.htm

David Fitzgerald

𐐙

𐐒𐐊𐐗 𐐎𐐆 𐐐𐐬𐐙𐐲𐐡𐐤:

𐐄 𐐐𐐬𐐤𐐄 𐐙𐐐𐐐 𐐒𐐊

𐐙 𐐙𐐎𐐐𐐒 𐐎𐐆 𐐐𐐬𐐙𐐲𐐡𐐤,

𐐙𐐎𐐐

𐐞𐐐𐐀𐐐𐐒 𐐐𐐀𐐒𐐊 𐐙𐐎𐐎𐐬 𐐙 𐐞𐐐𐐀𐐐𐐒 𐐎𐐆 𐐐𐐬𐐡𐐙.

———— ✦ ————

[Deseret Alphabet paragraphs — not transliterated]

𐐐𐐬𐐙𐐲𐐡𐐤.

~~~~~~~~~~
𐐓𐐐𐐐𐐞𐐐𐐐𐐞𐐐 𐐒𐐊 𐐞𐐐𐐐𐐙 𐐞𐐐𐐐, 𐐞𐐐𐐙.
~~~~~~~~~~

𐐞𐐐𐐙 I.

NEW YORK:
PUBLISHED FOR THE DESERET UNIVERSITY
BY RUSSELL BROS.
1869.

All four books were advertised for sale in the *Deseret News*. The first primer sold for fifteen cents, the second for twenty cents. Part one of the proposed three-volume BOM set cost seventy-five cents, while the complete family edition Book of Mormon went for two dollars. It appears they sold poorly; entire boxes of the unsold primers were found in the late 1950s and sold for fifty cents each.

An 1860 $5 gold piece from the LDS mint. The inscription reads "Holiness to the Lord" in the Deseret Alphabet. Source: Deseret Assay Office (Deseret Mint), Salt Lake City, Utah Territory

After just a year, the *Deseret News* was no longer advertising the sale of Deseret Alphabet books. During the 1870s the alphabet was mentioned less and less until interest in it had virtually disappeared. [ccxlviii]

Today, traces of the Deseret Alphabet can be found on a few gold coins minted in Salt Lake City, in surviving personal letters, diaries, and meeting minutes, engraved on a tombstone in Cedar City, Utah, and on the websites of its fans. However, it does remain the official alphabet of the Republic of Molossia, a fictional but quite real micronation whose territory is comprised of about 6 acres near Dayton, Nevada. [ccxlix] No, really.

Guide to the Deseret Alphabet:
Source:
http://www.utlm.org/onlineresources/deseretalphabet.htm

***

For further reading:

God is Not a Good Investment Advisor:
http://www.businessweek.com/articles/2012-07-10/how-the-mormons-make-money#p1

Lying for the Lord:
"Mormon Leader Admits Exaggerating Stories," Richard R. Robertson, *The Arizona Republic*, Feb. 16, 1991

"Dunn in the Name of God!" Jerald & Sandra Tanner, *Salt Lake City Messenger*, No. 78, June 1991, http://www.utlm.org/newsletters/no78.htm

---

Endnotes: Chapter 8

[cci] We really have to read that again: "Astronomers and philosophers have, from time almost immemorial until very recently, *asserted the moon was uninhabited, that it had no atmosphere*, etc. *But recent discoveries, through the means of powerful telescopes, have given scientists a doubt or two upon the old theory*." Astronomers—Ha! What do *they* know?
[ccii] Oliver B. Huntington, *The Young Woman's Journal*, 1892, vol. 3, pp. 263-64
[cciii] *Journal of Discourses*, vol. 13, p. 271, July 24, 1870
[cciv] Richard Packham, "Why I Left the Mormon Church" http://packham.n4m.org/whylft.htm
[ccv] Ostling, p. 198
[ccvi] ibid.
[ccvii] Brodie p. 280
[ccviii] ibid.
[ccix] ibid., p. 367
[ccx] ibid.
[ccxi] First Presidency letter of November 5, 1996, quoted in David E. Sorensen, "The Doctrine of Temple Work," *Ensign*, Oct. 2003, p. 56
[ccxii] Letter to all temple presidents from the First Presidency, May 22, 1968; archived in "Research Notes on LDS Temples:

Temple Clothes," *New Mormon Studies CD-ROM: A Comprehensive Resource Library,* San Francisco, Smith Research Associates, 1998

ccxiii"Garments & Temple Clothes," http://www.ldsendowment. org/clothing.html

ccxiv ibid.

ccxv David John Buerger, *The Mysteries of Godliness,* San Francisco: Smith Research Associates, 1994, pp. 147-148

ccxvi "Garments & Temple Clothes," op.cit.

ccxvii Brodie, p. 281

ccxviii Church Handbook of Instructions, vol. 1 of 2 Salt Lake City: The Church of Jesus Christ of Latter-day Saints, p. 70

ccxix "Garments & Temple Clothes," op.cit.

ccxx I'm grateful to Steve Thoreson for bringing the point about Jesus/Jehovah to my attention.

ccxxi Harold B. Lee, *"Admonitions for the Priesthood of God", Ensign,* Jan. 1973

ccxxii Krakauer, p. 275

ccxxiii ibid .

ccxxiv ibid.

ccxxv "Most Utahns Ever Go Bust," Steven Oberbeck, *Salt Lake Tribune*, Jan. 11, 2006

ccxxvi "Feds: Mormon Bishop Ran Ponzi Scheme," *Connecticut Post*, March 27, 2012

ccxxvii "Val Southwick's Victims Tell Stories of Shattered Lives," Ben Winslow, *Deseret News*, Dec. 17, 2008

ccxxviii "Ponzi operator gets 10-year sentence," Tom Harvey, *Salt Lake Tribune,* Jan. 8, 2012

ccxxix "The Mormon Madoff: How Shawn Merriman Scammed Millions," Jenna Martino, CNBC.com (http://www.cnbc.com /id/47881681/The_Mormon_Madoff_How_Shawn_Merriman_ Scammed_Millions)

ccxxx "Former Stake President, Regional Representative... and Scam Artist" http://utahsecuritiesfraud.co,m/2010/08/12/ former-stake-president-regional-representative-and-scam-artist/

ccxxxi "Mormons Deny Kleenmaid Links After Damning Audit," Natasha Bita, *The Australian*, May 18, 2009 ccxxxii "Judge Scolds, Sentences 5 For Mortgage Fraud," Linda Thomson, *Deseret News*, April 3, 2009

ccxxxiii "Investors believed in Giles County businesses," Mike Gangloff, *The Roanoke Times*, October 3, 2008

ccxxxiv "Immigrants Deported After Exposing Scam," UPI.com, May 11, 2009

ccxxxv "Father, Son Used Mormon Faith to Lure Investors In $220M Ponzi Scheme, SEC Says," Halah Touryalai, *Forbes.com*, December 16, 2011

ccxxxvi "Alpine Man Accused of Widespread Investment Scam," Pamela Manson, Lisa Schenker, and Dawn House, *The Salt Lake Tribune*, May 27, 2009

ccxxxvii "A Fraud Played Out on Family and Friends" By William Yardley, *The New York Times*, May 26, 2011

ccxxxviii "Swindler Sentenced to 40 Years," *Spartanburg Herald-Journal*, Nov. 14. 1984

ccxxxix The *Wall Street Journal*, Nov. 9, 1983

ccxl *New Era*, August 1975, page 7ff

ccxli Sources: "Mormon Leader Admits Exaggerating Stories," Richard R. Robertson, *The Arizona Republic*, Feb. 16, 1991; "Dunn in the Name of God!" Jerald & Sandra Tanner, *Salt Lake City Messenger*, No. 78, June 1991

ccxlii Brodie, p. 211

ccxliii Hay, Dan, "How Religion Holds the BSA Hostage," Illini Secular Student Alliance; www.illinissa.com/2011/12/how-religion-holds-bsa-hostage.html

ccxliv Mark Eddington, "What Happens if Scouts Must Admit Gays?" *Salt Lake Tribune,* April 26, 2000

ccxlv "Mormon Influence, Imagery Run Deep Through 'Twilight'" Angela Aleiss, *Huffington Post*, June 2, 2010; updated May 25, 2011

ccxlvi Bigler, p.56

ccxlvii "The Deseret Alphabet Died With Brigham Young," by Vania Grandi, *Salt Lake Tribune*, Dec. 2, 2000, p. D8

ccxlviii Richard G. Moore, "The Deseret Alphabet Experiment," in *Religious Educator* 7, no. 3 (2006), pp. 63–76

ccxliv See the official website of the Republic of Molossia at: http://www.molossia.org

Part Three

Skeletons in the Mormon Closet

Chapter 9

Book of Mormon Problems

Holy books of all religions share an interesting flaw: whenever you read their Word of God™ too closely, inconsistencies and other simple human errors appear. This problem keeps the apologists busy coming up with plenty of creative ways to explain away all the mistakes—no, no, not mistakes, the "apparent difficulties." This time-honored theological industry's goal is to make their scripture as fact-proof as possible. The only way to penetrate this armor (or maybe I should say get this ostrich to pull its head in the sand) is to keep hammering away at the layers of rationalizations and *ad hoc* defenses). So with apologies for the overkill, here are even more reasons to reject the Book of Mormon.

What a Load

Before we drop the plates, author David Persuitte and others have pointed out one fundamental glitch in Joseph's Book of Mormon story: the weight of the "Golden Plates". Some witnesses said the gold plates weighed about 30 lbs., others 40 or 60 lbs., though Emma Smith could easily lift them when she was dusting the table around them.

Joseph's mother said at one point when he was in the process of moving the plates from one hiding place to another to keep them safe from their greedy neighbors, he wrapped them in a linen frock and tucked them under his arm and traveled three miles through the woods, leaping over obstacles, repeatedly fighting off three different attackers and sprinting home at full speed:

"The plates were secreted about three miles from home... Joseph, on coming to them, took them from their secret place, and, wrapping them in his linen frock, placed them under his arm and started for home.
"After proceeding a short distance, he thought it would be more safe to leave the road and go through the woods. Traveling some distance after he left the road, he came to a large windfall, and as he was jumping over a log, a man sprang up from behind it, and gave him a heavy blow with a gun. Joseph turned around and knocked him down, then ran at the top of his speed.
"About half a mile further he was attacked again in the same manner as before; he knocked this man down in like manner as the former, and ran on again; and before he reached home he was assaulted the third time. In striking the last one he dislocated his thumb, which, however, he did not notice until he came within sight of the house, when he threw himself down in the corner of the fence in order to recover his breath. As soon as he was able, he arose and came to the house. (He) was still altogether speechless from fright and the fatigue of running."

But if the gold plates were as big as Joseph said they were—each six inches wide and eight inches long, in a stack nearly 6 inches thick—then the Book of Mormon would have had a total volume of 288 cubic inches. The density of gold is 0.69 lbs/cubic inch, which means the little box containing the gold plates that so many of Joseph's followers claim to have examined and casually hefted would have weighed over 198 pounds.
Since this damning point has come to light, LDS apologists have tried to backpedal. Some tried to suggest that there could have been "air spaces" between the individual

plates that lightened the load, but not even other Mormons have bought that lame attempt. Others suggest that maybe the gold plates were really only gold-plated gold plates, but even this downgrade wouldn't make the weight issue go away, since it still has young Joseph lugging over 50 lbs. under his arm during his dramatic chase scene. At the bottom of the barrel, some have tried to float the idea that God gave Joseph Smith superhuman strength to lift them, but if you're going to say this, you may as well throw up your hands and admit that the story makes no sense.

Angels in America

Much like Joseph's First Vision, the later visitation from the angel Moroni came with some odd questions. For instance, did the angel actually make a supernatural appearance—or was it all just in Joseph's head? Before 1830, all Mormon sources refer to it as a dream. [ccli]

And *was* the angel named Moroni? Before 1835 the angel had no name at all, but as late as the 1850s several LDS publications, including the 1851 edition of *The Pearl of Great Price* (p. 41, see below) gave the angel's name as *Nephi*, not Moroni. Even the original handwritten manuscript of the *Pearl* dictated by Joseph Smith shows that the angel was originally called "Nephi," and that a later editor has written the name "Moroni" above the line. All evidence indicates that this change was made after Joseph Smith's death. [cclii]

son. When I first looked upon him I was afraid, but the fear soon left me. He called me by name and said unto me, that he was a messenger sent from the presence of God to me, and that his name was Nephi. That God had a work for me to do and that my name should be had for good and evil among all nations, kindreds, and tongues; or that it should be both good and evil

Account of Joseph's first vision in the 1851 edition of the *Pearl of Great Price* (pg. 41), showing the angel's name as Nephi, not Moroni.

Original handwritten manuscript of the *Pearl* dictated by Joseph Smith. Note the angel was originally called "Nephi," (line 3); a later editor has written the name "Moroni" above the line.

Source: History, 1839-1856, Volume A-1, Page 5, *The Joseph Smith Papers.* Salt Lake City, UT: Church Historian's Press. 2008

Joseph's own mother, Lucy Mack Smith, also said the angel's name was Nephi (*Biographical Sketches*, 1853, p. 79). The 1878 edition of *The Pearl of Great Price* removed the name of Nephi altogether and inserted Moroni in its place. [ccliii]

Another funny thing about Nephi: The most common man's name in the Book of Mormon (and the title of four of its fifteen books) is "Nephi." Mormons might be happy to learn that there is historical evidence for the name; it appears in the Biblical Apocrypha book of 2 Maccabees (1:36). Unfortunately, it's not the name of a person, but a place name.

Correcting the Most Correct Book on Earth

Despite God himself calling the Book of Mormon "the most correct of any book on earth" and personally dictating to Joseph every single word and letter, the first editions have embarrassing spelling and grammar errors. None of Joseph's transcribers had a firm grasp of punctuation; when the manuscript went to press, there were hardly any commas, periods or capital letters. So the typesetters took it upon themselves to decide how to break up the sentences. As a result, out of the first two hundred sentences, one hundred and forty began with "And." [cliv]

It's also a bit ironic calling the Book of Mormon the most correct book on earth, since the book opens with an apology for being poorly written right on the title page. Ever since the first edition, Church editors have continued to make substantial alterations to their scriptures for over 180 years. In their book *Changes in Joseph Smith's History*, famed LDS critics Jerald and Sandra Tanners remark that the Church added or deleted over 62,000 words that Smith himself had written. If LDS editors hadn't fixed his mistakes, the ancient Nephites would have sounded a lot more like Tom Sawyer and Huck Finn. The church didn't just correct the pervasive grammar and spelling errors, but cleaned up Freudian slips like changing the title page so that Joseph Smith appeared as the translator, not the author of the Book of Mormon!

Other changes were more significant, coming in response to changes in church doctrine or simply out of embarrassment—or in some cases, both—such as verses like 2 Nephi 30:6, which claimed with a straight face that sinful dark-skinned races who repented would become "white and delightsome people." Today it says they will become "pure and delightsome" instead. And the changes have probably not come to an end.

Even today, after nearly 200 years, there are still several bizarre BOM passages that make no damn sense as written, waiting for a clever Mormon editor to fix them. One is in the book of Ether, where a newly-decapitated villain remains surprisingly active: "And it came to pass that after he had smitten off the head of Shiz, that Shiz raised up on his hands and fell; and after that he had struggled for breath, he died" (Ether 15:31). Or when Jacob, an ancient Hebrew-American in the 5th century B.C.E., bids the reader farewell in French, saying "Brethren, *adieu*" (Jacob 7:27).

This isn't to say there aren't good features of the Book of Mormon. For instance, the book's pacing improved as the writing went along; the Lord inspired fewer boring sermons in favor of more adventure stories. Joseph's biographer Fawn

Brodie praised his creative talents—albeit maybe a bit backhandedly:

"To belittle his creative talent is to do him as great an injustice as to say that he had no learning—a favorite Mormon thesis designed to prove the authenticity of the book. His talent, it is true, was not exceptional, for his book lacked subtlety, wit, and style. He was chiefly a tale-teller and preacher. His characters were pale, humorless stereotypes; the prophets were always holy, and in three thousand years of history not a single harlot was made to speak. But he began the book with a first-class murder, added assassinations, and piled up battles by the score. There was plenty of bloodshed and slaughter to make up for the lack of gaiety and the stuff of humanity." [cclv]

King James Fan Fiction

Another conspicuous shortcoming with the BOM is Joseph Smith's plagiarism from the King James Bible. Whenever he ran low on creative juice, he made up for it by letting his ancient American prophets quote the Bible—about 25,000 words in the *Book of Mormon* come straight from the Old Testament, with another two thousand from the New Testament. [cclvi] And even when he wasn't copying text verbatim, there were plenty of less obvious borrowings. For instance, of the 350 names in the BOM, over a hundred come directly from the Bible, and over a hundred others are simply slightly altered biblical names. [cclvii]

Joseph's desperation to give his *Book of Mormon* suitably biblical flavor resulted in some profoundly awkward prose. As Mark Twain aptly noted:

"Wherever he found his speech growing too modern—which was about every sentence or two—he ladled in a few such Scriptural phrases as "exceeding sore," "and it came to pass," etc., and made things satisfactory again. 'And it came to pass' was his pet. If he had left that out, his Bible would have been only a pamphlet." [cclviii]

Twain wasn't kidding. Paradoxically, reading the Book of Mormon could make a great drinking game: the phrase "and it came to pass" appears over two thousand times. Steve Well's terrific site Skeptic's Annotated Book of Mormon (http://skepticsannotatedbible.com/bom/index.htm), painstakingly lists out all of the instances of "and it came to pass" in the BOM, as well as each example of the exceedingly high usage of the word "exceedingly."

And once you also factor in all the cribbed stories from the Old and New Testaments, the Book of Mormon might as well be called Biblical fan fiction. Observe a few examples:

Book of Mormon	Kings James Bible
The beautiful daughter of Jared dances before the King, pleases him, and is coached to ask for her father's head as a reward:	The beautiful daughter of Herodias dances before the King, pleases him, and is coached to ask for John the Baptist's head as a reward:
*And now, therefore, let my father send for Akish, the son of Kimnor; and behold, I am fair, and **I will dance before him, and I will please him,** that he will desire me to wife; wherefore if he shall desire of thee that ye shall give unto him me to wife, **then shall ye say:** I will give her if ye will **bring unto me the head of my father, the king.**"* (Ether 8:10)	*But when Herod's birthday was celebrated, **the daughter of Herodias danced before them and pleased Herod.** Therefore he promised with an oath to give her whatever she might ask. So she, **having been prompted by her mother,** said, "**Give me John the Baptist's head** here on a platter."* (Matthew 14:6-8)

Alma and Amulek are freed from prison by an earthquake that handily also frees them from their chains:	Paul and Silas are freed from prison by an earthquake that handily also frees them from their chains:
*... and **the earth shook mightily, and the walls of the prison were rent in twain,** so that they fell to the earth... And Alma and Amulek came forth out of the prison, and they were not hurt... And **they straightway came forth out of the prison; and they were loosed from their bands; and the prison had fallen to the earth...*** (Alma 14:27-28)	*Suddenly **there was a great earthquake,** so that **the foundations of the prison were shaken;** and **immediately all the doors were opened** and **everyone's chains were loosed.*** (Acts 16:26)

Beloved Lamoni gets deathly sick. But the prophet Ammon assures all that although he stinks, he really only sleeps, and he shall rise again. When Ammon asks Lamoni's queen, "Believest thou this?" she replies, "I believe" and so Lamoni rises again.

*¹And it came to pass that **after two days** and two nights they were about to take his body and lay it in a sepulchre...²Now the queen... said unto him... others say that he is dead and that he **stinketh**, and that he ought to be placed in the sepulchre...⁸And he said unto the queen: He is not dead, but he **sleepeth** in God, and on the morrow **he shall rise again**; therefore bury him not. ⁹And **Ammon said unto her: Believest thou this?** And she said unto him: I have had no witness save thy word, and the word of our servants; nevertheless **I believe** that it shall be according as thou hast said...¹²And it came to pass that **he arose**, according to the words of Ammon...*
(Alma 19:1-12)

Beloved Lazarus gets deathly sick. But the prophet Jesus assures all that although he stinks, he really only sleeps, and he shall rise again. When Jesus asks Lazarus' sister, "Believest thou this?" she replies, "I believe" and so Lazarus rises again.

*⁶When he had heard therefore that he was sick, he abode **two days** still in the same place where he was.¹¹... after that he saith unto them, Our friend Lazarus **sleepeth**; but I go, that I may awake him out of sleep... ²³Jesus saith unto her, **Thy brother shall rise again**. ²⁴Martha saith unto him, I know that **he shall rise again** in the resurrection at the last day.²⁵Jesus said unto her... whosoever liveth and believeth in me shall never die. **Believest thou this?** ²⁷She saith unto him, Yea, Lord: **I believe**...³⁹Jesus said, Take ye away the stone. Martha, the sister of him that was dead, saith unto him, Lord, by this time he **stinketh**: for he hath been dead four days... ⁴³And when he thus had spoken, he cried with a loud voice, Lazarus, come forth. ⁴⁴And **he that was dead came forth**...*
(John 11:6-44)

In a dramatic conversion story, Alma and his men are traveling about, persecuting the church, when suddenly an angel of the Lord comes down from heaven. They are so scared they fall to the ground. He asks, "Why persecutest thou the church of God?" and strikes Alma dumb.

*¹⁰And now it came to pass that while he was going about to **destroy the church of God**... ¹¹as they were going about rebelling against God, behold, **the angel of the Lord appeared unto them**; and he descended as it were in a cloud; and he spake as it were with a **voice of thunder**, which caused the earth to shake upon which they stood; ¹²And so great was their astonishment, that **they fell to the earth**... ¹³Nevertheless he cried again, saying: Alma, arise and stand forth, for **why persecutest thou the church of God?**... ¹⁹And now the astonishment of Alma was so great that **he became dumb**...*
(Mosiah 27: 10-19)

In a dramatic conversion story, Paul and his men are traveling about, persecuting the church, when suddenly the Lord comes down from heaven. They are so scared they fall to the ground. He asks, "Why persecutest thou me?" and strikes Paul blind.

*¹And Saul, yet breathing out threatenings and **slaughter against the disciples of the Lord**...³And as he journeyed, he came near Damascus: and suddenly there **shined round about him a light from heaven:** ⁴And he **fell to the earth**, and heard a voice saying unto him, **Saul, Saul, why persecutest thou me?** ⁸And Saul arose from the earth; and when his eyes were opened, he saw no man: but they led him by the hand, and brought him into Damascus. ⁹And he was three days **without sight**...*
(Acts 9:1-9)

We could keep playing this game all day. The prophet Aminadi (Alma 10:2) interpreted mystical writing on the temple wall placed there by the finger of God, just as Daniel did in the Old Testament (Daniel 5:5-29). The BOM book of Mosiah (20:1-5) tells the story of the daughters of the Lamanites, who gathered in Shemlon to perform their celebratory dances, before some Nephites spied on them and burst out of the bushes to cart them off as wives; not to be confused with the OT book of Judges (21:21), which tells the story of the daughters of the Israelites, who gathered in Shiloh to perform their celebratory dances, before some Benjaminites spied on them and burst out of the bushes to cart them off as wives.

Both books share miracles, be it God appearing as a pillar of fire (Exodus 13:21 / 1 Nephi 1:6), godly men able to withstand being engulfed in flames (Daniel 3:15-25 / Helaman 5:23), or calming storms (Matthew 8:23-27 / 1 Nephi 18:8-21), or casually raising the dead (Matthew 10:8 / 3 Nephi 19:4), or just being instructed by the Lord to build a big boat (Genesis 6:14 / 1 Nephi 17:8 & Ether 2:16).

Bible Anachronisms

Many of the Biblical borrowings are particularly interesting because they demonstrate that either Joseph was copying from the King James Bible, or that the ancient Mormon prophets had a time machine. In his 1999 essay for the Secular Web, "The Bible in the Book of Mormon,"[cclix] Curt van den Heuvel has noted that the BOM, though supposedly written between 600 B.C. and 421 A.D., has 400 full and partial New Testament verses from the King James Version. In addition, he has listed close to one hundred words and phrases, which always, or almost always, appear in the Book of Mormon in a uniquely KJV context, implying that these words are the result of biblical quotations, not the coincidental, independent thoughts of two authors.

Some of the other mistakes van den Heuvel has found are huge, such as quotes that appear long before their sources were written. For example, several times in First and Second Nephi (e.g., 1 Nephi 22:15; 2 Nephi 26:4), speakers in the BOM quote or allude to a passage from the Old Testament prophet Malachi (4:1-2). The problem is that Lehi and his family supposedly left Jerusalem before the Babylonian conquest and exile. Malachi, however, was a post-exilic prophet who came much later. Other anachronistic mistakes like this show up when New Testament verses are quoted centuries before the first century: Matthew 3:10 is quoted in Alma 5:52; 1 Corinthians 15:53 is quoted in Mosiah 16:10; and Romans 8:6 in 2 Nephi 9:39.

Often the BOM even contains the same unique features (including translation errors) as the 1769 edition of the King James version that Joseph Smith used. For example, van den Heuvel notes there are 17 full chapters from the Old Testament book of Isaiah quoted in the BOM's book of Mosiah. If you compare chapter 53 of Isaiah and chapter 14 of Mosiah, you'll find that all the italicized words in Isaiah are copied word for word in Mosiah. But... those italicized words were added by the King James translators in 1611 for clarification and easier reading in English. How does the LDS Church explain their presence if Joseph Smith *didn't* copy out of the King James Bible?

Speaking of Isaiah, while nearly one-third of the entire book of Isaiah is quoted in Mosiah, the quotations from Isaiah are not exact. Joseph claimed the differences were because the Book of Mormon reflected the original, non-corrupted text of Isaiah. So when the discovery of the Dead Sea Scrolls was announced, Mormons were delighted and looked forward to the ancient scrolls vindicating the Book of Mormon's version... needless to say, that did not happen. [cclx]

Ironically, it was a faithful Mormon scholar who discovered that the BOM's errors were unique to the 1769 KJV Bible Joseph Smith used. In 1986 Dr. Stan Larson, a New Testament studies professor in the LDS church translation department compared the best texts of the Sermon on the Mount with 3 Nephi. He was shocked to realize that the particular errors of the 1769 Bible proved that Joseph was paraphrasing from that edition, not translating from gold plates. Thanks to his discovery, Larson was forced to resign.[cclxi]

To Be or Not to Be Plagiarized, That is the Question

Even traces of William Shakespeare have been found in the BOM. On the evangelical website saintsalive.com, [cclxii] Dr. Dean Maurice Helland has found elements from Hamlet in stories from the BOM books of 1 & 2 Nephi.

The Book of Mormon prophet Lehi, supposedly speaking around 600 B.C., speaks of "the cold and silent grave from whence no traveler can return" (2 Nephi 1:14). It's difficult to deny this is anything but a rewrite of this line from Hamlet's famous "to be or not to be" soliloquy: "...death, the undiscovered country from whose bourne no traveler returns" (Act 3, Scene 1).

Hamlet and Book of Mormon hero Nephi share an even weirder coincidence. Nephi is ordered by the "Spirit" to kill Laban (I Nephi 4:10-12). Hamlet is also visited by a spirit, his father's ghost, who orders him to kill his uncle (Act 1, Scene 5).

Another connection with Shakespeare is the odd fact that Joseph Smith slipped the French word "*adieu*" into the Book of Mormon (Jacob 7:27). This word choice becomes more understandable once you see how often the expression appears in almost all of Shakespeare's plays.

Who Really Wrote the Book of Mormon?

A common LDS apologist claim is that Joseph Smith was just a simple homespun country boy on the American frontier, far too ignorant to write anything as wondrous as the Book of Mormon (much like the Muslims who argue that Muhammad was far too illiterate to write the noble Koran). But the fact is, the Book of Mormon isn't all that wondrous to begin with, and by all indications, he certainly didn't write it all by his lonesome.

First of all, he was hardly raised in some howling frontier wilderness; D. Michael Quinn has documented the extensive number of books available to him in the libraries and bookshops of Palmyra. [cclxiii] Joseph appears to have plagiarized primarily from the Bible itself, but several other sources have been identified. And let's not forget, even the original parts of the BOM aren't all *that* original. Right from the beginning, people were criticizing Joseph's magnum opus for showcasing typical, pedestrian ideas that were in vogue at the time. One of his contemporaries, Alexander Campbell, criticized the Book of Mormon as a collection of "every error and almost every truth discussed in New York for the last ten years." [cclxiv]

View of the Hebrews

It also appeared to have an awfully lot of content in common with earlier books of half-baked archeology, such as Rev. Ethan Smith's *View of the Hebrews: The Ten Tribes of Israel in America*, which *also* speculated that the American Indians descended from ancient Israelites who migrated to the New World—and was published in 1823, 7 years before the BOM, less than 100 miles from Joseph Smith's parents home.

In 1922, a prominent Mormon scholar, B. H. Roberts, was startled by the troubling similarities between the plot and other details of the two books, and carefully listed out an impressive number of their parallels. (He also found evidence that Joseph Smith borrowed a great deal from still other books readily available to him, such as Josiah Priest's *Wonders of Nature and Providence*). As he put it [cclxv]:

"It has been pointed out in these pages that there are many things in the former book that might well have suggested many major things in the other. Not a few things merely, one or two, or a half dozen, but many; and it is this fact of many things of similarity and the cumulative force of them that makes them so serious a menace to Joseph Smith's story of the *Book of Mormon's* origin..."

Unsurprisingly, his findings were squelched and never published, but after his death, copies began to circulate surreptitiously.

It strains credibility to try to suggest the many obvious similarities are due to mere coincidence: Both books open with multiple references to the destruction of Jerusalem; both describe Hebrew prophets coming to ancient America; both depict ancient America as the home of advanced, highly civilized nations. Both books copy extensively and almost exclusively from Isaiah—and from the same passages in Isaiah! Both books make the argument that it was the destiny of the United States to gather together these lost children of Israel and bring them to Christianity in these last days before Christ's second coming.

Rev. Ethan Smith focused on the mysterious Aztec god Quetzalcoatl, who was said to have been white-skinned and bearded, and taught peaceful arts; the same god whose return the Aztecs were awaiting when Cortez appeared. Rev. Smith saw Quetzalcoatl as a type of Christ; Joseph took the notion one step further and turned these legends into echoes of Christ actually appearing in the New World. The occasional crucifixes found in Indian mounds seemed to validate his theory; it would be years later before archeologists proved they were from the French and Spanish, not Indians (Incidentally, Quetzalcoatl himself was supposed to have died in 1208 A.D., so he was almost a thousand years too late to be Jesus—and besides, it's only in Spanish accounts that he had white skin; in Aztec iconography, his face is black, sometimes with yellow stripes and a red mouth.)

View of the Hebrews played up the symbolism of "the stick of Joseph" being one day united with "the stick of Ephraim"—which Rev. Ethan Smith interpreted as referring to the Jews and the lost tribes of Israel; Joseph Smith's first advertisements for the Book of Mormon proclaimed it to be "the stick of Joseph taken from the hand of Ephraim." Ethan Smith had even excitedly described copper breastplates removed from Indian mounds, and the white buckhorn buttons fastened to them, as being "in resemblance of the Urim and

Thummim," an idea Joseph Smith certainly ran with.

Apologists deny that Joseph ever heard of *View of the Hebrews* before he wrote—sorry, translated—the Book of Mormon. But it's hard to take this refusal to admit the obvious as anything but stonewalling. When Joseph was editor of the church paper the *Times and Seasons*, he published the story of the long-buried book [clxvii] —and listed Ethan Smith as the original source! Two weeks later in the June 15th issue, he published a long extract from Alexander von Humboldt quoted in Elias Boudinot's *A Star in the West*, two of many contemporary writers who were proposing a Hebrew origin of the Indians.

And if any doubt remained, it just so happens that Oliver Cowdery, who helped Joseph finish the book after he stalled out on the project, attended the Congregational Church of Poultney, Vermont, where Ethan Smith was pastor for several years—during the same time that the reverend was writing *View of the Hebrews*. [cclxviii]

Manuscript Found

Around the time Rev. Ethan Smith was studying for his ministry at Dartmouth College in Hanover, New Hampshire, another divinity student at the same school was also preparing to become a fellow Congregational minister. His name was Solomon Spalding (sometimes spelled Spaulding), and he *also* authored a historical novel that dealt with American Indians originating from lost tribes of ancient Israelites. Like the Book of Mormon, his book *"Manuscript Found"* was presented as a translation of a cache of ancient texts discovered hidden under a stone, in a stone box, in rural northeastern America. And there were more intriguing similarities in plots, descriptions and styles between them. Both books described the ancient Americans domesticating horses and elephants, and larger, "useful" animals like mammoths and "mammoons" in Spalding's story, and "cureloms" and "cumons" in the BOM. Vernal Holley complied an extensive list of other parallels between the two books, available online as part of Dale

Broadhurst's information site on early Mormonism. *cclxix*

Spalding died in 1816 without his book ever seeing print. When the Book of Mormon was published, Spalding's widow, friends and family were shocked by the similarities between it and his unpublished manuscript. But how could Spalding's unpublished work have been plagiarized? As it turned out, years before, Spalding had left a transcript of the manuscript with a local printing shop for publication. The publication was delayed until he could write a preface. But during the wait the manuscript disappeared. Spalding had suspected the thief was a man that "was always hanging around the printing office" *cclxx*—a fellow named Sidney Rigdon...

After years of stonewalling, Rigdon finally issued a blanket denial of all such allegations. He called Spalding's widow a liar, proceeded to call all his other critics liars or adulterers, and not only denied that that he took the manuscript from the print shop, he denied that he had ever heard of Spalding. He even denied there ever was such a shop (not a very successful strategy, since there was plenty of evidence it existed). To make matters worse for the Mormon leader, other witnesses reported seeing "a large manuscript" in Rigdon's study, which he said was "a romance of the Bible," and that "a Presbyterian minister named Spalding, whose health had failed, brought this to the printer to see if it would pay to publish it." *cclxxi*

There's much more to the debate of whether Spalding's manuscript was employed in the construction of the BOM, but Rigdon's ham-fisted attempt at a denial certainly doesn't score any points for his side, and the Spalding-Rigdon theory would explain some mysteries, such as what Rigdon meant when he threatened if he wasn't given control of the Saints after Joseph's death, he would "expose the secrets of the church."

The Golden Pot

German Romance writer E.T.A. Hofmann is best known as the author of the fantasy novelette *The Nutcracker and the Mouse King*, which became immortalized as Tchaikovsky's ballet *The*

Nutcracker. But devout fourth-generation Mormon historian Grant H. Palmer has shown that one of Hofmann's other stories, "The Golden Pot," which came out in English in Palmyra a few years before the BOM, shows an uncanny series of parallels with four* of Joseph's personal accounts of finding the "Golden Plates":

Hofmann's story of finding *The Golden Pot* opens with Anselmus, a young man meditating on the errors and follies of his past life. Smith's account of finding the "Golden Plates" begins with him as a young man meditating on the errors and follies of his past life. Both receive a sudden vision of brilliantly shining spirit beings from an ancient civilization (ancient Atlanteans for Anselmus, ancient Americans for Joseph) that causes them a physical shock. Both are called on to translate ancient records.

The next morning, each set out to where their guides instructed them, both thinking about the riches they will soon have. Both quickly encounter an evil force which means to stop them, both fight with their diabolical opponent, but both are thwarted because their motives are not pure. Later that evening, both have a third vision, and are told more about their respective ancient civilizations. They also both learn that their messenger is a direct descendent of the founders of Atlantis/the Nephite civilization, the last archivist of his race, and is now a "Prince of Spirits."

The next day, both receive a fourth vision while lying down under a tree by "a green sward." There both go into deep thought and appear ill, in their visions the message is repeated and unfolded deeper and more clearly. Later, both are severely chastised for not engaging in their work. Because of their failure, both are told that they will have to wait for a year before resuming their mission. Both are told that their fiancée must accompany them on the next fall equinox to insure their success.

* The four come from his 1832 letterbook; his 1835 diary; his dictated 1838 version now canonized as LDS scripture in the *Pearl of Great Price*; and an 1842 version Joseph dictated to the *Chicago Democrat*'s editor John Wentworth. In addition, Grant compared accounts from the Smith family and acquaintances such as Brigham Young, Orson Pratt, etc.

Both make visionary trips to their spirit guide, and this time the door opens without difficulty, and both walk through many chambers, including large and spacious rooms, where, though no window or source of light could be seen, both find dazzling light illuminating a glittering treasure, including Egyptian artifacts, and a marvelous seer device, kept separate from the rest.

Both soon begin to work on the translation, and quickly forget about riches. Both suffer a setback around the time of the fall equinox. While their fiancée prays for them, from midnight on the Equinox until dawn, each fends off a flock of howling demons who wound him. But each passes their test.

Both describe their ancient records, and both marvel over their strange characters, which are in both cases some unknown kind of quasi-Arabic writing. Both set to work translating using their mystical tools, but each soon finds they can do the work by divine inspiration alone, hardly having to look on the original at all, and so both are able to come up with a perfect translation of their wonderful book. See Palmer's excellent book *An Insider's View of Mormon Origins* (pp.135-174) for a more detailed comparison of the similarities between the stories told about *The Golden Pot* and the "Golden Plates".

Pilgrim's Progress

Of the more than 60 religious books and pamphlets Puritan preacher John Bunyan wrote through his prolific career, it's his none-too-subtle allegory *The Pilgrim's Progress* that immortalized him. That book, written in 1678, made Bunyan the most read and memorized author of the late seventeenth century, and Christians the world over have loved it for upwards of 200 years. By the time the Book of Mormon was coming together, *Pilgrim's Progress* was America's most popular book (next to the Bible). And perhaps unsurprisingly by this point, critics have long noticed parallels between the two books.

Some superficial parallels between the two books were spotted early on. As early as 1831, Eber Howe's take-no-prisoners exposé *Mormonism Unvailed* noted that unusual place names in *Pilgrim's Progress* like "Desolation" and "Bountiful" reappear in the Book of Mormon. But discoveries like these were barely scratching the surface.

Mormon researcher William L. Davis [cclxxii] reports that Bunyan scholars have identified "fingerprints" of his writing style. In his stories, he would take assorted narrative elements, concepts and ideas from a variety of biblical and secular literary sources and then do a mash up with events from his own life and imagination. Bunyan's characteristic blend of old and new story elements have enabled scholars to identify Bunyan's unique style in his recombined tales. Significantly, several of these distinctive literary fingerprints have turned up all over the Book of Mormon.

One striking example is the story of the prophet Abinadi in the book of Mosiah (11:20-18:1)—a story with over a dozen remarkable similarities to that of the Christian martyr "Faithful" in *Pilgrim's Progress*:

The Pilgrim's Progress	The Book of Mormon
The two pilgrims, Faithful and Christian, arrive at the wicked city of Vanity Fair.	The prophet Abinadi arrives at the wicked city of Lehi-Nephi.
Their presence causes a disturbance among the citizens, and the pilgrims are bound and thrown into prison.	His preaching causes a disturbance among the citizens, and the prophet is bound and thrown into prison.
The leader of the city assembles a group to examine the pilgrims.	The leader of the city, King Noah, assembles a group of false priests to examine Abinadi.
The prisoners are "brought before" the town leaders and put on trial.	Abinadi is "brought before" the religious leaders and put on trial.

They accuse Faithful of being a "madman,"	They accuse Abinadi of being "mad,"
of stirring up contention among the people, and	of stirring up contention among the people, and
of slandering the town leaders.	of slandering the town leaders.
Faithful speaks "boldly" in his defense, but to no avail.	Abinadi speaks "boldly" in his defense, but to no avail.
The trial leader condemns Faithful to be "slain" and "put to ... death."	King Noah condemns Abinadi to be "slain" and "put to death."

Faithful is then "scourged,"	Abinadi is then "scourged,"
and finally, burned at the stake.	and finally, burned at the stake.
Thus, Faithful "seals" his "testimony" with his "blood."	Thus, Abinadi "seals" his "testimony" with his "blood."
But Faithful's teachings and martyrdom convert a witness, Hopeful,	But Abinadi's teachings and martyrdom convert a witness, Alma,
who becomes a main character in the story.	who becomes a main character in the story.
Other converts follow and they leave the wicked city,	Other converts follow and they leave the wicked city,
"entering into" a "covenant" to follow Christ.	"entering into" a "covenant" to follow Christ.

Bunyan's story of Faithful's martyrdom and Hopeful's conversion was itself a reworking of the New Testament story of the first Christian martyr Stephen and the conversion of Paul in Acts 7-9, along with elements—often in identical or very similar words—from John Foxe's massive sixteenth-century tome *The Actes and Monuments of these Latter and Perillous Days, Touching Matters of the Church*, better known to us as *Foxe's Book of Martyrs*.

Bunyan's particular signature blend of Acts and *Actes* with his own newer material forms a unique narrative pattern. And even though lurid-but-uplifting martyr stories are common in Christian tradition—in fact, a trademark Christian literary genre—no other martyr story in literary history follows the specific string of elements in Bunyan's story as closely as Joseph's story of Abinadi. Not only that, but the parallels work on multiple levels: both stories share the same underlying structural framework and often employ identical language to express ideas and describe events. As Davis points out, the stories of Abinadi and Faithful are far more similar to each other, both in content and expression, than *West Side Story* is to its narrative source, Shakespeare's *Romeo and Juliet*. To put it another way, the Mormon story of a prophet purportedly martyred in 148 B.C. is in lockstep with a seventeenth-century allegory, itself based in part on a sixteenth-century Protestant reboot of traditional Catholic martyr tales...

Davis adds that many of Bunyan's other books, tracts and pamphlets also play a significant role in the Book of Mormon, including *Pilgrim's Progress (Part 2), Grace Abounding, A Few Sighs from Hell, Holy War, The Life and Death of Mr.*

Badman and several others. Like *Pilgrim's Progress*, these lesser-known texts also show extensive parallels with the Book of Mormon, often by unique characteristics shared only by Bunyan and Smith. Davis notes that Bunyan's *Holy War* may have been an even bigger source to Joseph than *Pilgrim's Progress*, citing a serious number of unmistakable parallels:

"In fact, based on my years of extensive research and discoveries, *Holy War* provides what may be the most comprehensive collection of parallel narratives bridging the Book of Mormon to Bunyan's texts: battles between light- and dark-skinned combatants to the point of annihilation, siege warfare and battle strategies, seditious factions and civil strife, secret cabals attempting to seize government control, righteous men who are heroic captains of war, and even a personal visitation of Jesus Christ and his establishment of a righteous society. The parallel narratives are ubiquitous and systemic, appearing with sustained consistency throughout the entire narrative of the Book of Mormon."

Examining Davis's case, it's difficult, if not impossible, to dismiss the conclusion that John Bunyan was a major influence on Joseph. As Davis points out, "Indeed, reading the *Book of Mormon* is tantamount to reading John Bunyan's many works condensed into a single volume."

All the King's Sources

We may never be able to parse out all the various sources that went into the mix that comprises the Book of Mormon, but one thing is very clear: many of the plot points, themes and motifs found in the BOM were shared by plenty of other writers and would-be writers of his time. There was no shortage of materials for Joseph to either draw on, or to plagiarize from...

***

For further reading:

Grant Palmer, *An Insider's View of Mormon Origins*, (Salt Lake City: Signature Books, 2002)

David Persuitte, *Joseph Smith and the Origins of the Book of Mormon*, 2 Ed., Jefferson, NC: McFarland & Co., 2000

MormonThink.com has a wealth of well-researched essays on the origins of the Book of Mormon. For more on the Spalding-Rigdon theory, see Craig Criddle's "Sidney Rigdon: Creating the Book of Mormon." (see Appendix C of Persuitte's *Joseph Smith and the Origins of the Book of Mormon* for arguments for and against the Spalding-Rigdon theory)
http://www.mormonthink.com/mormonstudiesrigdon.htm#35

Curt van den Heuvel, "The Bible in the Book of Mormon"
http://www.infidels.org/library/modern/curt_heuvel/bom_bible.html

---

Endnotes: Chapter 9

[ccl] *History of Joseph Smith by His Mother, Lucy Smith*, pp.107-108
[ccli] See "Moroni Was A Dream", http://www.i4m.com/think/history/moroni_dream.htm

[clii] See "Did Joseph Smith see Nephi or Moroni?" http://mormonthink.com/nephiweb.htm

[ccliii] Whipple, p.125.

[ccliv] Brodie, pp. 53-54

[cclv] ibid, p. 62

[cclvi] ibid, p. 58

[cclvii] ibid, p. 73

[cclviii] Twain, *Roughing It*, University of California Press, 2003

[cclix] Curt van den Heuvel, "The Bible in the Book of Mormon" 1999 http://www.infidels.org/library/modern/curt_heuvel/bom_bible.html

[cclx] Ostling, p. 272

[cclxi] ibid., pp. 272-273

[cclxii]http://saintsalive.com/resourcelibrary/mormonism/book-of-mormon-problems-by-dr-dean-helland

[cclxiii] Ostling, p. 271

[cclxiv] Cited in Arrington and Bitton, *The Mormon Experience*, p. 33, originally appeared in the Plainsville Ohio *Telegraph*, March 15, 1831

[cclxv] Roberts, *Studies of Book of Mormon*, pp.240-242

[cclxvi] Larson, p. 19

[cclxvii] *Times and Seasons*, June 1, 1842; Nauvoo, IL, Vol III, pp. 813-814

[cclxviii] Brodie, pp. 46-48, 50

[cclxix] See Dale Broadhurst's site at: http:/www.solomonspalding.com/docs2/2001vern.htm

[cclxx] See Rebecca J. Eichbaum's 1879 statement at: http://www.solomonspalding.com/docs/Eich1879.htm#1879a

[cclxxi] Davis, Scales, and Cowdrey, 1977, p.105

[cclxxii] Davis, William L., "Hiding in Plain Sight: The Origins of the Book of Mormon," *Los Angeles Review of Books,* October 30, 2012, http://lareviewofbooks.org/article.php?id=1135

Chapter 10

Lying in Ruins:
Problems with Mormon Archeology

A thousand years ago, a tiny band of Vikings sailed westward into the New World. They landed at Newfoundland, set up scrappy, lonely little farmsteads, traded with the local natives, sometimes had run-ins with them, and all too soon, were lost to history. How do we know this? Because these tiny, short-lived settlements left clear and undeniable evidence: metalwork, buildings, Norse inscriptions and more.*cclxxii*

According to the Book of Mormon, just 600 years earlier, two great nations, spanning the entire American continent, with fortified cities and populations in the millions, clashed in an apocalyptic battle fought with horse-drawn chariots, steel swords and scimitars. That final battle was the death-knell of the sophisticated, literate, Bronze Age Christian civilization that had dominated North America for over a millennium. The victors descended into barbarian savagery. How much evidence did all that leave?

Mormons love to dance, and you will never see them dance faster than when they try to explain away the lack of physical evidence for their singular version of history. They even have an organization dedicated to just that: the Foundation for Ancient Research and Mormon Studies (FARMS), headquartered at, and fully funded by, Brigham

David Fitzgerald

Young University. Unfortunately, their success rate leaves something to be desired. LDS President Joseph Fielding Smith, Jr., great-nephew of Joseph Smith, perhaps said it best when he wrote that, in his opinion: "the Lord does not intend that the Book of Mormon, at least at the present time, shall be proven true by any archeological findings." *cclxxiii* I couldn't agree more. At this point, I suspect you won't be too shocked to hear that not a single person, place or event unique to the Book of Mormon has ever been proven to exist. Mormon archeology is an oxymoron.

But just in case there's any doubt, here are just a few of the chains of evidence to show it:

1. Genetics

American Indians are really Hebrews, at least, according to the Book of Mormon, which has ancient Israelites coming over to the New World in two main migrations. The Jaredites came over after the confusion of tongues at the Tower of Babel (What? You thought that was just a myth?), and the Lehites and Mulekites left Jerusalem around 600 B.C.E. to come to America. The good Lehites become the Nephites and the bad Lehites became the Lamanites; God cursed them with dark skin to make them easier to tell apart. What's more, Mormons claim Polynesians are also descended from a Nephite shipbuilder, Hagoth, who sailed "into the west sea" around 54 B.C.E. with a fleet of settlers, never to be seen again (Alma 63:5-8). How the white-skinned seafaring Nephites became dark-skinned Pacific Islander Lamanites is an unexplained mystery, but you can bet it has to do with sin...

Up until recent years, the introduction to the Book of Mormon described the Nephites and the Lamanites as "the two great civilizations" of the Americas, and added, "After thousands of years, all were destroyed except the Lamanites, and they are **the principal ancestors** of the American Indians." But since they have failed to find any evidence of this, LDS scholars have backed off from the notion that the

Lamanites were the only survivors of the two great civilizations that gave rise to the Native Americans, and the introduction has been quietly changed to now read: "...they are **among the ancestors** of the American Indians."

Currently, church apologists prefer to suggest that the Lamanites were *not* the primary ancestors of all American Indians after all; instead, they were just a small nation that blended in with the indigenous population—blending in so well that they left no trace of themselves, apparently. But besides flatly contradicting both the angel Moroni, the Book of Mormon and matter-of-fact statements from church authorities for over 180 years, even this back-pedaling revisionist explanation fails.

Molecular genealogists construct DNA family trees of ancestors and through these, have been able to track human migrations all over the world, from the very earliest to the most recent. The research shows that Native Americans and Polynesians do share a common ancestry—but not from Israel. Both groups are Asian. The ancestors of the various American Indian groups came from the vicinity of southern Siberia; they began migrating across the Bering Strait over 14,000 years ago (long before the date Mormons assign to the Tower of Babel). The Polynesians originated in southeast Asia, emerging 30,000 years ago in waves of migrations. The most recent was within the last 3,000 years and spread throughout the Pacific. [cclxxiv]

Ironically, one of the scientists who has done the most to reveal these problems is molecular biologist Simon Southerton, the author of *Losing a Lost Tribe: Native Americans, DNA, and the Mormon Church,* and a former LDS bishop. He explained why he left the church:

"I was amazed at the lengths that FARMS went to in order to prop up faith in the Book of Mormon. I felt that the only way I could be satisfied with FARMS explanations was to stop thinking.... The explanations of the FARMS researchers stretched the bounds of credibility to the breaking point on almost every critical issue." [cclxxv]

2. Linguistics

We can trace the eastward migration route of Pacific Islanders through linguistics as well, simply by observing the patterns of how words change in languages as they developed from Asia throughout Polynesia. Linguistic studies also show that there were no Native American words for common BOM items like chariots, swords, coins, silk, etc. No place names (Zarahemla, Shimnilom, Gid, Omner, Gimgimno, Zeezrom), names of ethnic groups (Mulekites, Nephites, Lamanites, Ammonihahites, Jacobites, Jaredites, Josephites, et al.) or personal names (Nephi, Noah, Aminadab, Gidgiddoni, Samuel, Zelph) from the Book of Mormon have ever been found in any native languages. Nor have any linguistic connections been discovered between any Native American languages and ancient Hebrew or Egyptian. And needless to say, even though Nephite civilization supposedly endured for over a millennium, no writings have ever been found, apart from the Book of Mormon.

Linguistics also points out glaring errors in the Book of Mormon. To start with, Joseph claimed the language of the "Golden Plates" was not Hebrew but "Reformed Egyptian." No such language exists, either in North America or Egypt. His "translations" of ancient Egyptian papyri have not impressed genuine Egyptologists (see ch. 12). Joseph also made anachronistic mistakes, such as having ancient Judeans mention "the church" (1 Nephi 4:26), and including Greek names and terms like Jonas, Lachoneus, Timothy, and Alpha & Omega—even though there's no reason the BOM could have any Greek influences—or French, even though Jacob 7:27 ends with the phrase, "Brethren, *adieu*."

3. Botany and Zoology

Flora: As Frank Zindler has pointed out [cclxxvi], Smith assumed that the ancient Americans had the same kind of agriculture he had in upstate New York. So he had them growing wheat, barley, corn, and flax, and planting vineyards for wine, gathering figs, and being able to understand the symbolism of the olive-tree and the grapevine. Well, he got corn right, anyway. The other two major crops were squash and lima beans, supplemented by things like avocados, amaranth, acorns, potatoes, tomatoes, yuca root, etc.

You can search all you want in the Book of Mormon, but apart from corn, you won't find any mention of the crops actually raised in ancient America. Incidentally, we have numerous cases where these crops have been preserved in archaeological sites and are easily identifiable. They are also commonly portrayed on ceramics and in murals and sculptures. [cclxxvii] If ancient Nephites and Lamanites had been growing these crops for even a few decades, let alone over a thousand years, every soil sample taken in Central America should show traces of wheat, barley, and flax pollen. Pollen is one of the most indestructible natural objects known. [cclxxviii]

Fauna: Although Mesoamerican art abounds with animals like armadillos, bats, deer, jaguars, xoloitzcuintli (the Aztec hairless dog), turkeys, tapirs, coatimundi, agouti, spider monkeys, squirrels, and many more, Joseph Smith populated his Book of Mormon world with animals completely unknown in the New World: elephants, donkeys, bulls, cows, pigs, goats, oxen, sheep and horses. He also often mentions flocks, herds and shepherds.

Dogs did live in ancient America, but in the BOM dogs only appear in metaphors lifted from the Bible:

"Give not that which is holy unto the dogs." (3 Nephi 14:6, cf. Matt. 7:6)

"... people had turned from their righteousness, like the dog to his vomit." (3 Nephi 7:8, cf. 2 Pet.2:22)

Elephants? Elephants. Remains of extinct mammoths had been discovered recently, so in the 1830s it would have seemed plausible and remarkably prescient to say that the ancient Indians had domesticated pachyderms. But rural New York back then had no way to know that although horses originated in North America, they and the various American species of "elephants" went extinct during the late Pleistocene, 10,000 to 12,000 years ago, many thousands of years before Biblical times. None of these animals was around North America before the Spaniards.

And while some LDS apologists lamely tried to suggest that maybe Smith translated words for "deer" as "horse," "buffalo" as "oxen," etc., do they really think Joseph couldn't tell the difference between a deer and a horse? Especially considering he was translating "by the gift and power of God"? Equally strange is that Joseph also included imaginary animals:

"And they also had horses, and asses, and there were elephants and cureloms and cumoms; all of which were useful unto man, and more especially the elephants and cureloms and cumoms." (Ether 9:19)

What are these Dr. Seuss-sounding cureloms and cumoms? No one knows. LDS apologists have suggested that in this case, Joseph transliterated instead of translated the ancient words "curelom" and "cumom," so we can only guess what Joseph (or the Lord) was thinking, though that hasn't stopped Mormons from usually imagining them as mastodons or mammoths.

But no matter what you think about Joseph's translating ability, it is an archaeological certainty that no animal-drawn wheeled chariots were ever used in pre-Columbian America, for the simple reason that they didn't have any draft animals to pull them. The closest thing is the South American llama, but it was used to carry packs, not to pull chariots. Nor did it ever make it north of the Andes. And to clinch it, we have absolutely no evidence of bridges, roads, stables, bridles, saddles, etc. or of the domestication of any other draft animal, unless you count the dogs that dragged travois packs—but again, no one tries to argue they were pulling chariots, either.

4. Metallurgy and Textiles

Iron and steel are mentioned in many places in the Book of Mormon, which is doubly strange, since his ancient seafaring Hebrews come from a Bronze age culture. Smith has ancient Jaredites making steel swords in 2,500 B.C.E. – or, more than a millennium before ironworking (let alone steel making!) came to Mesopotamia. *cclxxix* We do have evidence for copper, silver and zinc mines and smelters in pre-Colombian America. *cclxxx* Metalsmiths in Peru—not Mesoamerica—worked with gold and silver by 1000 B.C.E., *cclxxxi* and with copper beginning around the year 500 C.E., but archeologists have never found any trace of iron metallurgy anywhere in Pre-Columbian America.

Frank Zindler notes:

"If millions and millions of people made and used weapons and tools of steel for a period spanning more than three millennia, not only should archaeologists find plentiful remains of swords, chariot axles, anvils, sickles, and many other iron-based artifacts, they should be finding the remains of steel mills all over the territory covered by Smith's cast of characters! It is perfectly conceivable that one might lose a steel sword. But how in hell can you lose a steel mill?!" *cclxxxii*

Even BYU Archaeologist Ray T. Matheny has laid out the problem forcefully. Metallurgy as described in the BOM is not just mere metalworking, hammering and shaping metals cold (like unsmelted meteoric iron). When the Jaredites "did molten out of the hill, and made swords out of steel" as the Book of Ether says (7:9; more steel swordmaking occurs in verses like 2 Nephi 5: 14-15), it would have required temperatures of 700° to 800° C, and involved a number of technological processes: smelting, casting, gilding, annealing, soldering and alloying.*cclxxxiii* To make bellows, breastplates, chains, plowshares, rods of iron, idols of silver, swords or iron tools (all of which appear in the BOM), all these processes are needed, but it's not even that simple:

"A ferrous industry is a whole system of doing something. It's not just an esoteric process that a few people are involved in, but ferrous industry. That means mining iron ores and then processing these ores and casting these ores into irons and then making steels and so forth—this is a process that's very complicated... In other words, society would have to be organized at a certain level before ferrous industry would be feasible.

"The technology of mining is problematical for the Book of Mormon. Where do you find iron ores in sufficient to create an industry?... No evidence has been found in the New World for a ferrous metallurgical industry dating to pre-Columbian times. And so this is a king-sized kind of problem, it seems to me, for so-called Book of Mormon archaeology. This evidence is absent." [cclxxxiv]

The Book of Mormon tells us that the Nephite cities were fortified, with enormous structures such as temples, synagogues, and sanctuaries (examples: Jarom 1:7; Helaman 3:14; 4 Nephi 1:7). For instance, the wicked Nephite King Noah built many elegant and spacious buildings ornamented with gold, silver, iron, brass, copper, and ziff (Mosiah 11:8). Incidentally, Helaman 3:7 reports ancient Nephites were also "exceedingly expert" with cement and built their houses out of it. We could ask where is the evidence for a civilization of fortified cities with enormous and richly ornamented buildings in precious metals, or villages of cement houses, or pre-Columbian iron and brass metallurgy, but the real question is, *what is ziff?* Only Joseph Smith knows.

Textiles

Ancient Mexicans were weaving cotton into cloth fabrics by the year 5000 B.C.E. But not only does the Book of Mormon never mention cotton, Smith has his ancient Israelites wearing linen and silk—some as early as 600 B.C.E. But since silk was a trade secret in China until the 6th century, he is 1200 years too early. Some LDS apologists have suggested that what the Book of Mormon calls "silk" was not *really* silk, but may have been some other silk-like fabrics, woven from things like rabbit fur or ceiba tree pod fibers. Honestly, this might not be a half-bad defense; since "silks" like these wouldn't be expected to survive, not finding any wouldn't be a deal-killer. But on the other hand, Joseph also had Jaredites wearing linen: "And they did have silks, and fine-twined linen; and they did work all manner of cloth, that they might clothe themselves from their nakedness" (Ether 10:24).

Linen is made from the fibers of the flax plant, an Old World species. The sharper readers will recall that flax wasn't grown in Pre-Columbian America, and we know that for the same reason we know that the Book of Mormon was wrong about the Nephites growing wheat and barley: because their pollen has never turned up in any soil corings. Again, Frank Zindler has pointed out that it's impossible for ancient Americans to have cultivated flax for linen for centuries without flax pollen accumulating yearly at the bottoms of lakes, swamps, and ponds; or in the ordinary soil samples taken by archaeologists. [cclxxxv]

So when apologists' only option is suggesting when the BOM says "silk," "flax" and "fine linen" it *really* means three other things completely, the whole defense starts to feel a bit ad hoc.

5. Numismatics

In the Book of Alma, our protagonist Alma takes a break in the story to give a lesson on Nephite money. Why he feels the need to tell his readers how their own money system works, or why he does so in the past tense, isn't clear—it's as if he's explaining for readers from the future...

"Now the reckoning is thus—a senine of gold, a seon of gold, a shum of gold, and a limnah of gold.

A senum of silver, an amnor of silver, an ezrom of silver, and an onti of silver.

A senum of silver was equal to a senine of gold, and either for a measure of barley, and also for a measure of every kind of grain.

Now the amount of a seon of gold was twice the value of a senine.

And a shum of gold was twice the value of a seon.

And a limnah of gold was the value of them all.

And an amnor of silver was as great as two senums.

And an ezrom of silver was as great as four senums.

And an onti was as great as them all.

Now this is the value of the lesser numbers of their reckoning—

A shiblon is half of a senum; therefore, a shiblon for half a measure of barley.

And a shiblum is a half of a shiblon.

And a leah is the half of a shiblum.

Now this is their number, according to their reckoning.

Now an antion of gold is equal to three shiblons."

(Alma 11:5-19)

Although the ancient Mesoamericans had gold and silver in abundance, they never made coins or evolved a money economy. They used jade beads, obsidian flints, even cacao beans as media of exchange. But they never minted coins or create a standardized system of metal money. [cclxxxvii] But this didn't stop Joseph from acting like an eighth-grade Dungeon Master and inventing oodles of Nephite money. Do I really need to add that none of these coins have ever been discovered?

Gradually, these undisputed facts have percolated into general knowledge and now some LDS apologists act like they've known all along there were no coins in ancient Book of Mormon lands. According to FAIR, the Foundation for Apologetic Information and Research, a non-profit group of volunteer LDS apologists, "seeing 'coins' in the Book of Mormon occurs when readers apply their modern expectations and an inadequately close reading of the text." [cclxxxvii] Yes, or perhaps it's because the phrase "Nephite Coins and Measures" wasn't removed from the chapter heading for Alma 11 until 1981.

FAIR confidently states that the pieces of gold and silver described in the book of Alma are not coins, but "a surprisingly sophisticated system of weights and measures that is consistent with Mesoamerican proto-monetary practices." [cclxxxviii] This all sounds quite impressive... until you realize this "explanation" still doesn't explain why none of these "weights and measures" have ever been discovered, either—or you see that the text explicitly says they are measures for barley, since *barley* conclusively didn't exist in America. So despite all FAIR's smug assertions, it would appear the Book of Mormon's ancient Nephites had, in fact, not a barley-based, but a bullshit-based economy.

6. History (and Geography, and Archeology, and Sociology, and Anthropology...)

Mormon archeologist Thomas Stuart Ferguson's story pretty much says it all about BOM archeology.

For decades, the LDS faithful knew Ferguson as the church's big answer man: Founder of BYU's New World Archaeological Foundation, a beloved fireside lecturer and author of several books championing Mormon archeology. In college he developed a passion for Mesoamerican history and archeology, and how they related to Mormon beliefs. His girlfriend said he talked about the Book of Mormon so much and so excitedly she felt like she was going out with the Book of Mormon. [cclxxxix]

In 1946, brimming with confidence and zeal, he set off on his first archeological expedition with the goal of proving the Gentile critics wrong. He was determined to be the first to find solid physical evidence of Mormon history: the actual lands, cities and artifacts. He would spend the next 25 years in the attempt to prove Mormonism true.

The BOM mentions northern and southern lands (3 Nephi 6:2) connected by a "narrow pass" of land with an eastern and western sea on either side (Alma 50:34). Ever since Joseph Smith, church leaders had said this referred to North and South America. But why hadn't anyone ever found the remains of the once-mighty Nephite and Lamanite civilizations? As Ferguson saw it, the problem was that they were looking in the wrong place. The great ancient cities weren't in upstate New York— that would be ridiculous! They must have been in Central America.

Ferguson changed Mormon minds about the scale of BOM geography, showing that the church's traditional view couldn't possibly hold water, (even though Joseph Smith himself said so).He insisted on a much more limited view, confined to a small stretch of Central America. But after years of fruitless work, he finally admitted his own view was just as fatally flawed as the traditional view.

Ferguson's theories were pivotal in changing Mormon minds about where the action in the BOM takes place. As he picked apart the text for clues, Mormon geography continued to shrink. The traditional view that the Nephites and Lamanites dominated the entire western hemisphere obviously didn't pan out. He deduced from travel times between cities that the distances covered were only about 200-300 miles. And clearly the only logical place to search was Mesoamerica.

During the 1950s and 1960s his New World Archeological Foundation carried out professional fieldwork in and around Chiapas and the Yucatan. Ferguson searched tirelessly, always convinced that they were closing in on the truth. He knew Joseph Smith was a true prophet, and was excited that the next twist of the spade or slash of machete might uncover the inscription that would substantiate the record of the "Golden Plates" and "shake the entire world to its foundations." [ccxc]

After over fifteen years of searching, they had done fine archeological work—but they had utterly failed to find any Mesoamerican link to the "Golden Plates". Ferguson remained undaunted. He predicted that they would uncover Book of Mormon cities within the decade, and then everyone would know Joseph Smith was a genuine prophet who had told the truth. But there were just a few small puzzles to solve first... Such as:

1) In 1842, Joseph Smith raved over a newly published book, *Incidents of Travel in Central America*, which described the ruins of Palenque and other signs of Mayan civilization. He seized on the book as glowing corroboration of his history; just the very existence of Mayan cities like Palenque was enough to convince early Saints that they were the work of the Nephites and proof positive the "Golden Plates" were real.

Except... that the Book of Mormon says the final genocidal defeat of the Nephites by the Lamanites took place in the year 385. But archeologists agree Palenque was built after the year 600, some 215 years after the Nephites had supposedly been wiped out. In fact, Mayan civilization's golden age was only just revving up then; they would flourish for another five hundred years.

2) Also, Ferguson proposed that the Isthmus of Tehuántepec in southern Mexico was the "narrow pass" of land spoken of in the BOM—but to make this work, you have to cheat and tilt the map sixty degrees; otherwise the lands "northward" are "westward" and the lands "southward" are "eastward."*ccxci* In fact, if the BOM took place exclusively in a small portion of Central America, then there would have to be two hills of Cumorah: one somewhere in southern Mexico, the other in upstate New York. And how the "Golden Plates" managed to be taken thousands of miles to the north (let alone why anyone would bother!) remained a mystery.

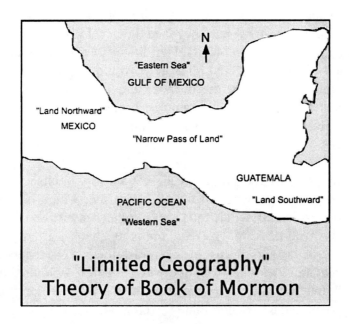

"Limited Geography"
Theory of Book of Mormon

Ferguson favored southern Mexico's Isthmus of Tehuántepec as the "narrow pass" described in the BOM, but this only works if you flip the map on its side, say there

were two hills of Cumorah, and posit that the prophet Mormon decided to carry the "Golden Plates" over 2,800 miles to go bury them in upstate New York.

3) Besides, throughout his career as prophet, Joseph Smith made it abundantly clear he wanted his followers to think the Book of Mormon lands stretched throughout North and South America. As he and his men traveled from Ohio to Missouri during the Zion's Camp expedition, he claimed they were "wandering over the plains of the Nephites"[ccxcii] and would regale them with the area's part in BOM history. According to the church's official history, when they stumbled across an Indian burial mound in southern Illinois containing a skeleton, Joseph (via a psychic vision of the past provided by the holy spirit) identified the skeleton as "a white Lamanite, a large, thick-set man, and a man of God. His name was Zelph ... (he) was known from the Hill Cumorah, or eastern sea to the Rocky Mountains." [ccxciii]

After ten more years of trying to solve conundrums like these, and still no trace of a connection between Mormon and Mesoamerican history, Ferguson was a changed man. By 1970, he was privately admitting "everything he had set out to prove in Central America/Mexico had proven to be wrong." [ccxciv] After a quarter-century of trying to uncover the tangible, uncontestable proof he knew was out there, he had realized "... you can't set the Book of Mormon geography down anywhere—because it is fictional and will never meet the requirements of the dirt archeology. I should say, what is in the ground will never conform to what is in the book." [ccxcv] Ferguson became a closet heretic, but never left the church he loved. Though disillusioned and an unbeliever, for the most part he kept his heresies to himself, speaking his mind only to select friends.

Today, LDS apologists studiously ignore the last fifteen years of Ferguson's life. They continue to play pin-the-Book of Mormon-lands on the map with one new proposed location after another (at least twelve and counting so far [ccxcvi]), but they just can't quite line up any of them with the real world. LDS president Joseph Fielding Smith expressed their frustration with a gem of theological sour grapes: that in his opinion "the Lord does not intend that the Book of Mormon to be proved by any archeological findings." [ccxcvii]

Meanwhile, Yale archeologist Dr. Michael D. Coe, one of the foremost authorities on the Maya, put it differently: "There is not a whit of evidence that the Nephites ever existed. The whole enterprise is complete rot, root and branch. It's so racist it hurts. It fits right into the nineteenth-century American idea that only a white man could have built cities and temples, that American Indians didn't have the brains or the wherewithal to create their own civilization." [ccxcviii]

***

For further reading:

"How Do You Lose a Steel Mill?" By Frank R. Zindler, http://nowscape.com/mormon/zindler1.htm

Stan Larson, *Quest for the Gold Plates: Thomas Stuart Ferguson's Archeological Search for the Book of Mormon* (Salt Lake City, Freethinker Press, 1996)

Simon G. Southerton, *Losing a Lost Tribe: Native Americans, DNA and the Mormon Church*, (Salt Lake City: Signature Books, 2004)

Endnotes: Chapter 10

[cclxxii] Southerton, p. 199
[cclxxiii] Smith, Joseph Fielding, *Answers to Gospel Questions*, vol.2, p. 196

[cclxxiv] Southerton, p.xii

[cclxxv] cited in Gruss, Edmond C., *What Every Mormon (and Non-Mormon) Should Know,* (2006), Xulon Press, p. 119

[cclxxvi] Zindler, "How Do You Lose a Steel Mill?" http://nowscape.com/mormon/zindler1.htm

[cclxxvii] Stan Larson, p. 239

[cclxxviii] Zindler, op. cit.

[cclxxix] ibid.

[cclxxx] ibid.

[cclxxxi] cited in Stan Larson, p. 197

[cclxxxii] Zindler, op. cit.

[cclxxxiii] cited in Stan Larson, p196

[cclxxxiv] ibid.

[cclxxxv] Zindler, op. cit.

[cclxxxvi] ibid.

[cclxxxvii] FAIRwiki, "Book of Mormon/Anachronisms/Coins"

[cclxxxviii] ibid.

[cclxxxix] Stan Larson, p. 2

[ccxc] ibid., p. 57

[ccxci] Ostling, p. 275

[ccxcii] Joseph Smith, Letter to Emma Smith dated June 4, 1834, *Personal Writings*, p. 324; spelling has been corrected

[ccxciii] *History of the Church,* 1948 ed., II: pp. 79-80

[ccxciv] Stan Larson, p.137

[ccxcv] ibid.

[ccxcvi] see Stan Larson, p. 8 for a listing of the twelve different proposed locations of just the "narrow strip of land" alone; the guesses range from the Isthmus of Panama to Costa Rica to the Bay of Honduras to Florida to various parts of central America to the strip between southwestern Lake Ontario and northeastern Lake Erie, and still others around the globe.

[ccxcvii] Ostling, op. cit.

[ccxcviii] cited in Hampton Sides, "This Is Not the Place," *Doubletake* Magazine/Spring 1999

Chapter 11

Greater than the Truth:
Mormonism's Ever-changing History

Mormon history has evolved just as much as its theology. For any group, a certain level of spin-doctoring and myth-making is understandable, perhaps even forgivable, when it's on the level of young George Washington chopping down a cherry tree or an apple falling on Newton's head causing an epiphany. The Miracle of the Gulls, when seagulls suddenly appeared in 1848 just in time to eat the horde of crickets devouring the LDS pioneers' first summer crop, may well fall under that category. Though it is a beloved story, celebrated in school plays, paintings and a monument in Temple Square, there is no evidence that the pioneers noticed anything remarkable at the time. Gulls were no strangers to the area, and their cricket-eating habits well known. Though things would certainly have been worse without the birds, the 1848 harvest was paltry; few if any seemed to think they had been miraculously saved. The real miracle occurred in 1853, when Apostle Orson Hyde told the story of the gulls at a General Conference and the legend began to grow from there. [ccxcix]

But the LDS church does more than foster sweet uplifting stories; at times the industrial-strength efforts toward sanitizing its wild and wooly history are unintentionally hilarious. In manuals like 1997's *Teachings of Presidents of the Church:*

Brigham Young, the portrayal of their subject apparently comes from a parallel dimension much like ours, except their Bizarro-Brigham was a gentle monogamist who never expounded the sexist, nationalistic and racist opinions that make modern LDS readers cringe in our world. Nor is there any hint of his more controversial notions, like the idea that Adam was God the Father, and Eve one of his wives. Nor does it bring up his own attempts at controlling church history. When Joseph's own mother, Lucy Mack Smith, wrote her *Biographical Sketches of Joseph Smith, the Prophet, and his Progenitors for Many Generations* (1853), Brigham did not approve of the book and ordered the printing destroyed. [ccc]

Even Mormon scripture, eternal and everlasting new covenants, and the restored sacred Temple rituals have all been altered or rewritten—and once such changes occur, historians are not supposed to notice that it hadn't been that way all along. [ccci] It's been left to outsiders and former Mormons to document just how pervasive the whitewashing has been, right from the very beginning. This rigid official policy of stonewalling against acknowledging embarrassing changes has had the unfortunate side effect of creating an underground market for trafficking in early Mormon documents and prior editions of church publications. And (again, as we'll soon see) this has repeatedly turned around to bite them.

For just one example, BYU Historian D. Michael Quinn acknowledges the only extensive comparison of changes to Joseph Smith's *History of the Church* in its various editions has been the work of longtime Mormon scholars Jerald and Sandra Tanner, both ex-Mormons and perhaps the most tireless critics of the church. Their research uncovered longstanding practices of editors, who "deleted evidence, introduced anachronisms, and reversed meanings in manuscript minutes and other documents which were detailed and explicit in their original form." [ccci] Quinn added that as far back as 1835, *Doctrine and Covenants* had also undergone extensive retroactive editing: reversing previous meanings, adding concepts and even whole paragraphs to the texts of previously published revelations. [ccciii]

"Idolizing the Truth"

Since 1908, the ominously named LDS "Correlation Committee" has ensured that all church publications are in line with official policy and represent the official interpretations. It also sees to it that sensitive historical issues are frequently downplayed, avoided or denied. [ccciv] Mormon educators are required to present whatever is the current acceptable, faith-promoting official view of church history, according to perennial Apostle Boyd Packer in an infamous 1981 speech entitled "The Mantle is Far, Far Greater Than the Intellect." Speaking at a symposium of church educators, Packer issued some rather startling marching orders, including these four Orwellian "cautions" that all teachers of "Faithful History" must heed:

1) "There is no such thing as an accurate, objective history of the church without consideration of the spiritual powers that attend this work."
2) "There is a temptation... to want to tell everything, whether it is worthy or faith-promoting or not. Some things that are true are not very useful."
3) "In an effort to be objective, impartial, and scholarly, a writer or a teacher may unwittingly be giving equal time to the adversary... In the Church we are not neutral. We are one-sided. There is a war going on, and we are engaged in it."
4) "The fact that something is already in print or available from another source is no excuse for using potentially damaging materials in writing, speaking or teaching: Do not spread disease germs!"

But perhaps Apostle Packer's finest moment was this revealing comment, in which he expressed his annoyance with those who, as he put it, "*idolize the truth*":

"I have a hard time with historians because they idolize the truth. The truth is not uplifting; it destroys. I could tell most of the secretaries in the church office building that they are ugly and fat. That would be the truth, but it would hurt and destroy them. Historians should tell only that part of the truth that is inspiring and uplifting." *cccvi*

Needless to say, directives like these have made Mormon studies a precarious undertaking for scholars, especially for those on the staff of Brigham Young University. Many leading Mormon historians, including Quinn, have aroused the ire of Apostle Packer, which is not hard to do, as it turns out. In Quinn's case, this eventually cost him his tenured professorship at BYU, his temple recommend, and eventually his church membership. Fawn Brodie, who wrote the definitive biography of Joseph Smith, *No Man Knows My History*, pulled no punches and was excommunicated for it. First Counselor J. Rueben Clark Jr. had the *Deseret News* publish his critique of the book, despite the fact he declined to actually read it. Juanita Brooks, author of *Mountain Meadows Massacre* (see below), avoided excommunication, only to be blacklisted and have the church squash a film project based on her book. Linda King Newell and Valeen Tippetts Avery wrote a sympathetic biography of Emma Smith; this seemingly innocuous act irked Church authorities enough to ban them from speaking publicly in church meetings for a year.

Even Richard Bushman, a committed believer who held both ward and stake offices, took flack for his biography *Joseph Smith: Rough Stone Rolling*. Though he presented Smith's claims at face value, he also substantiated Joseph's dealings with folk magic and didn't shirk from describing his multi-marital exploits. He also portrayed Smith as sometimes vindictive, abusive, unduly authoritarian and foolish. When asked if his book would shake his fellow believer's faith, Bushman answered that while it might not be appropriate to discuss the Prophet's character flaws in Sunday school class, factual candor had its place. Otherwise, for believers raised on a view of Smith as perfection personified, "The disconnect can damage young Latter-day Saints who learn later in life that they have not been given the whole story on church history."*cccix*

Richard Packham can relate: As a sixth-generation

Mormon who finally grew disillusioned with the church and left, he says this is not an isolated phenomenon: "After having read and heard hundreds of former Mormons tell their reasons for leaving the church, I find that by far the most frequent reason given, and often the only reason, is: 'The church lied to me!'" [cccx]

The September Six

During a CNN interview with Larry King (Sept. 8, 1998), LDS President Hinckley gave a chilling word of advice to Saints who had problems with doctrine: "They can carry all the opinion they wish within their heads... but if they begin to try to persuade others, then they may be called in to a disciplinary council." This was no idle threat, as dissident Saints had already found out the hard way exactly five years before.

Sunstone, an independent magazine, has been an outlet for liberal, intellectual and dissident voices in Mormonism since 1975, and holds annual symposia for free and frank discussion of church issues. Neither venue has always been appreciated by church authorities; in the late 80s and early 90s they issued a "Statement on Symposia" as well as veiled warnings against "alternate voices" that made prospective *Sunstone* contributors and symposium speakers think twice. But the harshest blow came in a single month, September 1993, when six different leading Mormon intellectuals came under fire and were convicted in church tribunals of various serious crimes. The "September Six" were:

Prof. D. Michael Quinn had long been known for his excellent history work investigating topics the Church leadership had hoped to keep buried. In a 1985 article, he had exposed Mormon leaders' surreptitious continuation of polygamy after they publicly repudiated it in 1890. His landmark 1987 book *Early Mormonism and the Magic World View* shed light on the folk-magic and occult roots of Mormonism. Neither of these endeared him to church authorities, but the last straw came when he wrote an article claiming that Joseph Smith had effectively given women the priesthood, as well as an essay on Church repression entitled "150 Years of Truth or Consequences About Mormon History."

Avraham Gileadi wrote a conservative book on the Second Coming, which was duly vetted and published by the church's own Deseret Book Company. This did not stop church leaders from directing him to stop promoting his views, or from excommunicating him, even after he complied—and even though he was never told just which of his opinions was supposed to be heretical... Feminist **Maxine Hanks** was excommunicated for advocating women priesthood and putting undue focus on our Mother in Heaven. **Lynne Kanavel Whitesides**, then president of the Mormon Women's Forum, was disfellowshipped, a slightly lesser punishment, for the same offenses.

Salt Lake City attorney and author **Paul Toscano**, a longtime harsh critic of the church, co-founded The Mormon Alliance in 1992 in order to call attention to the LDS hierarchy's entrenched elitism, white-washing of Mormon history and growing problems with intellectuals, gays and women. Following his Sunstone Symposium address entitled "All is Not Well in Zion: False Teachings of the True Church," he was brought before a church court and excommunicated for apostasy and false teaching. His wife **Margaret Toscano** would have been the seventh of the September Six, but her own excommunication was delayed until 2000.

Lavina Fielding Anderson was never told exactly what led to her being drummed out of the church, but it isn't hard to guess: She has been a leader of the suspiciously-feminist Mormon Women's Forum and active in the Mormon Alliance, and in 1992, she delivered a paper at a Sunstone Symposium documenting over one hundred cases of church repression against intellectuals. After she did a follow-up article, church members sent her information on a hundred more such cases. As one commentator noted, rather than being removed for heresy, she suffered church discipline for revealing information on church discipline. *cccxi* Her most shocking bombshell was that the Mormon leadership engaged in covert intelligence upon its membership, secretly keeping tabs on individuals' writings, LTEs, quotes in the media, and public activities. Anderson took a courageous stand against this, saying "We must protest, expose, and work against an internal espionage system that creates and maintains secret files on members of the church." *cccxii*

Big Brother is Excommunicating You

The First Presidency later admitted it had indeed long been running just such a monitoring operation on the Saints: the "Strengthening Church Members Committee" (SCMC), led by two apostles, justified by Joseph Smith's command that the church should document "abuses" against them (D&C 123). No other major religion spies on its own members this way. And the six were only the tip of the iceberg, the most visible victims of a wider crackdown on dissent. The careers of several other journalists, historians, and BYU faculty members all came to a premature halt within two years following the September Six's expulsion. *cccxiii*

What's more, the SCMC had been in operation long before this. Leonard Arrington, the official LDS Church Historian for nearly a decade (1972-1982), was a distinguished scholar and a beloved figure both inside and out of Mormon circles. His first run-in with church leaders was caused by a 1959 article in the premiere issue of *BYU Studies* in which he uncovered evidence that early Mormons treated the Word of Wisdom more as a suggestion than a commandment. The journal was suspended for a year, but Arrington survived that scandal to have an impressive teaching career. In 1970, the church realized they needed a historian to manage their massive archives, and it soon became apparent that the position should be in the hands of a professionally trained historian. In 1972, Arrington was asked to take the reins— the first and only credentialed historian to take the position of official Church Historian, the only one who was not also a General authority.

In the beginning it looked like exciting times were ahead for the church history department... they weren't. Arrington was surprised to find that the index card for one of his own books had been marked with an "a" for "anti-church" by the former librarian. It was a sign of things to come. Apostle Boyd K. Packer objected to the new department's "orientation toward scholarly work" and their inclusion of negative details in church histories, and clamped down. New publication projects were soon stalled by opposition from above. Arrington was troubled to observe ongoing anti-intellectualism from the church hierarchy, especially efforts from his superiors to remove all the scholars from the department. One historian after another fell under suspicion, was transferred, or was blacklisted outright.

Micro-management worsened until in 1977, Arrington was informed that a subcommittee of Apostles Hinckley, Peterson and Packer would personally investigate all publications coming from the church historian's office. New projects were derailed and shelved. In 1979, Arrington learned the SCMC had arranged for two BYU students to spy on Arrington's classes and report back weekly. He only discovered this because after two weeks, one of the students came and confessed to him. [cccxiv] Three years later, Arrington received a letter informing him that he had been released from his duties. The release was not publicly announced, and in a Soviet-worthy move, his portrait was quietly removed from the gallery of church historians in the east wing hallway of the Church Office Building. After nearly a decade of service, Leonard Arrington had been officially disappeared.

As for the September Six, Avraham Gileadi was allowed to rebaptize in 1996. Maxine Hanks had to wait almost twenty years to be allowed back in 2012. The rest linger in ecclesiastical limbo. Just as she has all her life, Lavina Anderson continues to faithfully—but silently—attend services every Sunday—but not as a member of the Mormon church. Richard and Joan Ostling reported her status: "By order of her stake president and his advisors, she is no longer a church member and is forbidden to enter the temple, to fill any ward post, to receive the sacrament, or to speak or offer prayers during worship. Her eternal temple "sealings" to her husband and son have been suspended. It is unclear whether and on what terms she will ever be able to undergo rebaptism and resume her place in the LDS church." [cccxv]

We Don't Talk About it: Two Incidents the Church Would Rather You Forgot

Mainstream Christianity had an 1,800 year head start on Mormonism, and even it has never managed to whitewash over all the discrepancies, anachronisms, contradictions and flat-out errors that infest its scriptures. The Book of Mormon suffers from the same problems, but these are exacerbated by the unfortunate timing of its arrival in an age of mass-printing and better methods of preserving historical documents. The church's beginnings are so recent that Mormonism had no place to hide. For the first centuries of Christianity, we have almost no artifacts or manuscripts, but there is a wealth of information on Joseph Smith and the early Mormon church— an embarrassment of riches, as it turns out. The church has always tried to maintain a firm proprietary lock on the telling of its own history, and discourages the flock from looking too deep into the primary source materials of their own faith. But no matter how many documents and artifacts the church manages to safely squirrel away out of sight in the vaults of their Historical Dept., too much is already out of their hands— the lid on Pandora's box blew open long ago.

Here are two of the biggest events you'll never find in "faith-promoting history."

The Mormon Inquisition

By 1856 it seemed that God was displeased with his chosen people. They had failed to turn Utah Territory into either an independent nation of their own or a full-fledged state. A two-year drought and plagues of locusts had ravaged their crops and threatened them with starvation. Desperate economic conditions had combined with their worst winter yet to make their misery complete. Brigham Young considered abandoning the Great Basin altogether.

But instead, he blamed the victims and decided the best course of action was to whip the church into shape. So he unleashed a witch-hunt on the faithful and swore that all backsliders would be "hewn down." [cccxvi] All who wanted to remain Saints had to "consecrate," that is, deed their property, to the President of the church. [cccxvii] He also brought the doctrine of blood atonement into full flower. "I want their cursed heads cut off that they may atone for their sins," [cccxviii] he raged to the Council of Fifty. An "orgy of recrimination and rebaptism" followed as the Saints turned on each other to save themselves from Brigham's new Inquisition, driven by his second counselor, Jedediah Grant, who became known as "Brigham's Sledge Hammer."

Jedediah Grant looks so gentle and harmless, but "Brigham's Sledge Hammer" carried out the Mormon version of the Spanish Inquisition. Jedediah saw to it that

many of the church's own members were killed in order to save them. "We have those amongst us that are full of all manner of abominations, those who need to have their blood shed..."

Hammer Time

Today, Jedediah's grisly cultural revolution goes by the lofty name of the Mormon Reformation. LDS apologists refer to it as "a period of rejuvenated emphasis on spirituality." Grant had kicked off the spiritual campaign by advising sinners to "appoint a committee to attend to their case; and then let a place be selected, and let that committee shed their blood," because, as he said, "We have those amongst us that are full of all manner of abominations, those who need to have their bloodshed, for water will not do, their sins are of too deep a dye."[cccxix]

Those Mormons who tried to escape Utah were hunted down and killed. One was William R. Parrish, an elderly Saint of high standing. Accused of "growing cold in the faith," [cccxx] he tried to take his family to California, but Brigham's enforcers, the "Avenging Angels," caught them before they had gotten far, and slit his throat.

In Manti, Mormon Bishop Warren Snow led a party and went after a young man whose only crime was to be engaged to a girl the bishop wanted to take as a plural wife. The bishop accused him of sexual misconduct, so the gang castrated him "in a brutal manner, tearing the chords (sic) right out," a witness reported, "and then took the portion severed from his victim and hung it up in the schoolhouse on a nail, so it could be seen by all who visited the house afterwards." [cccxxi]

News of terrors and slayings like these spread through the territory—but not in the Church-run *Deseret News*, which kept a lid on the wave of violence. And even though the identities of the perpetrators were common knowledge in every Mormon settlement, no one was ever brought to justice. The season of bloody violence raged on until Jedediah burned himself out, dying suddenly of typhoid on December 1, 1856 (His son Heber, born just nine days earlier, would grow up to become the seventh president of the church).

The Reformation groaned on for another year or so without its chief scourge. But even its worst terrors were eclipsed by what was about to occur the following year.

The Mountain Meadows Massacre

In 1857, one of the worst atrocities in American history occurred, ironically enough, on 9/11. The Fancher-Baker party, a wagon train of Arkansas emigrants, was passing through the peaceful green Mountain Meadows, Utah Territory, heading for a new home in California. They would never get there.

The emigrants' timing couldn't have been worse, for a variety of reasons. First, they had the bad fortune of traveling during the so-called "Utah War," when tensions were strained to the breaking point between Washington and Salt Lake City. The president had already sent the U.S. Army marching towards Utah to quell what appeared to be a theocratic rebellion; the Saints were terrified that the troops were coming to annihilate them.

In fact, it wasn't the army they should have been afraid of; their worst enemies were right at home, inflicting the Reformation upon them. Like Mao's cultural revolution, it turned them against themselves, and had sharpened their paranoia and xenophobia and instilled desperate, slavish loyalty to their leaders. Brigham Young had been ratcheting up his rhetoric to hell-fire hot and using their fears to shore up his own considerable power. He riled them up into a fortress mentality: their enemies would never be able to kick them out of Utah. They would have their vengeance on their persecutors. He would lift his sword and slay those who wished to destroy his people. No mercy to the Gentiles.

This was the welcome the Fancher party received when they arrived at Salt Lake City. Before the current crisis, emigrant trains like theirs were a welcome sight; they provided much-needed goods and paid top dollar for fresh supplies and animals. But now, Brigham had forbidden any commerce or fraternization with any outsiders. A number of Mormon apostates hoping to escape Utah had also joined their party; they explained that the Saints who broke that rule paid for it with beatings or expulsions. There was nothing for them here. When they rode on, many envious eyes had watched them go; they were the richest wagon train any of them had seen pass through the territory, and the Saints were desperately poor these days.

While the Fanchers struggled on to the south, desperately low on supplies, their fate was being sealed in Salt Lake City. A propaganda campaign against them was launched and the rumors took off from there: The emigrants were from Arkansas (where beloved apostle Parley Pratt had just been murdered by a jealous husband whose wife he had stolen). No, they were from hated Missouri; they were kin to Joseph Smith's killers; they were some of his killers; they were bragging how they killed the prophet; they carried the very gun that killed him. Once the wagon train finally reached the Mountain Meadows, they gave a sigh of relief. For the first time in weeks of traveling past unfriendly Mormon territory, they had at last come to a spot of safety where they could rest and recuperate for a few weeks before making the last leg of their journey.

On the morning of Monday, September 7, 1857, [cccxxii] the camp was waking up to the gentle clatter of cookware, and the smell of fresh-brewed coffee and roasting game. Years later, Sarah Baker said what happened next. "While eating breakfast of rabbit and quail for breakfast a shot rang out and one of the children toppled over." Then bullets were flying everywhere. Seven men were killed instantly, along with many of their horses and mules tied to the wagons and unable to escape. Several others were seriously wounded in that first volley, including the three-year-old Sarah and their captain Alexander Fancher, who was hit in the throat and went down, helpless. His 25-year-old cousin Matt Fancher jumped in to take command just as a great howl rose up and a mass of attackers in warpaint charged them.

The Arkansans (including one of the women) returned

fire, killing at least one attacker and shattering the knees of two of the Paiute warchiefs. The rest quickly retreated, and the two sides exchanged gunfire for another half hour. When the shooting let up, the emigrants circled the wagons and dug in as best they could. Their situation was grim; they were surrounded and cut off from the only stream. A siege began.

After a sleepless, bitter cold night, Tuesday brought a long day of sporadic sniper fire. Off in the distance, they could hear the enemy rounding up their cattle herd. Near at hand they could hear the groans of their wounded. By Wednesday most of the wounded had died, and the survivors knew if the siege wasn't lifted soon they were doomed. The enemy gunfire started up even stronger than before; it was clear that their attackers' forces had increased. The smell of rotting corpses and animal carcasses in the hot sun was unbearable. The lack of food and water was taking its toll. Desperate and hoping to appeal to their enemies' humanity, they dressed two little girls in spotless white and sent them out with a bucket to fetch water. Both were shot dead in an instant.

That night the party decided their only hope was to risk a run to seek help, and sent out two of the men under cover of darkness. They slipped out, leading their horses, planning to mount up after a safe distance and riding for help from the wagon train following theirs. Later that night, one of them returned, wounded. They had found a campfire where they had expected the other wagon train. When his companion dismounted, described the attack and pleaded for their help, one the listeners stepped up and shoved a pistol in his chest, shooting him dead on the spot. He wheeled his horse around and was shot as well, but he was able to ride back to camp. No one was going to help them.

Thursday morning two men made a desperate run to the stream; miraculously, they got back through a hail of bullets with two buckets of water. Two others left camp to chop firewood while dodging bullets. That night, the group decided to risk another attempt to get help, or at the very least, let the world know what had happened. They chose the three best scouts, who would have to make a grueling trek across the

Mojave Desert. After emotional goodbyes, the trio slipped out without drawing fire. They would never see them again, and never know that the three men were tracked down and within 5 days all had their throats slit before ever reaching help. The last man seems to have crossed as far as 150 miles on foot before being caught and killed.

On Friday morning, September 11th, the remaining survivors were alone except for their unburied dead and dying. A third of their men were gone. Exhausted, out of food and water, and nearly out of ammunition, too, they huddled under cover, waiting for the gunfire to return, but the morning remained eerily still. They knew it would take a miracle to get out alive.

And then a miracle arrived.

A large body of men came up the road, waving an American flag and a white flag of truce. Young Matt Fancher walked out to meet with them, and was told they were there to negotiate a cease-fire. A man rode up and dismounted, flashing secret Masonic signals to convey his solidarity. He introduced himself as John D. Lee, a federal Indian agent, American military officer and a major in the Mormon militia. He was here to help. The local Paiute Indians had gone "hog wild" on the warpath, and he was trying to broker an end to the attack. The Mormons would escort them all to safety—but in return, the Arkansans would need to surrender their rifles, provisions and cattle; nothing less would satisfy the bloodthirsty redskins.

The reaction was mixed. Many in the party were overjoyed, but some of the men glared at the Mormon officer with deep distrust. Undaunted, Lee continued to coax them to surrender for another three or four hours, and in the end promised them everything would be returned once they were safe in Cedar City. Still a heated minority argued against giving up the weapons. They urged Matt not to be a fool, that if they gave in they were all dead men; even their dying leader Alexander Fancher gasped one final order: "Good God no, Matt!"

It's unknown if the ex-Mormon refugees in their party were among those who didn't trust the offer, but it seems likely. But the emigrants really had no choice. Even though the rescue offer sounded dodgy, they were down to their last handful of ammunition and worn out, dying of hunger and thirst. In the end, the members of the Fancher party resigned themselves to the thought that even though they were perhaps going to be robbed, at least they'd be alive.

They were divided up into three groups. First to head out were the wounded men and women together with the youngest children, who went in one of the wagons; all the rifles were placed in another. A quarter mile behind the wagons followed the uninjured women and the older children. After they had gone about a mile and disappeared from sight, the men were marched out in a single-file column, led by John Higbee, a Mormon major on horseback. They marched along until they came up to a waiting company of the Nauvoo Legion. When they reached the troops, the Arkansans smiled, waved and gave a cheer of thanks to their rescuers, and an armed Mormon soldier fell in line alongside each of them. They continued on to a flat open patch surrounded by oak brush, At that point, the major fired a shot in the air and called out "Halt! Do your duty!"—and each Mormon guard turned and shot the emigrant man next to him.

Most of the men died instantly; those who didn't tried to run and were picked off by a second volley or chased down by horsemen bringing up the rear. The ex-Mormons among them got a special treatment; they were also blood atoned with Bowie knives. "Higbee, I wouldn't do this to you," one of them pleaded to the commander, who he recognized from Cedar City. "You would have done the same to me or just as bad," Higbee responded as he cut the man's throat.

Up the road from them, the women and children screamed at the sound of the gunfire and tried to flee. "From the survivors went up such a piercing, heart-rending scream—such a shriek of blank despair—then the flight of all except one young woman, who sprang to Lee, and clung to him for protection," read one account. The wagon drivers began shooting the wounded. Sally Baker, one of them, reported: "One of the Mormons ran up to the wagon, raised his gun and said, 'Lord my God, receive their spirits. It is for Thy Kingdom that I do this.'" She watched as he shot the men next to her, and as the wagon driver beat a 14-year-old boy to death with the butt of a gun.

Jack Baker, holding four-year-old Nancy Huff in his arms, was shot dead. She watched as her mother was shot in the forehead next, and then saw two sisters, Ruth and Rachel Dunlap, aged 14 and 16, run for their lives. Some lurid reports, difficult to verify, said they were caught, raped and stripped of their clothes, and that they pleaded to Lee for their lives, promising they would love and obey him, but he killed them. Vina Baker, Jack's pretty black-haired daughter, was led away out of sight. Nancy also saw all the other teenage girls being killed while begging to be spared.

One eyewitness described "children clinging around the knees of the murderers, begging for mercy and offering themselves as slaves for life could they be spared. But their throats were cut from ear to ear in answer to their appeal." Two dozen women and fifty older children were killed. Traditional reports said most of the women were hacked or beaten to death. From the forensic evidence of at least 28 victims, many were shot, some from behind, execution-style, though at least one woman was shot in the face.

Nancy Huff was gathered up along with about eighteen other of the youngest children and waited while the Mormons decided what to do with them. Saints had a horror of committing the sin of shedding "innocent blood," that of a child under the age of eight, but they were even more concerned about any credible witnesses old enough to testify. One of the girls was about ten years old; they decided she knew too much and shot her in front of the others.

All in all, around 140 men, women and children were killed, most within about three minutes. Until the Oklahoma City bombings in 1995, it remained the worst civilian atrocity in American history. Lee would always claim he never personally killed anyone that day; he filled his book *Confessions* with self-serving stories of how he only reluctantly took part in the massacre, forced by his duty, and heroically and single-handedly saved several of the children from being killed by his own men or their Indian allies. Today it is disputed whether any Indians actually participated at all after the first day or two of the siege. What's not in dispute is that many of the attackers were Mormons dressed up as Indians with faces covered in warpaint, and that afterwards all the Mormons stood together to make a blood oath: tell no one what really went on, under pain of death, and lay blame for the whole massacre on the local Paiute Indians alone. They ended their words with a blessing from one of the bishops. Amen.

Nancy Huff was 4 years old at the time of the massacre. The youngest daughter of six children, she was the only member of her family to survive.

They had stripped the bodies of any goods and clothing. The loot was taken to the Cedar City tithing office to be sold at public auction. The bloodstained clothing lay in the cellar for weeks before close-mouthed Mormon women washed and mended it. Two years later, the horrible smell still lingered.

The children were also divvied up. The leaders got first choice of their favorites, then if there were any left over, the soldiers could request one. Lee called dibs on one of the boys, a girl, and possibly another infant. The rest went to be raised in local Mormon families. In the meantime, they were all taken to the ranch of a local Mormon, Jacob Hamblin, for safekeeping. Hamblin's wife came out of her house as they arrived that night, drawn by the shrill cries of the traumatized children. She was horrified to find their clothes were wet with the blood of their parents and their own wounds. One child died as they arrived; a one-year-old girl lost her left arm. All of them continued shrieking in terror and anguish all night long, inconsolable.

As for the remains of the victims, some were lightly covered with dirt, but the majority was left to rot. A week later, travelers found scattered corpses lying where they had fallen, all nude except for a torn stocking on the foot of one. The eyes were picked out by crows, and packs of wolves and coyotes returned again and again to eat the corpses. When investigators came two years later, bleached skulls and bones were still strewn about everywhere, and women's hair hung in detached locks and masses from the sage bushes.

News of the massacre soon hit the papers across the country, and few seemed to be buying it as an Indian attack; one San Francisco paper dubbed it "the Mormon Massacre" and appealed to the federal government to punish them. Ironically, the only paper in Utah territory, the LDS house organ *Deseret News*, made no mention of it at all until months later, and then only to deny that any Mormons were involved. The church issued denials at once, sending out letters blaming the Paiute Indians. The church's claims were countered within days. The front page of *The New York Times* fingered John D. Lee as the instigator of the massacre.

**Cover of the August 13, 1859 *Harper's Weekly* depicting the
site of the Mountain Meadows Massacre when
investigators returned two years later.**
**"The scene was one too horrible and sickening for language
to describe. Human skeletons, disjointed bones, ghastly
skulls and the hair of women were scattered in frightful
profusion over a distance of two miles."**
(from the 1859 report)

In 1859, newly arrived federal Judge John Cradlebaugh
convened a federal grand jury to investigate crimes in the
territory, starting with the murder of William R. Parrish and
others during the Reformation. Other cases included the
execution-style murders of six California emigrants, the
castration and murder of another apostate, and other blood
atonement slayings committed by Joseph Smith's Danite
bodyguard Porter Rockwell.[cccxxiii] He also began to get first-
hand testimony of the massacre. Cradlebaugh was deeply
religious, open-minded and sympathetic to the Mormons as a
persecuted religious minority, but soon came to the conclusion
that the church was mired in all these horrific murder cases and

the involvement went all the way to Brigham Young himself.

For weeks Cradlebaugh struggled to bring justice to the troubled territory. He had to strive to secure protection for intimidated and threatened witnesses frightened for their lives. He also had to battle his own grand jurors who refused to return indictments. It soon became clear to him that they were participants in the very crimes he was investigating and he dismissed them in disgust, saying:

"I always supposed that I lived in a land of civil and religious liberty...but I regret to say that the evidence... clearly proves that, so far as Utah is concerned, I have been mistaken in such supposition. Men are murdered here. Coolly, deliberately, premeditatedly murdered—their murder is deliberated and determined upon by church council meetings, and that, too, for no other reason than that they had apostatized from your church, and were striving to leave the territory." [cccxxiv]

The gentle acceptance of the Mormons Judge Cradlebaugh had brought to Utah was gone, replaced with a conviction that the church was guilty of murder and despotism and a fiery passion to bring them to justice. He issued bench warrants that sent a stampede of church officials and corrupt civil officials running for the hills.

The Indian Superintendent and his marshals set out to retrieve survivors of the massacre. They began by investigating the site itself. They were experienced frontier lawmen and veterans of battle, but the scattering of human remains from slaughtered women and children left them sickened and shaken. Soon afterwards, they tracked down Jacob Hamblin, who repeated the official story: all the surviving children had been captured by Indians. The lawmen were in no mood for lies; they raised their rifles and pistols at his head and said, "Produce them or we will kill you." [cccxxv] Hamblin quickly delivered the orphans. They were in poor condition: filthy, half-starved, half-naked and their eyes diseased from neglect. Only the two oldest boys remembered their full names. None of the looted property was ever recovered, though there were

Mormon ladies who wore their fine new outfits with pleasure, and Brigham Young himself was very proud of his fine carriage, formerly in the Fancher's wagon train.

In May of 1861, Brigham and his entourage stopped at Mountain Meadows and stopped at the rock cairn that had been built there by U.S. soldiers as a monument to the victims. Atop the peak of the cairn stood a heavy wooden cross engraved with "Vengeance is mine: I will repay, saith the Lord." Young regarded it for a moment, then read the inscription aloud with a slight change: "Vengeance is mine, saith the Lord: I *have* repaid." He gave a Danite signal by raising his right arm, fist to the sky. His men understood. A horseman lassoed the cross and pulled it down, dragging it until it splintered to pieces. The others set to work and five minutes later not a single stone was left of the memorial. [cccxxvi]

But Brigham wouldn't be able to sweep the massacre under the rug quite so easily; though years passed, he could never shake the accusations that he masterminded the killings. Mark Twain was one of the journalists who wouldn't let the matter drop and wrote up a list of eight damning pieces of evidence: the Mormon participants who confessed to Judge Cradlebaugh; Brigham's failure as superintendent of Indian affairs to report the incident in a timely fashion; the mass flight of participants fleeing Judge Cradlebaugh's investigation; the blackout of the incident in the church-owned *Deseret News*; testimonies of the local Indians, Indian agents, other federal officers, and the surviving children; and finally, the rather blatant simple fact that the victims' children and all their stolen property were in Mormon hands.

The LDS church authorities did everything they could to delay the inevitable and shake off the investigation, stonewalling and throwing up one obstacle after another, for years. After it became abundantly clear that no one was buying the Indian story, the church switched tactics and began saying that the massacre was the work of a small band of rogue Mormons acting alone. But it was too late in the game to try to head off the investigation.

Brigham Young was never able to shake the allegations that he orchestrated the Mountain Meadows Massacre; but he was able to stymie the investigation for 17 years and prevent the prosecution of any of the actual murderers except his adopted son, John D. Lee—the only one executed for the massacre.

It would take 17 years for anyone to be brought to justice for the massacre. The investigation was delayed by the Civil War, which Brigham watched with delight, hoping North and South would destroy each other. In 1874, nine of the Mormon leaders of the massacre were indicted at last. In the end, out of all the participants, only one ever made it to a court of law: the man who lured the Fancher party to their deaths, John D. Lee. After two trials, he was convicted and sentenced to death. Lee was devastated to be made the scapegoat and during his final months in jail wrote a bitter exposé (actually, four conflicting and contradictory ones). On March 23, 1877, Lee was taken back to Mountain Meadows for the last time. A firing squad executed him at the massacre site.

His family claimed that Lee had said before his death, "If I am not guilty, Brigham Young will die within one year! Yes, within six months." On August 23, three months to the day after Lee's execution, Brigham gorged himself on green corn and peaches and became deathly ill. He suffered for six days and then died. According to the *Deseret News*, his final words were "Joseph! Joseph! Joseph!" (According to his biographer M.R. Werner, his actual last words were "I feel better.") [cccxxvii]

The LDS church has long since stopped denying that Mormons were involved in the massacre. But after more than 150 years, the church is still arguing over who was responsible. When the truth came out about the massacre (and even before), the participants were pointing fingers at everyone else. Today the only real debate left is, did Brigham Young order it? Naturally, the Saints have never been comfortable admitting that their beloved second president could have been responsible and LDS historians like Glen Leonard continue to insist that he was out of the loop and shocked by the massacre, turning a blind eye to any inconsistencies in the official story.

For instance, as evidence that Brigham was innocent, they point to the story that as soon as he heard about the siege he dispatched a rider at once with a letter telling Lee and the others not to harm the travelers, a letter that sadly, arrived too late. But this clever attempt at an alibi is a catch-22 for Brigham—why would he need to send special orders *not* to kill innocent travelers?

Utah historian Juanita Brooks was the first to write a comprehensive account of the massacre. A descendant of Mormon participants, Brooks argued that Brigham's incendiary rhetoric provoked the attack, and that he was clearly was "an accessory after the fact" for obstructing the investigation, but stopped short of calling him the chief culprit. With the surfacing of more evidence, recent historians aren't quite so reluctant. Will Bagley, another historian brought up in the LDS church, spoke out in the 2007 PBS special "The Mormons," to say that even if Brigham managed to effectively (but not completely) cover his tracks, he couldn't erase the evidence of his involvement afterwards: "What we do know is the cover-up. The cover-up can be very clearly documented—and it is not ambiguous, it is absolutely clear, that this event was purposely distorted, and misrepresented, and hidden."

After having studied the events of the massacre for a decade in great detail, Bagley remains convinced Brigham issued the orders. Nothing happened in Utah that he did not know about. The church regarded his orders as divine commands; if he wanted the murderers brought to justice, it wouldn't have taken 17 years—not that Brigham ever made an attempt to track down the murderers. On the contrary, at Lee's trial, the prosecution gave a blistering closing argument: that the Mormon Church had not simply failed to investigate, but had thrown every impediment in the way of the investigation. The massacre was no isolated fluke. It was the logical culmination of a long process. It was a deliberate act of vengeance and a political message to demonstrate that the Mormons controlled the route to the west. It was ordered from the top.

The Mountain Meadows Massacre was a crime of true believers, acting on the orders of a leader who considered himself above the law, who believed the end justified the means, who expected and got unquestioned obedience, and who fully expected to get away with it—and to a great extent, he did. "I am haunted by that story," says Mormon historian Melvin T. Smith. "Not only because my people and my church were involved, but because as a true believer I could understand how they could do it; and because I sense that I might have been involved, as the true believer I was, had the time and circumstances been right." *cccxxviii*

***

For further reading:

For more on the Mountain Meadows Massacre:

Will Bagley's *Blood of the Prophets* (Norman: Univ. of Oklahoma Press, 2004)

Juanita Brooks' *The Mountain Meadows Massacre* (Norman: Univ. of Oklahoma Press, 1950)

Sally Denton's *American Massacre* (New York: Knopf, 2003)

Endnotes: Chapter 11

ccxcix Ostling, p. 246
ccc ibid., p. 254
ccci Tanner, *CiJSH*
cccii from "On Being a Mormon Historian and Its Aftermath" in Smith, *Faithful History*, pp. 69-112
ccciii ibid.
ccciv Ostling, p. 251

[cccv] from "The Mantle is Far, Far Greater Than the Intellect," speech to Church Educational System Religious Educator's Symposium on August 22, 1981. Reprinted in *BYU Studies*, 21, no. 3 1981, pp. 259-277

[cccvi] in *Faithful History: Essays on Writing Mormon History*, p. 103

[cccvii] Ostling, p. 254

[cccviii] ibid., pp. 254-263

[cccix] ibid., p. 263

[cccx] Richard Packham, "Why I Left the Mormon Church" http://packham.n4m.org/whylft.htm

[cccxi] Ostling, p. 360

[cccxii] ibid.

[cccxiii] ibid., p. 364

[cccxiv] ibid., p. 261

[cccxv] ibid., p. 358

[cccxvi] Denton, p. 105

[cccxvii] Bagley, p. 52

[cccxviii] Denton, p. 106

[cccxix] Bagley, p. 51

[cccxx] Denton, op.cit.

[cccxxi] Bigler, p. 132

[cccxxii] The sources for this section include the account of survivor Sarah Baker, Will Bagley's *Blood of the Prophets* and Sally Denton's *American Massacre*.

[cccxxiii] Denton, p. 190

[cccxxiv] ibid, p.191

[cccxxv] Bagley, p. 219

[cccxxvi] Brooks, p. 183. Ironically, one of Brooks' own ancestors was present at the scene.

[cccxxvii] Bagley, p. 322

[cccxxviii] ibid., p. 378

Chapter 12

Forgery and The Mormon Church

One particular Achilles' heel that seems unique to Mormonism is their vulnerability to archeological fraud. In general, mainstream Christians don't have as much invested in holy relics. Of course, the Catholic and Orthodox traditions have a long and venerable history of treasuring bits and pieces of their saints—including as many as 18 different holy prepuce, i.e., foreskins of Jesus; and as Erasmus of Rotterdam joked, enough splinters of the Holy Cross to build several buildings. Still, when hoaxes like the Shroud of Turin or the Ossuary of St. John turn out to be fakes (and they always do...), it's not necessarily a deal-killer. But what makes Mormon doctrine so special is that Joseph seems to never have realized archeologists were already learning to read ancient Egyptian. So he continued to put smoking guns in his mouth throughout his career. Here are three of the biggies:

Kinderhook Plates

In 1843, six brass, bell shaped plates were discovered in a burial mound in Kinderhook, Illinois, resting upon the breast of a decomposed human skeleton that the excavators thought must have stood nine feet tall. Each plate was four inches long, nearly two inches wide at the top and nearly three inches wide at the bottom, and had a hole near the small end. The plates hung upon a ring of iron wire with clasps; the rings and clasps were so oxidized and decayed that they crumbled to dust upon touch.

The plates themselves were completely encrusted with rust. The discoverers washed them with soap and water and scrubbed them with a wool cloth, but without success. But when they finally treated the plates with a dilute mixture of sulphuric acid, ancient inscriptions were revealed plainly. The curiously shaped plates were engraved with an unknown type of hieroglyphic characters.

Two Mormon elders were among the spectators at the unearthing of the artifacts. One declared that the Lord had directed them to witness the digging and suggested taking them to Joseph Smith to see if he could translate the mysterious engravings. So they did, and naturally, he could indeed translate them. He told them the engravings were very like those of the Book of Mormon plates, and they told the story of an ancient Jaredite. He likely meant to run a complete translation of the plates, but things fell apart and he was killed before ever having the chance to turn the plates into any more Mormon scripture. He did, however, translate a portion of them and offered this brief synopsis:

"I have translated a portion of them, and find they contain the history of the person with whom they were found. He was a descendant of Ham, through the loins of Pharaoh, king of Egypt, and that he received his kingdom from the Ruler of heaven and earth." [cccxxix]

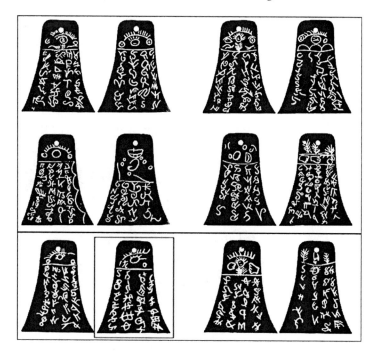

**The six Kinderhook plates (front and back of each)
Plate No. 5 (bottom left hand corner) was rediscovered in
1962.
Drawings appeared in *History of the Church* and the
Nauvoo Neighbor.**

Though an Illinois man came forward 36 years later and admitting that the plates were forgeries made by himself and two other men to trick Joseph Smith, the church continued to assert that they were genuine. Mysteriously enough, however, the actual plates had disappeared during the Civil War. And for nearly a century all six plates remained lost. Then in 1962, a BYU Professor rediscovered one of the original Kinderhook plates in the stacks of the Chicago Historical Society Museum, mislabeled as one of the original gold plates of the Book of Mormon, ironically enough. Welby W. Ricks, President of the BYU Archaeological Society, was delighted; he was certain the plates were genuine and proved Joseph Smith to be "a true prophet and translator of ancient records by divine means." He had nothing to hide, announcing "all the world is invited to investigate the truth which has sprung out of the earth not only of the Kinderhook plates, but of the Book of Mormon as well."*cccxxx*

Photo of Kinderhook Plate No. 5 (Compare with the drawing on previous page)

From Utah Lighthouse Ministries
(http://www.utlm.org/onlineresources/kinderhookplates.htm)

Accordingly, in 1980 permission was granted to make some very sophisticated electronic and chemical analysis of the plate, which verified that it was indeed one of the genuine original Kinderhook plates, not some modern forgery—and unfortunately for Ricks, that the genuine original plate was also a genuine fake, made of a 19th century metal alloy.

Reaction from LDS apologists changed swiftly to keep up with current events. They went from proudly crowing that Joseph Smith had been vindicated, to insisting that the rediscovered plate was a modern forgery of one of the genuine, original plates, and when that option was removed, completely flip-flopped by saying that yes, the plates had always been a forgery, but that Joseph Smith had not been fooled for a second. But Joseph's own statement on record and multiple attestations of the wonderful testimony of the Kinderhook plates for years in different church publications (and still available ^{cccxxxi}) makes you wonder who do they think they're fooling?

Book of Abraham

In 1835 Joseph Smith obtained some Egyptian papyri along with several mummies from a traveling showman. From these Egyptian writings Smith claimed to translate one of the cornerstones of Mormon scripture, the *Book of Abraham*, which he said were the "writings of Abraham while he was in Egypt, called the Book of Abraham, written by his own hand, upon papyrus" (see introduction to the *Book of Abraham* in *The Pearl of Great Price*). Since 1880, by unanimous vote of LDS authorities, the Book of Abraham has been canonized as official scripture of the LDS Church.

But as early as 1856, critics were challenging Joseph's "translation." For instance, in one illustration, he identifies two individuals as "King Pharaoh" and "Prince of Pharaoh"—but both are clearly females! In 1912, an Episcopal bishop sent copies of the three facsimiles from *The Book of Abraham* to some of the world's leading Egyptologists, and asked each to independently assess Joseph's interpretations. The verdict was unanimous: each one replied that Joseph's clumsy translation was sheer nonsense.

Book of Abraham facsimile no. 3.
Joseph identified figure 2 (far left) as "King Pharaoh" and figure 4 (middle) as "Prince of Pharoh, King of Egypt". In reality, figure 2 is the goddess Isis and figure 4 is the goddess Maat.

Photo: www.bookofabraham.com

Mormon apologists responded by protesting that less than one-seventh of the whole *Book of Abraham* was represented by the facsimiles. Before the experts could dismiss the entire book as bogus, there would have to be a fair test of Joseph's true translating ability. And the only way to do that would be for them to examine the original Book of Abraham papyrus.

Unfortunately—or maybe, luckily—there was no way for anyone to do that. After Joseph was killed in 1844, the original Egyptian papyrus had become his (first) wife Emma's property. When she broke with Brigham Young and the church, the papyrus stayed with her until she eventually donated it to a museum in Chicago. When the museum burned down in the Great Chicago Fire of 1871, everyone naturally assumed the original *Book of Abraham* text had been lost forever. The argument over the translation seemed to be at a stalemate.

At least until the original papyrus turned up safe and sound again in 1967, complete with Joseph Smith's handwritten notations!*cccxxxii* Needless to say, there was no contest. Egyptologists immediately identified the twelve fragments as portions from three different common Egyptian funerary manuals. It doesn't contain any information about Abraham or his religion—in fact, all fragments clearly date after 500 B.C., some 1500 years after Abraham's time—but rather is a collection of spells and incantations to help the deceased through the perilous journey in the afterlife.

One text is the "Book of Breathings" for the priest Hôr, son of the priest Osorwer and the lady Tikhebyt. The other two are "Books of the Dead," belonging to the lady Amon-Re Neferirnub, and Ta-Shere-Min, daughter of Nes-Khensu, *cccxxxiii* as well as directions for burying the texts with the mummy.

Incidentally, the *Book of Abraham* is a source for several important LDS doctrines like including humanity's pre-mortal existence, the plurality of gods, and the ability of good Mormons to become gods themselves. It's also the one and only reference to god's favorite planet—or is it a star?—Kolob. Sorry, Kolob.

The Greek Psalter Incident

In 1842, Dr. Henry Caswell, an Episcopal minister visiting from England, decided to go undercover and try to expose Joseph Smith as a fraud. He succeeded admirably. Armed with a Medieval Greek psalter (a book containing the Psalms and often other devotional material), Caswell arrived in Nauvoo, dressed down to avoid being recognized as a clergyman. Since Joseph had translated the Book of Mormon from "Reformed Egyptian" and the Book of Abraham from Egyptian papyri, the minister wanted to see what he thought about this ancient Greek manuscript. He made it known that he wanted to show Joseph Smith a very wonderful book which had lately come into his possession, and quickly attracted an audience of onlookers, who oohed and awed when he unwrapped the 600-year-old book with its worm-eaten oak covers, discolored parchments and mysterious characters:

"... after a long silence, one person wiser than his fellows, declared that he knew it to be a revelation from the Lord, and that probably it was one of the lost books of the Bible providentially recovered. Looking at me with a patronizing air, he assured me that I had brought it to the right place to get it interpreted, for that none on earth but the Lord's Prophet could explain it, or unfold its real antiquity and value. 'Oh,' I replied, 'I am going to England next week, and doubtless I shall find some learned man in one of the universities who can expound it.' To this he answered with a sneer, that the Lord had chosen the weak things of the world to confound the mighty; that he had made foolish the wisdom of this world; and that I ought to thank Providence for having brought me to Nauvoo, where the hidden things of darkness could be revealed by divine power."*cccxxxiv*

News of Caswell's amazing book spread fast, and when he was granted an interview with Joseph next day, a crowd of excited and curious Mormons came out to see what the Prophet would make of it.

"I met Joseph Smith at a short distance from his dwelling, and was regularly introduced to him... He led the way to his house, accompanied by many elders, preachers, and other Mormon dignitaries. On entering the house, chairs were provided for the prophet and myself, while the curious and gaping spectators remained standing. I handed the book to the prophet, and begged him to explain its contents. He asked me if I had any idea of its meaning. I replied, that I believed it to be a Greek Psalter; but that I should like to hear his opinion. 'No' he said; 'it ain't Greek at all, except, perhaps, a few words. What ain't Greek, is Egyptian; and what ain't Egyptian, is Greek. This book is very valuable. *It is a dictionary of Egyptian hieroglyphics.*'

"Pointing to the capital letters at the commencement of each verse, he said: 'Them figures is Egyptian hieroglyphics; and them which follows, is the interpretation of the hieroglyphics, written in the reformed Egyptian. Them characters is like the letters that was engraved on the "Golden Plates".' Upon this, the Mormons around began to congratulate me on the information I was receiving. 'There,' they said; 'we told you so—we told you that our prophet would give you satisfaction. None but our prophet can explain these mysteries.'"

To be fair, Caswell was probably exaggerating Joseph's hick accent and bad grammar, though the first editions of the Book of Mormon show some pretty horrendous language gaffes, too. Caswell says Joseph then tried to get the psalter from him, saying it was of no use to him, since he couldn't understand it. When Caswell refused, Joseph asked him how much he would be willing to sell it for. He curtly replied that his price was higher than they would be willing to pay, and when the Mormons pressed him, Caswell told them he would not sell it to them for many hundred dollars. At that, they insisted he lend it to them until their prophet had time to translate it, promising him to keep it under the utmost security. Caswell coolly declined, and instead asked Joseph to show him his famous collection of Egyptian papyri and give his translation of them. Joseph took Caswell and the disappointed crowd into his office and produced the Egyptian texts, but:

"...he did not appear very forward to explain the figures. I pointed to a particular hieroglyphic, and requested him to expound its meaning. No answer being returned, I looked up, and behold! The prophet had disappeared. The Mormons told me that he had just stepped out, and would probably soon return. I waited some time, but in vain: and at length descended to the street in front of the store. Here I heard the noise of wheels, and presently I saw the prophet in a light wagon, flourishing his whip and driving away as fast as two fine horses could draw him. As he disappeared from view, enveloped in a cloud of dust, I felt that I had turned over another page in the great book of human nature." (pp.35-37)

After Joseph's hasty retreat, the remaining Mormons asked Caswell if he had been satisfied by their Prophet's ability to translate his book; he told them on the contrary, Joseph had proved his own ignorance most effectually. He went on to inform them that what Joseph had declared to be a dictionary of Egyptian hieroglyphics, written in similar characters as the Book of Mormon no less, was in fact a copy of Psalms, written in ancient Greek, and asked "Now what shall I think of your prophet?" They were confounded by this uncomfortable revelation, until one of them at last said, "Sometimes Mr. Smith speaks as a prophet, and sometimes as a mere man. If he gave a wrong opinion respecting the book, he spoke as a mere man." More than 150 years later, LDS apologists still haven't come up with a better defense for this embarrassing debacle, or been able to respond to Caswell's brilliant retort:

"Whether he spoke as a prophet or as a mere man he has committed himself; for he has said what is not true. If he spoke as a prophet, therefore, he is a false prophet. If he spoke as a mere man, he cannot be trusted, for he spoke positively and like an oracle respecting that of which he knew nothing." [cccxxxv]

Isn't that handy? As one commenter on MormonThink.com aptly put it: "When Joseph speaks and leads others to assume he is speaking as a prophet then he needs to be accountable for what he says. It's very convenient to say Joseph speaks as a man whenever he's proved wrong and as a prophet whenever his statements can't be proven right or wrong or haven't been proven one way or the other yet."[cccxxxvi]

Joseph Smith, Non-Prophet

Joseph pulled the exact same stunt with the Greek Psalter as he did with the Kinderhook Plates and the Egyptian *Book of Abraham* papyri: He got his hands on an ancient text that presumably no one could translate, and told everyone that *he* could. And in all three cases, he was getting his translations from out of the exact place where they later turned around and bit him.

As MormonThink.com speculates, it's interesting to imagine what would have happened if Rev. Caswell had taken his Greek Psalter gambit one step further by going ahead and giving Joseph the book and telling him he thought it was a religious text? Would Joseph have cranked out yet another ancient source of Mormon scripture—at least, until the true contents became exposed?

As damaging as these three embarrassments were, even these paled compared to the massive PR debacle that would come later. During the 1980s, the LDS church was rocked by a series of scandals that frankly, one would think would have been enough to finish them for good. But then again, the Catholic Church is still around…

The Hofmann Affair

In the early 80s, Mark William Hofmann, a sixth-generation Mormon, started discovering a flood of early LDS documents, one after another. Some the church publicized, others they bought secretly and put a lid on. The first was the "Anthon Transcript," which Hofmann claimed to have found stuck inside the pages of a seventeenth-century Smith family Bible. It appeared to be the original chart written by Joseph Smith himself of the "reformed Egyptian" characters from the "Golden Plates" that Martin Harris had taken to Prof. Anthon (see ch. 2). The Church went gaga and paid over $20,000 worth of artifacts in trade for it.

Hofmann soon became a professional antiquities dealer full-time. He claimed to have an entire network of tipsters, had tracked down modern descendants of early Mormons, and had gone through collections of nineteenth-century letters that had been saved for their postmarks rather than for their contents.

Soon he had a reputation for discovering previously unknown documents with great historical significance—some *very* significant.

In 1981, Hofmann showed up at LDS headquarters in Salt Lake City and tried to sell a letter to the LDS Church's chief archivist. The letter claimed that Joseph Smith's son, not Brigham Young, had been personally appointed by the Prophet to be his successor. You'll remember, back in the day, the church split over the issue of who would succeed Joseph Smith. The Missouri-based Reorganized Church of Jesus Christ of Latter Day Saints was the splinter group which had always claimed that Joseph Smith's line were the real successors, but they never had written proof—until now. So when the LDS church archivist balked at his price, Hofmann offered it to them instead.

This set off a scramble to acquire the letter. Hofmann finally traded it to the Utah church for over $20,000 in antiquities so they could bury it. But then... he turned around and also leaked the news to the *New York Times*, so the LDS Church was forced to confirm the discovery and publicly present the document to the RLDS Church.

Hofmann continued this fun and lucrative game over and over during the early 80s, producing new discoveries and playing the anxious church presidency like a fiddle. As one commentator put it, he discovered "a lever to exercise enormous power over his church," a power to "menace and manipulate its leaders with nothing more sinister than a sheet of paper." *cccxxxvii*

No one outside a small handful of men in the LDS church's leadership circle can say for certain just how many documents Hofmann sold to them during his run—because they kept many of the purchases hushed up—but they have admitted to buying at least 445 items from Hofmann. These included: a letter from Joseph Smith's mother to her sister, describing the origin of the Book of Mormon and including material that appeared to come from the lost 116 pages of the "Plates of Lehi" Joseph first translated (which in reality were probably burned by Martin Harris' wife Lucy) ; a letter from two of the Three Witnesses, each giving a personal account of their visions; and most intriguing—and disturbing—of all, the "Salamander letter." This was a letter that claimed that Smith had been treasure hunting and practicing black magic five years after his first vision, and that it had not been the angel Moroni who first appeared to him, but a devious spirit in the shape of a white salamander.

As in other cases, Hofmann sold it secretly to high-ranking church officials for thousands of dollars, gave his word that no one else had a copy, and then as soon as it was safely buried deep in the forbidden recesses of the LDS Historical Dept., secretly leaked its existence to the press, so that the church was forced to release the letter to scholars for study... despite having already denied it existed or that they had it in their possession. What a fun game!

What ratchets the already-entertaining story up a notch is that all these controversial documents were actually forgeries created by Hofmann. It would eventually turn out that of the 445 documents he sold them, forensic analysis revealed 107 were forgeries. In other words, nearly 1 in 4 were fakes. His plan was to embarrass the church as much as possible, and to get rich doing it. But it would take a shocking turn of events before the church found out.

In 1985, during a secret meeting with Second Counselor Gordon Hinckley (at that time, the real leader of the church, since the octogenarian president Ezra Taft Benson had become increasingly enfeebled from dementia, blood clots in the brain and strokes), Hofmann said that he had discovered a cache of documents that was potentially devastating to the church: the long-lost personal papers of excommunicated LDS apostle William McLellin. A close friend of Joseph's and a prominent early church insider, McLellin (or M'Lellin) was one of the original twelve Mormon apostles who broke with Joseph in 1838 over the church's banking fraud debacle. The McLellin collection was three large crates full of journals, early revelations, damaging affidavits from people like Emma Smith, records, church writings, and important artifacts like Egyptian papyri fragments including the original Facsimile #2 papyrus from *The Pearl of Great Price.*

Hofmann claimed that the collection painted a picture of the early church very different from traditional LDS history. He told them he had an option to buy the potentially dangerous find, but it would expire soon and there were other buyers interested. If they acted fast, he could acquire it quietly and sell it to them for $185,000. The church agreed and surreptitiously arranged the payment. But once he had the money, he failed to hand over the documents—repeatedly. Eventually the church lost patience with him and demanded that he either fork over the McLellin collection or the $185,000. This would be difficult for Hofmann, since he had lied about getting a lead on the McLellin purchase, hadn't the foggiest idea where the real McLellin collection was and hadn't gotten around to the Herculean task of forging three crates' worth of books and artifacts.

He had bitten off more than he could chew. When his schemes began to unravel, he panicked, and went from forger to murderer. He started by killing two people with homemade bombs, hoping both to prevent discovery of an earlier forgery, and to put an end to the McLellin deal. A third bomb exploded in his car, seriously injuring him and tipping the police off. They found evidence of a forgery-making workshop in his house, and he was sentenced to life in prison. Ironically enough, the nihilist ex-Mormon apostate Hofmann is today a cellmate with fundamentalist Mormon blood atonement double-murderer Dan Rafferty, whose grisly slaying of his sister-in-law and infant niece are the focus of Jon Krakauer's book *Under the Banner of Heaven.*

If you needed bonus irony, here it is: six months after Hofmann's arrest, LDS officials were mortified to discover that the real McLellin collection *had been in their possession the whole time*. The church had secretly acquired the papers in 1908 and hidden them away in the Historical Dept. so deep that the cache had been forgotten. Church leaders were so embarrassed by their blunder they didn't admit the mistake for six years—even though it would have aided in the police's murder investigation. The church had paid out $185,000, and

Hofmann had murdered two people, all over a set of documents the church already had all along.

As several commentators have noted, Hofmann could never have gotten away with his scams without the Mormon Church's special blend of paranoia and obsessive protectiveness of their history. Though Mormons are told their leadership has "the keys of discernment," the much touted divine ability to judge character and detect falsehood, the Hofmann forgeries showed the Mormon leaders were not only easy to dupe, but eager to spend thousands of dollars—over $900,000 in antiquities and cash—to cover up what they thought was concrete proof that their religion was founded on fraud.

***

For further reading:

Charles Larson, *By His Own Hand Upon Papyrus: A New Look at the Joseph Smith Papyri*, Institute for Religious Research, 1992. Includes a full-color foldout of both Joseph Smith's "Book of Abraham" papyri and his untranslated "Book of Joseph" papyri.

Kevin Mathie's excellent online site "Examining the Book of Abraham" gives a great breakdown of the Book of Abraham texts. (www.bookofabraham.com)

Lindsey, Robert. *A Gathering of Saints: A True Story of Money, Murder, and Deceit*, Simon & Schuster, 1988

Sillitoe, Linda and Roberts, Allen. *Salamander: The Story of the Mormon Forgery Murders* (2nd. Ed.), Salt Lake City: Signature Books, 1989

Endnotes: Chapter 12

[cccxxix] *History of the Church*, vol. 5, p. 372

[cccxxx] Welby W. Ricks, *The Kinderhook Plates*, cited in "Joseph Smith and the Kinderhook Plates" by Jerald and Sandra Tanner, http://www.utlm.org/onlineresources/josephsmithkinderhookplates.htm

[cccxxxi] For instance, see Joseph Smith's statement printed in *History of the Church*, p. 372; link available on the MormonThink.com website: http://www.mormonthink.com/hc372to379.htm

[cccxxxii] Brodie, pp. 422-23

[cccxxxiii] Palmer, p.29

[cccxxxiv] Caswell, pp. 20-21

[cccxxxv] Caswell, pp. 43-44

[cccxxxvi] http://mormonthink.com/greekweb.htm

[cccxxxvii] Lindsay, p. 298

Part Four

Tomorrow
is a Latter Day:
The Future of
Mormonism

Chapter 13

Tomorrow is a Latter Day

The Future of Mormonism

Don't believe in evolution? Then you should look at the constantly mutating world of Mormonism for a prime example. From its earliest days, the LDS church has struggled with the problem of schisms and splinter groups, to the point where the history of the Mormon movement comprises a half dozen major branches and by some counts almost 200 breakaway sects, some no larger than a single family. But today even the one true official, original and orthodox Utah Mormon faith is in danger of coming apart again. Jason "Dr. Shades," the creator of MormonInformation.com has discussed how a theological rift has been steadily dividing what he terms "Chapel Mormons," your average LDS members sitting in the pews, and "Internet Mormons," the Mormon apologists who are actively defending their faith against critics on the Internet (He is quick to add that of course Chapel Mormons can be found on the Internet and Internet Mormons can be found in the chapels—the terms simply refer to the areas where they typically promote their views). He asks: has the Church of Jesus Christ of Latter-day Saints split into two different religions (without even knowing it)?[cccxxxviii]

281

David Fitzgerald

Mormon vs. Mormon

According to Jason, Chapel Mormons tend towards fundamentalism and scriptural literalism, a position supported by church leaders. Internet Mormons, on the other hand, tend to temper their beliefs to fit modern science; they grant that traditional church answers may be in error and need new interpretations. They are quick to point out that their prophets and other early church leaders were fallible human beings capable of making ethically questionable statements or behaving badly.

To cite one of his examples, Brigham Young said that black skin was God's curse and those whites who "mix their seed" with blacks should be put to death on the spot. Mormons have a choice to make: was he speaking as God's prophet, or he was just expressing his own racist views? Chapel Mormons take a prophet's words at face value. They would defend Young and insist he was giving the flock the word of the Lord. We do not always know why God commands the things that he does—we must simply have faith that it was fulfilling his plan at the time. And besides, who are we puny humans to question God's ways?

Internet Mormons take the opposite approach and often view a prophet's words through the lens of his cultural context and his limited knowledge. They cut Brigham slack as a 19th century man, giving his own opinion, freighted with the prevailing prejudices and biases of his time. This nuanced approach is reasonable, but it certainly leaves something to be desired. For one thing, it admits that Mormonism is just another religion led and managed (if not created outright!) by human beings. They are also quick to point out that a prophet is only a prophet when he speaks in that role. Unfortunately, that convenient explanation doesn't answer how one is supposed to know when a church leader is speaking for God or just shooting his mouth off. And as Jason points out, the trick is getting tired fast:

"A typical apologetic ploy is the 'that was only his opinion' tactic. By reminding readers that Mormonism never claimed its leaders to be infallible, any controversial or repugnant teaching of yesteryear—such as the Adam-God doctrine—can be dismissed as being only the prophet's opinion. Nowadays, with knowledge of such historical items becoming more and more widespread, that tactic has been put into overdrive. Similarly, apologists are now spending a lot of time reminding readers that prophets in the Bible did and said many foolish things, so it would be absurd to hold modern prophets to a higher standard."

There are still more disagreements between the two camps just on the nature and role of prophets. Internet Mormons say the prophets don't tell the members what to believe. Chapel Mormons say the prophets *do* tell them what to believe—in fact, that's their job! Most if not all Chapel Mormons believe the prophet is always right about church doctrine when he declares it in General Conference—otherwise what's the point? Internet Mormons believe that the prophet can be mistaken about church doctrine, in General Conference or at any other time. How do you interpret the words of a Prophet? Can living Prophets override scripture with new revelation? Do the General Conferences and official Church publications count as gospel? Do the teachings of the Prophet apply to everyone, or are some people exempt? Both sides disagree.

When it comes to the word of the prophets, you will almost never hear a Chapel Mormon suggest any of them were dispensable. Internet Mormons, on the other hand, quite often dismiss troublesome statements or uncomfortable facts with "that's not necessary to my salvation." And the list of disagreements between the two sides of the divide, ranging from evolution vs. Adam and Eve, the age of the earth, New World archeology, the flood of Noah, the location of the Hill Cumorah, the process of translating the Book of Mormon, details of God's own mortal probation before he attained his divinity, his wife or wives, his own father, and more—they never seem to end.

Internet Mormons believe that their faith can and should go hand in hand with reason. They dismiss Chapel Mormons' literalism by chalking it up to their lack of education, naiveté and inability to grasp the sophisticated use of symbolism and metaphor in the scriptures. Evidently, God is such a poor communicator it takes a crack squad of linguists, historians, scholars, researchers and theologians to explain what he really meant to say. For their part, Chapel Mormons think their Internet Mormon brethren are prideful, liberal and lacking in faith. Seduced by science and worldly wisdom, they "lean unto their own understanding." Naturally, each side believes their interpretation is the correct one and the other is fundamentally misguided.

Which side will win? Like its evil twin Mormon Fundamentalism, Internet Mormonism continues to poach from mainstream Chapel Mormons. It's an interesting cultural struggle to keep an eye on. It's also fun to watch what Darwinian leaps it triggers and how the church leadership scrambles to keep up with the changes. But of course, becoming an Internet Mormon isn't the only option. Whenever a Saint is confronted with a doctrinal quandary or inescapable fact too thorny or too simple to ignore, explain away or compartmentalize, and their doubts reach that crucial, critical mass, they have a choice to make: They can become a Mormon apostate (hooray!) or the next best thing: a New Order Mormon.

New Order Mormons

Like the so-called "New Atheists," the "New Order Mormons" aren't really anything new, and New Order Mormonism isn't some separate new spin-off sect, but a shift in attitude. They are the church members who accept that the Book of Mormon is a wonderful work—of fiction—and that Joseph Smith was many things, but a true prophet wasn't one of them. Yet despite rejecting some or all of the major LDS tenets, these heretic Saints aren't apostates; they want to stay in the church family that they grew up in and still love.

There are plenty of leading Mormon thinkers who have found themselves in this position, such as the disillusioned archeologist Thomas Stuart Ferguson, historian D. Michael Quinn, scholar and educator Sterling McMurrin, and feminist Lavina Fielding Anderson, to name just a very few. Many have been contributors to independent Mormon studies journals such as *Dialogue* or *Sunstone*, magazines that have long been an outlet for liberal and dissident voices in Mormonism.

Some in this camp prefer to call themselves "Humanistic Mormons," like those who founded the Society for Humanistic Mormonism in 2010. It serves the needs of those heretical freethinkers who still feel connected with the rest of Mormon culture and identity, even though they may self-identify as Atheists, Agnostics, Humanists, Transhumanists, Liberal Mormons, Cultural Mormons, Reform Mormons, Secular Mormons or Post-Mormons, and may even be disfellowshipped, resigned or excommunicated.

A 2009 Examiner.com article ("Is Mormon theology diverging into new directions?" [cccxxxix]) looked at all these trends in Mormonism and predicted that, at the end of the day, the LDS church can manage to hold together even with these competing perspectives—but only by watering down its message and historical claims:

"It's unlikely that we'll see any new schisms from any of this. New Order Mormons want to stay with the mainstream church, and apologists want to defend it, not reject it in favor of something better. Chapel Mormonism will likely shift gradually to slowly accept some of these new views or simply abandon its old views altogether. We're already beginning to see this. Church lessons will drop references to historical events or future predictions and instead just focus on Christ, raising a good family, making moral choices. By avoiding anything that would ground Mormonism in the physical world, the church can continue to grow and be 'true' without challenge."

Gay Mormons

Like many religions, the LDS church takes a hard stance against homosexuality. When California's Proposition 8 put a ban of same-sex marriage on the ballot, the Mormons joined forces with the Catholic Church to push it through. Prop 8's proponents estimated that about half of their nearly $40 million in donations came from Mormons, along with between 80% and 90% of the volunteers for early door-to-door canvassing. LDS church members were instructed to "do all you can to support the proposed constitutional amendment by donating of your means and time."

And yet, despite all the efforts from the church to fight against gay equality, paradoxically, Salt Lake City has a huge thriving gay community. So much so, that in 2012, gay and lesbian newsmagazine *The Advocate* raised eyebrows by naming Salt Lake City "the gayest city in the U.S." Though San Francisco is far and away still no. 1 by population, the new and somewhat unscientific *Advocate* poll established "per capita queerness" through other semi-serious indicators, like a city's number of gay bookstores, openly gay elected officials and semifinalists in the International Mr. Leather Contest.

And it may well be because they are in the heart of anti-gay Mormon Utah that Salt Lake City's LGBT community is so strong. Over 15,000 people attended Gay Pride Day in 2011. In Library Square, a map covered in pushpins was posted with the sign: "Where on your mission did you meet your partner?" Despite the hopeful signs, Utah remains a difficult place for gays and lesbians. Utah has a high and rising rate of homeless teens living on the streets after their families kicked them out for being gay.

Gay teens in Utah have also reported higher than national rates of harassment: 69% reported being verbally harassed, compared to 53% nationwide; and 27% said they are physically assaulted, compared to 17% nationwide. [cccxl]

Despite the church's historical opposition, some gay Mormons have tried to embrace both their sexual orientation and their faith. In the 1970s, gay Mormons who had been meeting secretly, began coming out of the closet to found support groups like Affirmation. The Church takes a slightly different tack with the group Evergreen International, which treats same-sex orientation as just another sexual problem to be overcome. In 1996, distinguished Mormon historian, BYU professor and one of the infamous "September Six" (see ch. 11), D. Michael Quinn, wrote *Same-Sex Dynamics Among Nineteenth-Century Americans: A Mormon Example,* and cited several examples of homosexuality in early Mormon circles, arguing that it was not always regarded as the grave sin it is today. He also let it be known he was openly homosexual, and that regardless of that (or his 1993 excommunication), he still considers himself a Latter-day Saint.

Like their rival Christian sects, the Mormon Church still has a tough struggle ahead of it as it wrestles with the issues of same-sex marriage, gay equality and the transgendered. But if it has any hope of staying relevant to its gay members and their loved ones, let me predict that after years of protracted and painful division, the beleaguered First Presidency will finally have a divine revelation to shake up the flock and put an end to its institutionalized homophobia, just like it finally did for the African-American priesthood ban in 1978, and polygamy in 1890.

Mormon For Life

Mormons have long thought of themselves as "a peculiar people," and for those born into the church, it's not uncommon to be a 6th, 7th or even 8th generation Mormon. The Saints have managed to cram an extraordinary amount of vibrant and turbulent history into less than two centuries. Mix in a record of persecution, add in large spoonfuls of justifiable paranoia, a somewhat micromanaging leadership and a sacred devotion to the family, and *voilà*—you have one of the most tightly knit populations on earth.

Many of those Mormons who find that they are no longer in step with their fellow Saints—the doubters, the feminists, the gays, lesbians, bisexuals and transgendered, the heretics and the rest—find that no matter what they go on to call themselves, or whether they ever set foot in a church again, and no matter how they feel about the general authorities, they will always be Latter-day Saints. Cultural Mormons have realized that "Mormon" is as much an ethnic group as a religion, giving Mormonism a staying power that other religions lack. Will there still be Mormons after there's no longer a Mormon church?

The End of Mormonism

In 1984, University of Washington sociologist Rodney Stark famously projected that the Mormon Church could reach 265 million members by the year 2080; he then revised his figures to 300 million by the end of the 21st century [cccxli], making it the biggest religious success story since Islam. Yale's Harold Bloom, author of *The American Religion,* has said if the LDS church growth rate continues, within sixty years, governing the United States will be "impossible without Mormon cooperation." [cccxlii] Are they right? Not a chance. Love it or hate it, the Church of Jesus Christ of Latter-day Saints in the 21st century is in the same boat as the rest of Christianity... and the boat is going down.

By all indications the Mormon Church has maxed out. Stark's optimistic forecast was based on their impressive 53 percent growth rate from 1940 through 1980, a rate they've have been unable to match in the three decades since. At one time it claimed to be adding 1 million members every three years. [cccxliii] Nowadays, in the age of the Internet, with its open dialogue across religious borders and easy fact checking, the LDS Church's rate of growth is primarily from children born into Mormon families. And according to the 2001 American Religious Identification Survey conducted by the Graduate Center of the City University of New York, the LDS church's net growth was zero percent: the number of new Mormons was matched by the number of people who had left it.

David G. Stewart Jr., an active Mormon, has been conducting research on LDS missionary work in 20 countries for 13 years, examining census figures, and analyzing published data. His findings do not bode well for the church; there are significant numbers of converts who drop out after baptism. "It is a matter of grave concern that the areas with the most rapid numerical membership increase, Latin America and the Philippines, are also the areas with extremely low convert retention," warned Stewart. "Latter-day Saints lose 70 to 80 percent of their converts." [cccxliv]

The number of new ordinations to the Mormon Priesthood gives an even more accurate picture of the retention rate. In 1994, BYU sociology professor Lawrence A. Young reported data from the church almanac showing the percentage of Mormon males who reached the rank of Melchizedek priesthood, broken out by country. In Utah, about 70% of all baptized males reached this level, but the U.S. average was 59% and in Canada, 52%. Overseas, those figures dropped off more dramatically still, down to a low of 19% in Mexico and 17% in Japan. [cccxlv]

In more impoverished regions of the globe, the church faces another difficulty: so-called "Rice Mormons." For instance, in Nigeria and Ghana, local LDS bishops distribute food, but as Elder James O. Mason, former African Area President put it, "we want the Africans to join because they believe the Book of Mormon is true." The church "does not want them to join for the wrong reasons." [cccxlvi]

Salt Lake Tribune reports that Utah's LDS population is only 62.4 %, with decreases occurring in every county. Based on dropout rates, only 41.6% of Utahns would be considered church-going Mormons.[cccxlvii] And there are millions of disenfranchised multi-generational Mormons who describe themselves variously as 'Jack Mormons', 'social Mormons', 'fringe Mormons' etc., who are categorized as 'inactive' by church census takers. As in other faiths, many converts drift away and become inactive, or even leave to join other religions, but their names remain on the church rolls except for the rare cases who formally request in writing that their names to be removed, or are excommunicated. [cccxlviii]

The *Salt Lake Tribune* [cccxlix] also cited Stewart's research indicating that the church's worldwide activity is about 35%, which means active, churchgoing membership is down to only around 4 million members—a far cry from the 13 million figure they like to tout. In other words, there are over three times as many as many inactive Mormons as there are active ones!

One last note: While the first draft of this book was being written, I was moved and delighted to see Reuters report on 150 ex-Mormons from Utah, Arizona, Idaho and further afield, who quit the church in a mass resignation ceremony in Salt Lake City on June 30, 2012 [cccl]. They gathered to sign a "Declaration of Independence from Mormonism" and collect their resignation letters before marching up to Ensign Peak, Utah's most sacred mountain. There, overlooking Salt Lake City, the Mormon Temple and church headquarters, they gave three loud shouts of "Freedom" before breaking into applause and hugs all around. I wish them all the best.

**

For further reading:

New Order Mormonism:

Dialogue and *Sunstone* are the two main Mormon intellectual magazines. http://www.sunstonemagazine.com/, http://dialogu ejournal.com/

Chapel vs. Internet Mormons: MormonInformation.com has links to several pages devoted to the topic, including a quiz to see if you are a Chapel or Internet Mormon, as well as other topics of interest to New Order Mormons.

Gay Mormons:

Affirmation, the organization for LGBT Mormons, has a website at: http://www.affirmation.org/

8: The Mormon Proposition (2010) is a documentary film described as "A scorching indictment of the Mormon Church's historic involvement in the promotion & passage of California's Proposition 8 and the Mormon religion's secretive, decades-long campaign against LGBT human rights."

Endnotes: Chapter 13

cccxxxviii http://www.mormoninformation.com/imvscm.htm

cccxxxix http://www.examiner.com/article/is-mormon-theology-diverging-into-new-directions

cccxl "Utah sees rise in LGBT teens becoming homeless" http://www.abc4.com/mostpopular/story/Utah-sees-rise-in-LGBT-teens-becoming-homeless/LboIk6v82UO7GErL4kRtsQ.cspx

cccxli "Keeping Members a Challenge for LDS Church" by Peggy Fletcher Stack, *Salt Lake City Tribune,* July 26, 2005; and Krakauer, p. 324

cccxlii Krakauer, ibid.

cccxliii For a critical breakdown of official LDS membership statistics, see also "Does the LDS Church really have 14 million members?" on the Mormon Information.com website: http://www.mormoninformation.com/stats.htm

cccsliv Stack, op. cit.

cccxlv Ostling, p. 220

cccxlvi ibid, p. 215

cccxlvii ibid, p. 388

cccxlviii ibid, pp. 220-221

ccxlix Stack, op cit.

cccl http://www.reuters.com/article/2012/07/01/us-usa-utah-mormons- idUSBRE86000N20120701

Chapter 14

Talking to the Ex-Mormons of the Future—Today!

This is Your Brain on Mormonism

Before you try to start up a dialogue with a Latter-day Saint, it's good to try to get an appreciation of the Mormon mindset first, of just what an all-encompassing part their religion plays in their lives. Most gentiles have no idea just how much Mormons have invested in their family, church and community. What's it like to be a Mormon today?

Being Mormon is more than just accepting a set of beliefs about heaven and hell and ancient American history. It's embracing rules for living that permeate every facet of one's life: your diet, your money, your language, your behavior, even your clothes and appearance. Mormons are to shun tattoos and piercings, though females are allowed a single pair of earrings. They must be good citizens, avoid debt and gambling (even the state lottery), and refrain from cursing. All church members are expected to be an outgoing, winsome ambassador for their religion at all times. Young Mormons are engrained with chastity and moral responsibility. They are told to "choose the right;" many wear "CTR" bracelets or necklaces to remind them. Mormon youth do not date before age sixteen. They are to shun porn and told masturbation is a sin and homosexuality is a choice—a wrong choice.

Time for Church—Again...

Time for church doesn't end at Sunday school for Mormons; it's a full-time occupation, 24/7. The church's demand on time is daunting. Members are asked not to work or study for school on Sunday. Sundays are dedicated to 3 hours or more of sacrament meeting, testimony meeting, and lesson classes for all ages. For an hour, sexes are segregated in priesthood and auxiliary meetings. During high school, Mormon students have pre-dawn religious classes every weekday. On top of that, extracurricular activities can include still more time commitments like Boy Scouts, stake choir rehearsal or Relief Society meetings featuring a Bishop-approved speaker or a potluck dinner.

Ward, stake and regional levels all offer a wide variety of church social opportunities for believers of all ages, including theatrical productions, youth orchestras, athletic competitions, choirs, mini-trek campouts, square dances and devotional or cultural "Fireside" evening talks by visiting scholars or General authorities [ccli]. But never on Mondays—Monday is sacred and set aside for Family Home Evening. Mormons are directed to shut out the world and gather with the nuclear family for one night a week for devotionals, instruction and wholesome family fun.

Mackenzie Solaro was born and raised in a large Mormon family. Her troubles began when she began researching early church history and after years of diligent study and prayer, ultimately left the church at age 25. "What I liked *least* about being Mormon was the time commitment," Mackenzie said. During her junior year of high school, she was president of the young woman's group for her ward. Here is what her typical week looked like:

SUN: Wake up early to read scriptures and pray with family. Get ready for church. Attend Sacrament meeting (1 hour), Sunday School (1 hour), Young Women's (1 hour), choir practice (1 hour), young women's presidency meeting (1.5 hours). Go home, eat, have scripture reading and prayer with family. Write in my journal, do my own scripture reading, say my own prayers. Bed.

MON: Get up at 4am to attend hour-long seminary (mandatory scripture study for high school kids, 35 minutes away from my home and high school) prior to school. Go to school. Come home, do homework, attend Family Home Evening, which happens every Monday. This is family religious time, and lasts about 2 hours. Write in my journal, do my own scripture reading, say my own prayers. Bed.

TUES: Seminary and school. Organize and attend a young woman's activity in the evening that takes approximately 2.5 hours. Home and homework. Family scriptures and prayer, personal scriptures and prayer.

WED: Same as Tuesday except I'm taking my younger sisters to church activities instead of going to mine.

THURS: Same as Wednesday except our Home Teacher (a pair of men assigned to our family) comes over for his monthly visit in the evening. We sit in the living room and listen to him read the monthly lesson and bear his testimony to us.

FRI: More seminary. And since I have just turned 16, I have a date with a Mormon boy in the evening. Even though we really like each other, we aren't allowed to date exclusively yet, so we alternate weekends with dating other people. We've been out ten times, but the farthest we've gotten is holding hands. We say prayers together at the start and close of the date.

SAT: No seminary, no school, but at night we have a church dance that LDS kids over 14 can go to. It's held in the cultural hall at church, which is basically a large carpeted basketball court with a stage. The DJ only plays popular music that doesn't have negative or violent lyrics. A local bishop chaperoning the dance goes around during slow dances inserting a large Bible between couples that are dancing too closely. He also owns a decibel meter and checks the noise levels periodically; 80 decibels is the limit, which in the large room means that you can barely hear anything. This is the social highlight of my week.

Mackenzie adds, "You can see how with this schedule, there's basically *zero* time to question Mormonism, much less think about anything else. You spend so much time 100% immersed in the lies, and having them reinforced by *everyone* around you, it's impossible to see them as such."

The Missionary Position

Don't let the smiles fool you: Those two squeaky clean-cut young elders on your doorstep have it tough. The two years of service as a Mormon missionary are often the most grueling, expensive, isolated, lonely and thankless of their lives. For the duration of their call, every aspect of their lives 24/7 is carried out in accordance with the rules prescribed in the little booklet that they carry in their shirt pocket: the "White Bible," better known as *The Missionary Handbook*.

Seven days a week, without exception, they get up at 6:30 a.m., get cleaned up, study the Missionary Gospel Study Program for 2 hours, and then go out to proselytize for 10 hours between 9:30 a.m. and 9:30 p.m. Lights are out at 10:30 p.m. sharp. There are no breaks on weekends or holidays; on the contrary, that's when they are instructed to proselytize as much as possible because that's when they find people at home.

One of the ironclad rules is "Never be alone." Missionary partners are joined at the hip. They are told to be loyal to their companion; to seek to be one in spirit and purpose and help each other succeed (but they are also expected to immediately inform their mission president if their companion doesn't obey the rules). Pray, study, plan your work with your companion every day, and take time at least once a week for companionship inventory. You must always address your companion as elder (or sister). You may not wake up before your companion nor stay up after they go to sleep. You *are* to sleep in the same bedroom as your companion; however, you *are not* to sleep in the same bed as your companion.

You are expected to keep your thoughts, words, and actions in harmony with the gospel message. This means, among other things, you cannot watch TV or listen to the radio (not even the news) or any unauthorized music. You may read only books, magazines or materials that are authorized by the Church. Don't debate or argue. Keep a regular journal.

Except for the companion they are yoked to at all hours, missionaries are quite isolated. Encounters with the opposite sex are extremely limited; dating or flirting is not permitted. They are to write to their parents once a week, less frequently to siblings and friends. No phone calls are allowed to family or friends, though in some areas, the mission president will make an exception to this rule and will allow two phone calls to your parents per year: one on Christmas and one on Mother's day.

And there are many more rules to follow: rules for dress and grooming, transportation, spending money, exercise and recreation (missionaries may play half-court basketball; they may not swim), housing, driving and biking, and other less obvious prohibitions (they may not handle firearms or explosives, or become involved in politics, music groups or adoption proceedings) and dozens more. If going door-to-door in shirt and tie witnessing to an overwhelmingly unreceptive audience 16 hours a day every day with the same person beside you every minute for two years doesn't sound like a total drag, remember you also have to smile the whole time, too. So when they show up on your doorstep with their Book of Mormon in hand, be kind.

Mission Control

As mentioned before, though the Latter-day Saints spend a massive amount of energy on missionary efforts, the truth is their worldwide growth has stalled. New converts simply aren't joining up at the rate they used to. But that's okay, because the church still is getting the people their missionary program targets: the missionaries themselves.

The real goal of the missionary program doesn't appear to be outreach to new converts, but retention of their own young people. Richard and Joan Ostling have noted that while the young people in other faiths are experimenting in college, sowing their wild oats and falling away from the church, young Mormons are gearing up more than ever to serve their church: "At an age when the youth of most religions are beginning to avoid church activities, Mormon youngsters are babysitting, mowing lawns and pumping gas after school to save the $375 per month they must someday deposit with the church to cover expenses when they serve a mission." [ccclii]

Their two years in the crucible may or may not win them any new converts, but it will bring them trials and tribulations to suffer, build character and leadership, and strengthen their bond to the church. It's a paradox of religious psychology— the more hardship the missionary is made to endure, the deeper they will entrench themselves in their religion. It *must* be true, because they're being persecuted for their faith. And the more they suffer for their faith, the deeper they commit themselves. Every bit of time and energy they expend makes it that much harder to ever admit that they are wrong—once they're in too deep and have paid too much to let all that blood, sweat and tears be for nothing... As the LDS church's *Lectures on Faith* says: "A religion that does not require the sacrifice of all things never has power sufficient to produce the faith necessary unto life and salvation."

But that's not to say it's impossible for even the most dedicated Latter-day Saint to deconvert. In fact, it happens all the time. Here's how you can help.

Talking to Mormons

As cookie-cut as Mormons may appear to be, every individual is different. Talking to a "New Order Mormon" or an "Internet Mormon" will be very different from talking to a "Chapel Mormon." The missionary who shows up on your doorstep is not only extremely likely to be a Chapel Mormon, but they are under a tremendous amount of pressure. Mormon Missionaries *must* return home with honor. Returning home early from a mission, due to sin or lack of faith, will severely demoralize and humiliate them. So first get to know your audience, be sensitive to their needs, try to determine the impact your ideas may have on their lives, and adjust your approach accordingly.

Keep in mind that you may well succeed in convincing a believer to renounce the error of their ways—but as my friend Greta Christina points out in her brilliant book *Why Are You Atheists So Angry?*, chances are it won't happen in single conversation:

"For most people, letting go of religion is a process. It takes time. And while other people can help with that process, ultimately it's something people need to do on their own. So if you're expecting to persuade someone out of their beliefs in a single conversation, you're going to be disappointed. Don't let that discourage you. Don't think of it as winning or losing an argument. Think of it as helping someone along, helping them move a little farther along their path. Think of it as planting the seeds of doubt. Or as nurturing seeds of doubt that are already there."

Just the fact that you are not already a Christian will put Mormon missionaries off balance; much of their game plan presumes that you already accept the basics of Christianity and take the Bible seriously. The LDS church's biggest successes outside the U.S. have all been in Catholic countries: Mexico, Brazil, the Philippines and Chile. Another disappointment for missionaries in talking to a heretic like you is that their favorite tactic won't work on you: Moroni's Challenge. Basically, it boils down to "fake it till you make it." Missionaries encourage would-be converts to pray to know the truth, assuring them that the Holy Spirit will give them the famous "burning in their bosom" as a guarantee that Mormonism is true. Needless to say, if you fail to receive a sign, it only means that you aren't doing it right...

Some Basics

1. Be friendly, be yourself. You may be one of the only people they get a chance to really talk with, and that puts you in a unique position to reach out to them. Think of yourself as an ambassador for science, reason and godlessness.
2. Remember that changing minds is an ongoing process. Don't try to slam-dunk an argument; plant the seed.
3. Avoid using curse words.
4. Don't try talking to a Mormon with a cigarette, or an alcoholic or caffeinated drink in your hand. That immediately disqualifies your argument.
5. Avoid debates. Members are instructed to avoid "the spirit of contention."
6. On a similar note, avoid snark, ridicule or going on the attack. Mormons have a hair-trigger persecution complex, honed by almost two centuries of dickish behavior from the outside world, and easily slip into "Help, I'm being persecuted!" mode if you're not careful. "Persecution" has a funny way of reinforcing religious faith for most believers, (especially most spoiled American mainstream Christians who really have no clue what genuine religious persecution is), so don't mock or attack them, or even say "you are wrong." If they think you are the enemy, the conversation is over.
7. A better approach is to be friendly, listen and ask questions. Who knows, you might realize that their religious world-view isn't as bad as you had assumed. You can still reject their beliefs, but you'll be in a much better position to at least know where they are coming from, and to better understand their needs/desires.
8. Respect the person, even if you can't respect their beliefs. If you fail to connect with someone as a fellow fallible human being, it's unlikely they'll want to pay any attention to what you might have to say—and really, why would they?
9. People care more about whether you are real than whether

you are perfect. If you get stuck, or don't have an answer, just say you don't know. If you make a mistake and get called out on it, admit it. A little willingness to acknowledge you could be wrong will go a long way.

10. Know your stuff. Faithful Saints spend more hours in church and reading scriptures than you do in front of the television. They have little patience for people who think they know their beliefs but actually misunderstand them. If you don't fully understand something, ask them about it. They'll be delighted to explain it to you.

11. You'll find you may have more of an impact by focusing on the joys of being an atheist rather than going on the warpath and just trashing Mormon beliefs. When you do tackle Mormon dogma and historical claims, do it with gentleness. Explain why you find problems with the claim in question, rather than just saying you reject it outright.

12. Tolerate their testimony. If you engage with any TBM (True-Believing Mormon/True Blue Mormon) for any length of time, you can rest assured sooner or later they will bear their testimony to you. This will involve a series of statements starting with "I know (the church/Joseph Smith/The Book of Mormon/blah, blah, blah) to be true." Often this will be accompanied by tears. Let them get it out of their system and then you can continue to engage in more productive conversation.

Finally: Remember, you can lead a horse to water but you can't make them think. Ultimately, they will be the ones who change their minds or not.

Some Helpful Approaches

Keep in mind that the Saints live, for the most part, in a Latter-day bubble. Mormons trust LDS-approved materials only. They are actively discouraged from seeking out information on the church from any other sources. Chances are they will not believe anything that does not come straight from a legit LDS source. Mormons get a great deal of mileage from sanctimoniously standing firm on being "the one and only true religion." Anything *you* have to say is due to your inability to fully understand the lofty truths of the faith.

So one of the best things you can do is to point them towards information on early church history using church-sanctioned sources. Don't show it to them yourself. Don't try to read it to them or email it to them. Don't try to debate with them. Instead, point them towards resources they can examine on their own. The Internet has an amazing wealth of material. One especially excellent site is **Mormonthink.com**, which is run by church members and critically examines and compiles an enormous number of controversial facts from impeccable church-sanctioned, first-hand sources.

Another good approach seems to be bringing up other religions and examples that are similar enough to their beliefs, way of life, or general religion model, and challenging *those* examples. For instance, one ex-Mormon acquaintance had things click when she was reading a book about cults, and recognized that her beliefs fit into the same mold. That book, by the way, was *Combating Cult Mind Control* (Park Street Press, 1990) by Steven Hassan, a respected authority on cults and an expert exit-counselor who was himself a former member of the Unification Church before his own escape. Hassan's book has been mentioned by several interviewees as a valuable resource to make believers examine the dynamics of their own faith.

At the risk of shameless self-promotion, here's another example: you could bring into question a central tenet of mainstream Christianity, such as: Did Jesus really exist, or was he just a mythical figure? Twelve years ago, I would have thought that was a crazy question...until I began looking into what we could really know for sure about what Jesus really said and did. The result was my 2010 book, *Nailed: Ten Christian Myths that Show Jesus Never Existed At All*, which points out ten ways the traditional view of Jesus fails the reality check. [cccliii]

David Fitzgerald

A Few Fun Questions to Ask

- "Just hypothetically speaking, if your religion *was* a hoax, would you want to know?"
- "How do you think the church would be different if it *wasn't* true? What do you think *that* church would look like?"
- "Can we talk about Mormon archeology?"
- "What convinced you to become a Mormon?" (follow-up question if they say they grew up in the church: "Have you ever wondered what religion you'd be if you hadn't been born in a Mormon family?")
- "Why is Mormonism so small compared to other major religions?"
- "Why did it take so long for Mormonism to be revealed?"
- "If all the sincere and god-fearing members of non-Mormon religions can be wrong about their faith, isn't that a sign that faith alone isn't a good enough guide to what's true or not?"

Again, see Greta Christina's book (esp. ch.12, "Is Atheist Activism Effective?") for a lengthy list of good topics to discuss with all kinds of believers, and good advice on strategy. Another good book for holding discussions like these is M. Guy Harrison's *50 Reasons People Give For Believing in a God.*

Losing My Religion

One common theme from interviews with former Mormons (or "Formons"[cccliv]) is that Mormonism is more than a religion; it is an all-encompassing world unto itself. And those that leave it can find themselves feeling like strangers in a strange land, alone for the first time in their lives:

"Leaving the Mormon Church was the hardest thing I've ever had to do. I had to choose between being honest with myself and others, or living up to expectations. I lost 99% of my

302

social life, my relationship with my family is likely permanently damaged, and I still have some leftover psychological issues thanks to the LDS church upbringing. I got out early enough in life that I'm a lot better off than most ex-Mormons. Those who went on missions, got married, had families before figuring it all out, tend to have even more issues than I ever did. Things are much better 13+ years later, but it was nasty for a very long time. I still occasionally have church-related nightmares." —Erin McBride

"When I left the Church, I was depressed for a couple of years, and I couldn't figure out why. I felt like I was going crazy. Mormonism teaches that the only way to be "truly" happy (Blegh, whatever that is...) is to be a member of the church. So when I left and felt so miserable, I always had it in the back of my mind that the reason was because the church was true and I was going against it. It never occurred to me that I was undergoing a form of post-traumatic stress disorder. I actually started going back to church a few months ago because I couldn't take the pain anymore, but after a while realized what was going on. I happened upon (an article about post-traumatic stress disorder) and it blew me away. That was exactly what I had experienced. I know a lot of ex-Mormons who were able to just leave the religion and were instantly happier than they'd ever been. However I think a lot of people, myself included, struggle to be happy after leaving."—Jenan Abbar

"My leaving Mormonism was a very long, sometimes painful journey of dealing with the cognitive dissonance between faith and evidence. Education and critical thinking are the best antidotes to the fantastical beliefs of Mormonism. Also, for Mormon women it is important to discover personal empowerment which can be found through feminism—the other "F-word" in Mormon patriarchal structure/culture."— Andrea Moore-Emmett

"The biggest no-no for atheists is to mock or over-trivialize the 'stupidity' of the beliefs or the 'ease' of walking away.

Chuckle in private, or amongst atheist-only audiences, sure, but not to their face. Even as an ex-mo, this pains me. People will jibe me, saying, "How could you believe all of that crazy stuff?" And frankly, it was easy to.

"The brainwashing in Mormonism is so incredibly deep. It's drilled into your head over and over from birth, and as a result, most Mormons exist in a complete altered state of reality. Exhibiting any semblance of critical thinking skills is labeled as "prideful." You learn to trust gaps in your understanding and to avoid asking questions—it becomes as second nature as breathing.

"Exiting the church is incredibly difficult. People are condemned for even *asking* the hard questions, and people are disowned by friends and families for exiting. Many atheists haven't experienced being intensely immersed in a brainwashed culture, so it's not for them to judge how difficult it is to wake up and walk away. Doing so means being willing to give up your entire life and everything in it that is dear to you."—Mackenzie Solarno

Mackenzie Solarno had some additional interesting insights on Mormon psychology and deconversion that are also worth repeating:

"Ultimately, if somebody is looking to lead someone out of Mormonism, I'm forced to quote Morpheus from the Matrix: 'I'm trying to free your mind, Neo. But I can only show you the door. You're the one that has to walk through it.' Just like you cannot talk an alcoholic out of being an alcoholic, you cannot talk a Mormon out of being Mormon.

"The psychology they've built in their brain to support their personal belief system is more complex than you can fathom. Picture a 30-foot tall tangled ball of Christmas lights. That's a Mormon's brain. You're not going to be able to untangle it for them. For most of us that wake up and exit, we have to spend a significant amount of time unraveling that mess.

"For me, this meant re-engineering my ENTIRE belief system. I didn't know who I was or what I believed anymore. What is moral behavior? What kind of person am I now? What is my place in the world? Some of these questions are so big and terrifying, having never faced them, that it's enough to immediately drive you back into the arms of Mormonism. For most ex-Mos, this rebuilding of identity and purpose is a multi-year process.

"So don't go in expecting you're going to point out some absurdities in the religion and get them to suddenly 'wake up'... You must let them find their own path out. Just show them the door."

Endnotes: Chapter 14

cccli Ostling, pp.186-7

ccclii Ostling, p. 218

ccclii And as long as we're pausing for a commercial interruption, my next book will be a follow-up to *Nailed* entitled *Jesus: Mything in Action*. It will take on the weaknesses and problems of the arguments some atheists and secular scholars make to argue that there was a strictly human Jesus.

cccliv Thanks to "Mr. Deity," (and a Formon himself) Brian Keith Dalton for inventing the term "Formon." You can catch him at www.mrdeity.com .

Select Bibliography

Abanes, Richard. *One Nation Under Gods: A History of the Mormon Church*
New York: Four Walls Eight Windows, 2002

Bagley, Will. *Blood of the Prophets*, Norman: Univ. of Oklahoma Press, 2004

Bigler, David L. *Forgotten Kingdom: The Mormon Theocracy in the American West, 1847 -1896*, Logan, University of Utah Press, 1998

Brodie, Fawn M. *No Man Knows My History: The Life of Joseph Smith*, New York: Vintage, 1995

Brooks, Juanita, *The Mountain Meadows Massacre*, Norman: Univ. of Oklahoma Press, 1950

Buerger, David John. *The Mysteries of Godliness*, San Francisco: Smith Research Associates, 1994

Bushman, Richard L. *Joseph Smith and the Beginnings of Mormonism*, Champaign: University of Illinois Press, 1984

Bushman, Richard L. *Joseph Smith: Rough Stone Rolling*, New York City, NY: Vantage, 2007

Caswell, Rev. Henry, *The City of the Mormons, or, Three Days at Nauvoo*, London: J.G.F. & J. Rivington, 1843

Compton, Todd. *In Sacred Loneliness: The Plural Wives of Joseph Smith*, Salt Lake City: Signature Books, 1997

Davis, Howard A., Donald R. Scales, and Wayne L. Cowdrey. *Who Really Wrote the Book of Mormon?*, Santa Ana: Vision House Publishers, 1977.

Denton, Sally, *American Massacre*, New York: Knopf, 2003

Gaunt, LaRene Porter and Smith, Robert A. "Samuel H. Smith: Faithful Brother of Joseph and Hyrum," *Ensign*, Aug. 2008

Hardy, B. Carmon. *Solemn Covenant: The Mormon Polygamist Passage*, Urbana, University of Illinois Press, 1992

Howe, Eber D. *Mormonism Unvailed*, Painesville, Ohio, 1834

Kimball, Spencer W. *The Miracle of Forgiveness*, Salt Lake City: Bookcraft, 1969

Krakauer, Jon. *Under the Banner of Heaven*, New York: Anchor, 2004

Larson, Stan. *Quest for the Gold Plates: Thomas Stuart Ferguson's Archeological Search for the Book of Mormon*, Salt Lake City: Freethinker Press, 1996

Lindsey, Robert. *A Gathering of Saints: A True Story of Money, Murder, and Deceit*, New York: Simon & Schuster, 1988

Matheny, Raymond. T. "Book of Mormon Archeology: Sunstone Symposium #6, Salt Lake Sheraton Hotel, August 25, 1984." Typescript, 1984, in the David J. Buerger Collection, Manuscript 622, Box 33, Fd 17, Manuscripts Division, J. Willard Marriott Library, University of Utah, Salt Lake City.

Metcalf, Anthony. *Ten Years Before the Mast*, Malad City, IN: 1888; New Haven Research Publications, 1967

Moore-Emmett, Andrea. *God's Brothel*, San Francisco: Pince Nez, 2004

Newell, Linda King and Avery, Valeen Tippetts. *Mormon Enigma: Emma Hale Smith*, Champaign, University of Illinois Press, 1994

Nibley, Preston. *The Witnesses to the Book of Mormon*, Salt Lake City: Deseret Book Co., 1968

Ostling, Richard N. and Joan K. *Mormon America: The Power and the Promise*, New York: HarperCollins, 2007

Palmer, Grant H. *An Insider's View of Mormon Origins*, Salt Lake City: Signature Books, 2002

Persuitte, David. *Joseph Smith and the Origins of the Book of Mormon*, 2nd Ed., Jefferson, NC: McFarland & Co., 2000

Quinn, D. Michael. *Early Mormonism and the Magic World View*, Salt Lake City: Signature Books, 1998

The Mormon Hierarchy: Origins of Power, Salt Lake City: Signature Books/Smith Research Associates, 1994

The Mormon Hierarchy: Extensions of Power, Salt Lake City: Signature Books/Smith Research Associates, 1997

Ray, Darrel W. *Sex & God: How Religion Distorts Sexuality.* Bonner Springs, KS: IPC Press, 2012

Roberts, Brigham H. *Studies of the Book of Mormon*, Salt Lake City: Signature Books, 1992

Smith, Lucy. *Biographical Sketches of Joseph Smith the Prophet and His Progenitors for Many Generations*, Liverpool, England, 1853

Smith, George D., ed. *Faithful History: Essays on Writing Mormon History*, Salt Lake City: Signature Books, 1992

Smith, Joseph Fielding. *Answers to Gospel Questions*, (5 volumes) Salt Lake City: Deseret Book Co., 1998

Southerton, Simon G. *Losing a Lost Tribe: Native Americans. DNA and the Mormon Church*, Salt Lake City: Signature Books, 2004

Tanner, Jerald and Sandra. *Changes in Joseph Smith's History*, Salt Lake City: Utah Lighthouse Ministry, 1965

The Changing World of Mormonism, Chicago: Moody Press, 1981

Van Wagoner, Richard S. *Sidney Rigdon: A Portrait of Religious Excess*, Salt Lake City: Signature Books, 1994

Vogel, Dan, ed. *Early Mormon Documents*, Salt Lake City: Signature Books, 1998

Vogel, Dan. "Rethinking the 1826 Judicial Decision," mormon scripturestudies.com/ch/dv/1826.asp

Whipple, Walter L. *An Analysis of Textual Changes in "The Book of Abraham" and in the "Writings of Joseph Smith, The Prophet" in the Pearl of Great Price*, Master's Thesis, Brigham Young University, 1959

Whitefield, Jim, *The Mormon Delusion*, Vol. 1-5, Raleigh, NC: Lulu Press, 2009

Wyl, Wilhelm. *Mormon Portraits, Joseph Smith the Prophet, His Family and His Friends*, Salt Lake City, 1886

Zindler, Frank, "How Do You Lose a Steel Mill?" http://nowscape.com/mormon/zindler1.htm

Further Resources

One of the hardest things about writing this book, besides trying to keep all the changing versions of Mormon history straight, was to *stop* writing it. There's an old writer's adage that says books are never finished, they're just abandoned. That certainly felt like the case with this one. Just when I thought I had finally uncovered every last juicy tidbit of Mormon wackiness in my research—surprise! I would stumble across some whole new cul-de-sac of crazy. Ancient Jaredite submarines! Magical Liahona compasses! Yet another jaw dropping quote from a church leader— It would take an *Encyclopedia Mormonica Merda* to sufficiently catalog the rich and seemingly never-ending wellspring of entertainment, wonder, comedy and tragedy that is Mormonism. Until then, here are some other treasure-troves of information and/or entertainment on Mormonism, in no particular order:

Television:

"The Mormons" PBS Website http://www.pbs.org/mormons/

The *South Park* episode "All About Mormons" (Season 7, episode 12). Yes, you heard that right. Trey Parker and Matt Stone nailed Joseph Smith's dodgy story of finding the BOM—and then took the LDS church to Broadway with the award-winning *The Book of Mormon*.

Online:

Mormonthink.org—The quality of information and discussions on this website are first-rate, and they cite from impeccable Mormon sources. I can't recommend it enough.

Utah Lighthouse Ministry—Ex-Mos turned evangelical Christians, for over half a century Jerald and Sandra Tanner have been the patron saints of Mormon critical investigation.

MormonInformation.com is a great site with links to a variety of LDS topics geared to Mormons who are wrestling with doubts.

Steve Well's Skeptic's Annotated Book of Mormon (www.skepticsannotatedbible.com/BOM/index.htm) is every bit as brilliant as his Skeptic's Annotated Bible. A fantastic reference.

Book of Abraham.com

Institute for Religious Research IRR.org

Rethinking Mormonism http://www.i4m.com/think/intro/

Translated-Correctly.com

HolyFetch.com the Mormon Urban Legends website

Cultural Mormon Cafeteria http://culturalmormoncafeteria. blogspot.com/

20 Truths about Mormonism http://20truths.info/mormon.html

Dale Broadhurst has complied an extensive collection of research materials on early Mormonism under various websites. His many collections can be found online at: http://sidneyrigdon.com/ DRB/host03.htm

And in no particular order, here are additional sites worth looking into:

www.iamanexmormon.com

www.postmormon.org

www.exmormonscholarstestify.org

www.mormonexpression.com
www.exmormonfoundation.org

www.reddit.com/r/exmormon

www.lifeaftermormonism.net

www.latterdaymainstreet.com

Essays:

Ken Clark, "Lying for the Lord," http://www.mormonthink.com/lying.htm

Richard Packham, "Mormon Lying," http://packham.n4m.org/lying.htm

Zindler, Frank, "How Do You Lose a Steel Mill?" A classic. http://nowscape.com/mormon/zindler1.htm

Books:

Former Mormon (for 43 years!) Jim Whitefield has an excellent five-volume book series, *The Mormon Delusion* (Lulu, 2009)

For just plain gonzo-level Utah nuttiness, check out Trent Harris' amazing little classic book *Mondo Utah* (Dream Garden Press, 1996)

While not specific to Mormonism, these excellent, accessible books are very helpful for atheists who are talking about atheism to religious friends. (and by the way, they also make great gifts for your religious friends, too...):

David Fitzgerald

Richard Carrier, *Sense and Goodness Without God*

Greta Christina, *Why Are You Atheists So Angry? 99 Things That Piss Off the Godless*
M. Guy Harrison, *50 Reasons People Give For Believing in a God*

Acknowledgements

Thanks to all of you who were so generous in offering so much help, information and support with this book:

Mo tiogar cogarnach, mo siombí marfóir, mo cárta fhiáin, my Dana Fredsti, first and always.

All the organizers, staff and attendees of Skepticon, the most awesome student-run secular event on the planet; the Secular Student Alliance and Center for Inquiry, all my fellow San Francisco Atheists, and all the global network of supportive fans of my first book, *Nailed: Ten Christian Myths That Show Jesus Never Existed At All*, for all your love, support and encouragement.

Huge thanks to the Mighty Don Havis and former Mormons Steven McIntosh, Andrea Moore-Emmett, Mackenzie Steele Solaro and Steve Thoreson for sharing a tremendous amount of their expertise with me.

Thanks also to Jenan Abbar, Ernesto "Ernie" Aranda, Amanda Brown, Ted Cox, Greg Davis, Samuel Foit, Julia Galef, Daniel Hay, Harald Illig, Erin McBride, Sara Moglia, Darrel Ray, Ben Roberts, the Society for Humanistic Judaism, and so many more for answering my endless questions.

Special thanks to those current Mormons, ex-Mormons and soon-to-be-ex-Mormons who generously shared their experiences and insights but for various reasons needed to remain anonymous.

Thanks for all the generous support from all of the book's Indiegogo contributors; especially all the contributors at Patron level and above, including: Lisa Brackmann, Brandon Christian, Contra Costa Atheists & Freethinkers, David Diskin, Carol Gallante, Sean Gillespie, Frank O. Glomset, Helen Kahn, Jason Korbus, David Madison, Gordon Maples, Bruce Martin, Eamonn McKay, Bobby Nelson, Andy Ochoa, Mick Phillips, Tara Schlotzhauer, Anne Stevenson, Patty Tweedle, and Jura master Michael A Vogt. And a huge shout out to my beloved Arch-heretics Larry Kaufman and Margaret Morgan (*Dziękuję bardzo!*).

Thanks also to the following podcasters:

David Smalley, Shayrah Akers and Daniel Moran of Dogma Debate Radio (http://www.dogmadebate.com)

Mick and Joe of Skeptic Fence (www.blogtv.com/people/skepticfence)

Jason Korbus and Bobby Nelson of Strange Frequencies Radio (www.strangefrequenciesradio.net)

JT Eberhard, Steven Olson and Christina Stephens of WWJTD?
(http://www.patheos.com/blogs/wwjtd/2012/12/wwjtd-podcast-5-david-fitzgerald/)

Dustin Williams and Wesley Bonetti of Atheist Nomads (http://www.atheistnomads.com)

Finally, thanks to the all-star team who got this book finalized:

Cas Fornalski - Cover Design
Matt Burns - Cover Illustration (www.theartfulmatt.com)
Judi Fennell - Manuscript Formatting www.formatting4U.com
Brittni Philippi- Maps
Susan Fink (Great-granddaughter of famous Mormon pioneer,

Bishop and Stake President Thomas E. Ricks) - Line Editor
Dave Smalley and Kishke Nelson – Audiobook Recording
(with apologies and thanks again to Dave Smalley for his
unintentional, but excellent, work as line editor, too!)
Additional special thanks to Mitchell Bender, Jim Whitefield
and Richard W. Wilson for making further corrections and
improvements.
And thanks to the ever-awesome Lauren Lane and Kaitlyn
Chandler for their Indiegogo pitch video!

Thanks again—I love you all!

-D

About the Author

David Fitzgerald is a writer, historical researcher and public speaker. He is on the Speaker's Bureau of both the Secular Student Alliance and Center for Inquiry, and lectures around the country at universities and national secular events. He is an audience favorite at Skepticon.

After actively investigating the Historical Jesus question for over ten years, he wrote the acclaimed history book *Nailed: Ten Christian Myths That Show Jesus Never Existed At All*, voted one of the Top 5 Best Atheist/Agnostic books of 2010 from AboutAtheism.com's Readers Choice Awards.

He has been called both "The Ferris Bueller of San Francisco" and "one of the busiest atheist activists in the Bay Area." In addition to serving on the board of San Francisco Atheists, Center For Inquiry-SF and the former Garrison-Martineau Project, he is also the Director/Co-Founder of both the world's first Atheist Film Festival and *Evolutionpalooza!*, the Bay Area's annual Darwin Day celebration. He lives in San Francisco with writer, producer and movie actress Dana Fredsti.

David says: "I welcome your comments, criticisms and especially corrections. William Strunk has a useful motto that has guided me well while writing this book: 'Understanding is that penetrating quality of knowledge that grows from theory, practice, conviction, assertion, error, and humiliation.'"

-DF

Contact me at: Everybodylovesdave@gmail.com

www.davefitzgerald.blogspot.com

If you like *The Complete Heretic's Guide to Western Religion,*
you'll also love:

Nailed

Ten Christian Myths
That Show Jesus Never
Existed at All

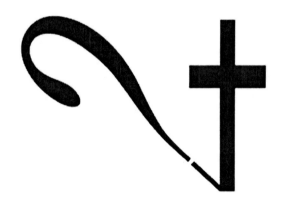

David Fitzgerald

**Voted one of the Top Five Best Atheist/Agnostic Books of
2010**
- About Atheism.com Reader's Choice Awards

Why would anyone think Jesus never existed?

Isn't it perfectly reasonable to accept that he was a real first century figure? As it turns out, no. ***Nailed: Ten Christian Myths That Show Jesus Never Existed At All*** sheds light on ten beloved Christian myths, and with evidence gathered from historians all across the theological spectrum, shows how they point to a Jesus Christ created solely through allegorical alchemy of hope and imagination, a messiah transformed from a purely literary, theological construct into the familiar figure of Jesus – in short, a purely mythic Christ.

See *Nailed's* page on Facebook for more information.

And stay tuned for *Nailed*'s follow-up book
Jesus: Mything in Action
coming soon!

Available from Amazon, Amazon.UK, Barnes & Noble, Smashwords and other online retailers.

Praise for *Nailed*:

"Fitzgerald's is possibly the best 'capsule summary' of the mythicist case I've ever encountered …with an interesting and accessible approach."

−Earl Doherty
author of *The Jesus Puzzle*

"Fitzgerald summarizes a great number of key arguments concisely and with new power and original spin. I really learned something from him. Recalls classical skeptics and biblical critics. A surprising amount of new material."

−Robert M. Price
author of *Deconstructing Jesus and The Incredible Shrinking Son of Man*

"David Fitzgerald reveals himself to be the brightest new star in the firmament of scholars who deny historical reality to 'Jesus of Nazareth.' His brilliance would have been sufficiently established had he done nothing more than illustrate and explain traditional arguments with a clarity and transparency never achieved…But he has done more. He has developed new arguments and insights as well..."

−Frank R. Zindler
editor of American Atheist Press
and author of *The Jesus the Jews Never Knew*

"Fitzgerald has hit the nail on the head…A nice, readable introduction to the top ten problems typically swept under the rug by anyone insisting it's crazy even to suspect Jesus might not have existed."

−Richard C. Carrier, Ph.D
author of *Not the Impossible Faith: Why Christianity Didn't Need a Miracle to Succeed* and the forthcoming *On the Historicity of Jesus Christ*

CPSIA information can be obtained
at www.ICGtesting.com
Printed in the USA
FFOW02n1334290216
21956FF